FANTAGRAPHICS PRESENTS

BLACK RIVER

by
JOSH SIMMONS

D1131428

Editor and Associate Publisher: Eric Reynolds
Book Design: Sammy Harkham
Production: Paul Baresh
Publisher: Gary Groth

FANTAGRAPHICS BOOKS, INC.
Seattle, Washington, USA

ISBN 978-1-60699-833-5

Library of Congress control number 2014957444

First printing: May 2015

Printed in South Korea

THANK YOU
Wendy, Luke, Jess, Jacq, Gary, Eric, Sammy, Seattle Comics Crew, and Jen

ALSO BY JOSH SIMMONS AND FANTAGRAPHICS
HOUSE
JESSICA FARM, VOLUME ONE
THE FURRY TRAP (short stories)

jhscomics.tumblr.com

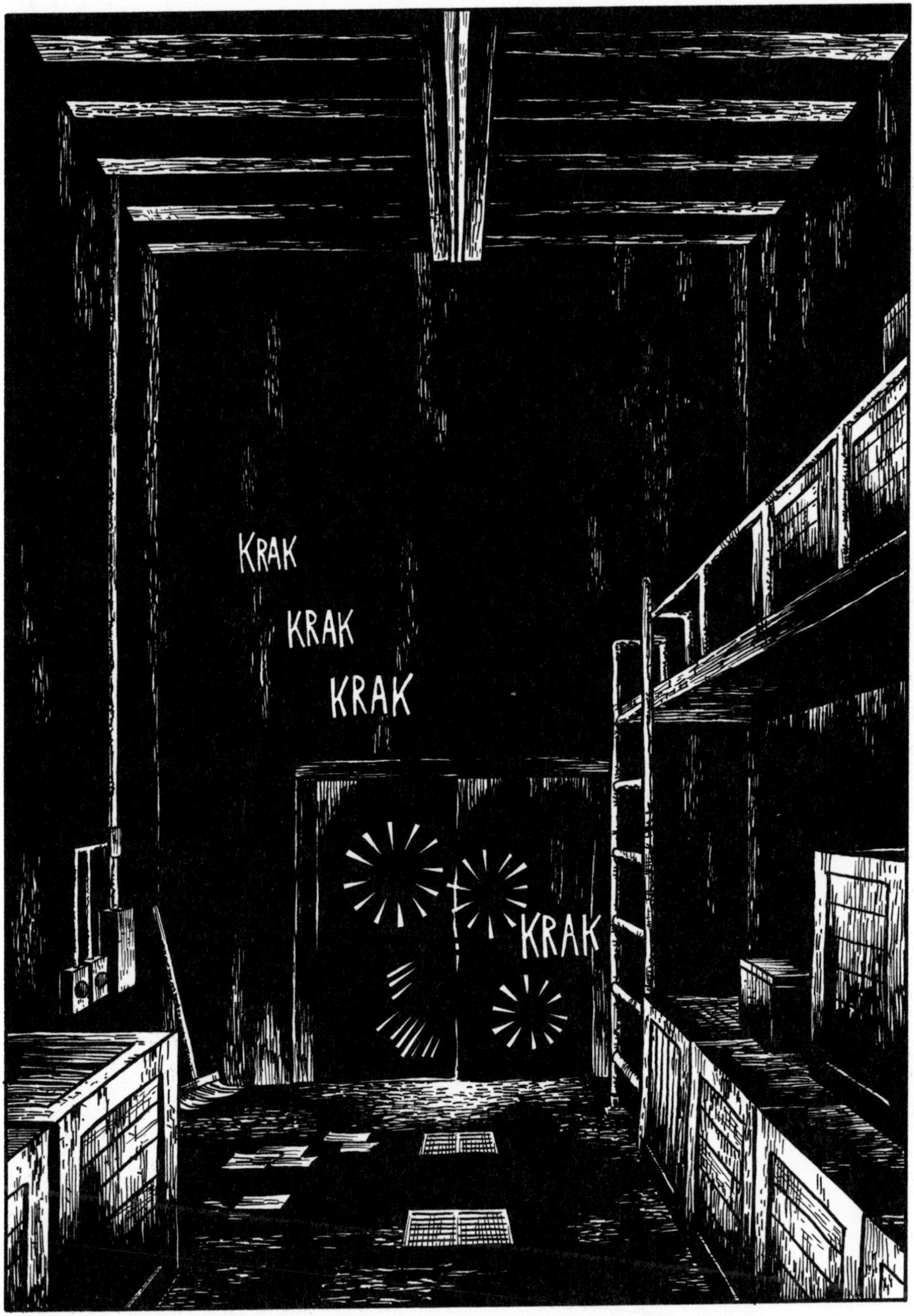
KRAK
KRAK
KRAK
KRAK

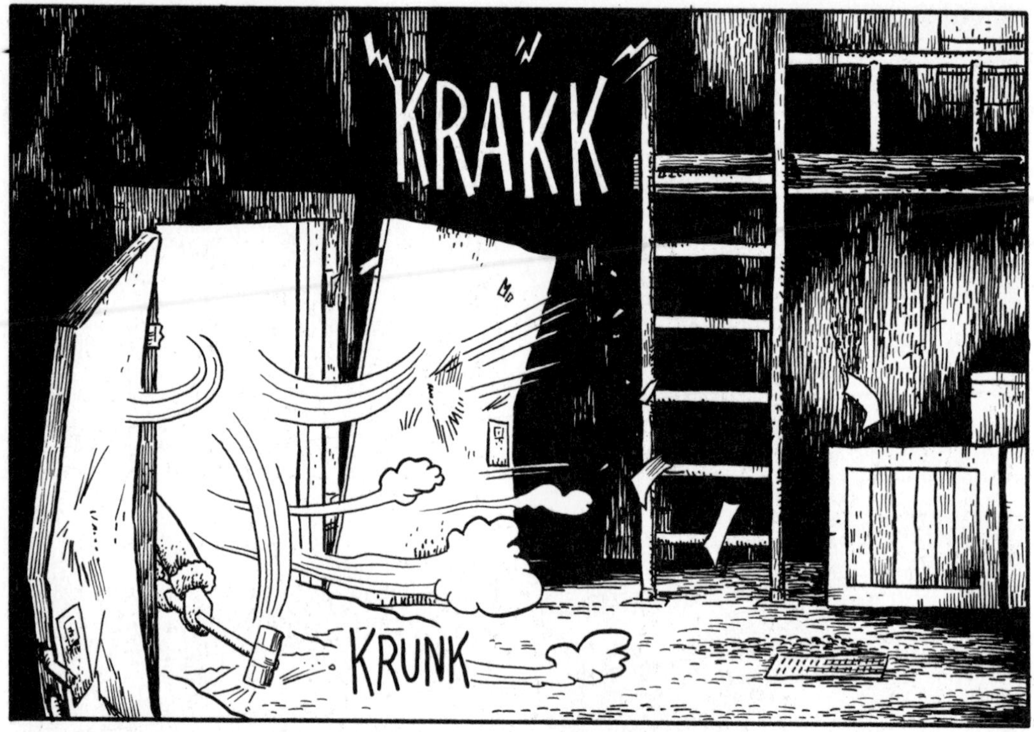
KRAKK
KRUNK

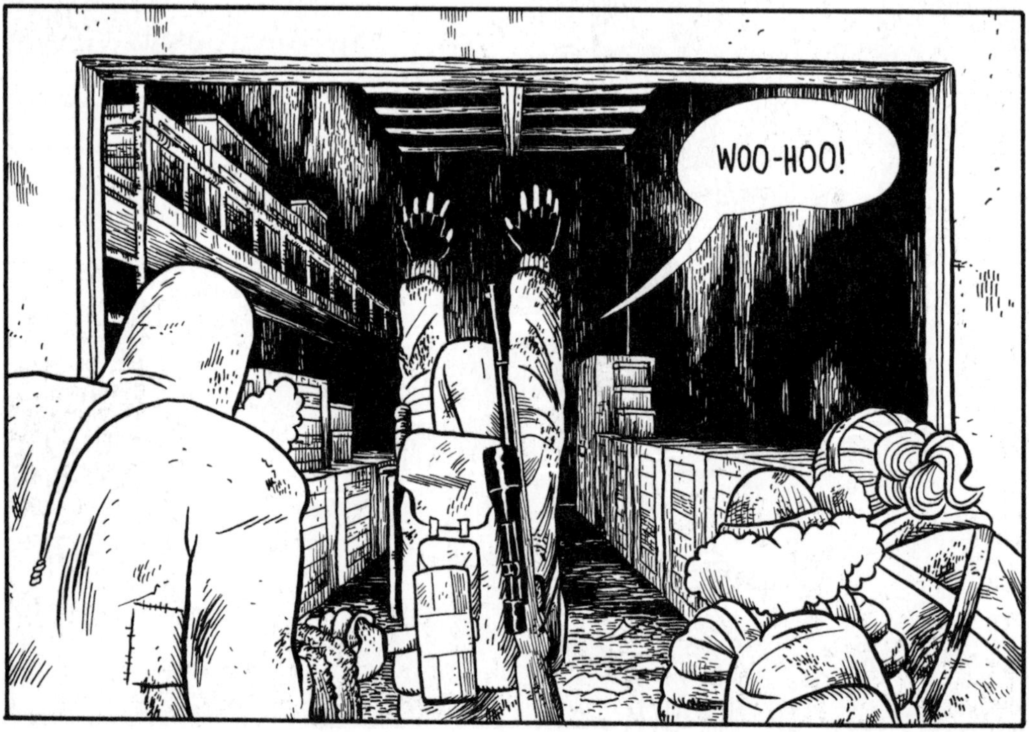
WOO-HOO!

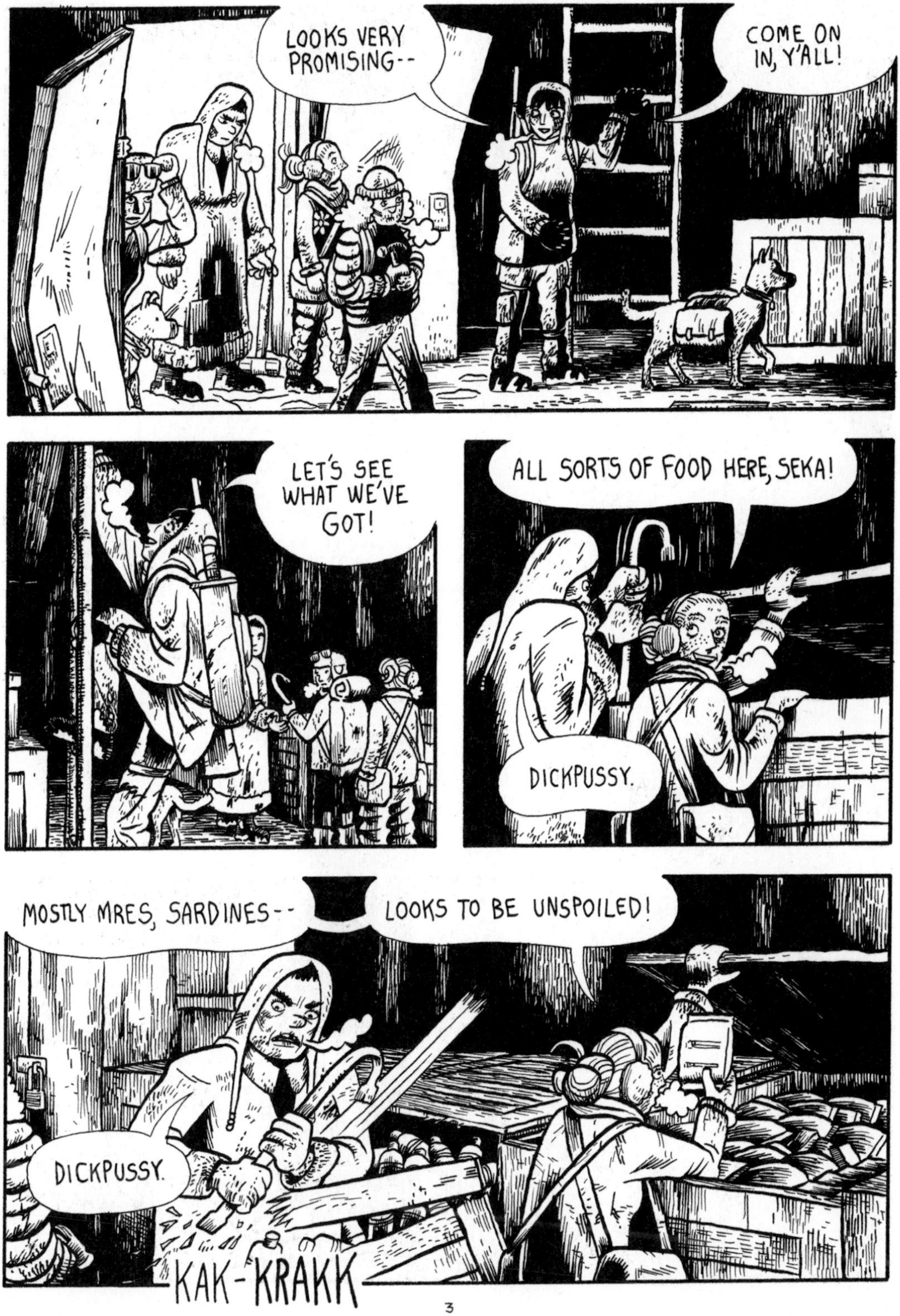

LOOKS VERY PROMISING--
COME ON IN, Y'ALL!
LET'S SEE WHAT WE'VE GOT!
ALL SORTS OF FOOD HERE, SEKA!
DICKPUSSY.
MOSTLY MRES, SARDINES--
LOOKS TO BE UNSPOILED!
DICKPUSSY.
KAK-KRAKK

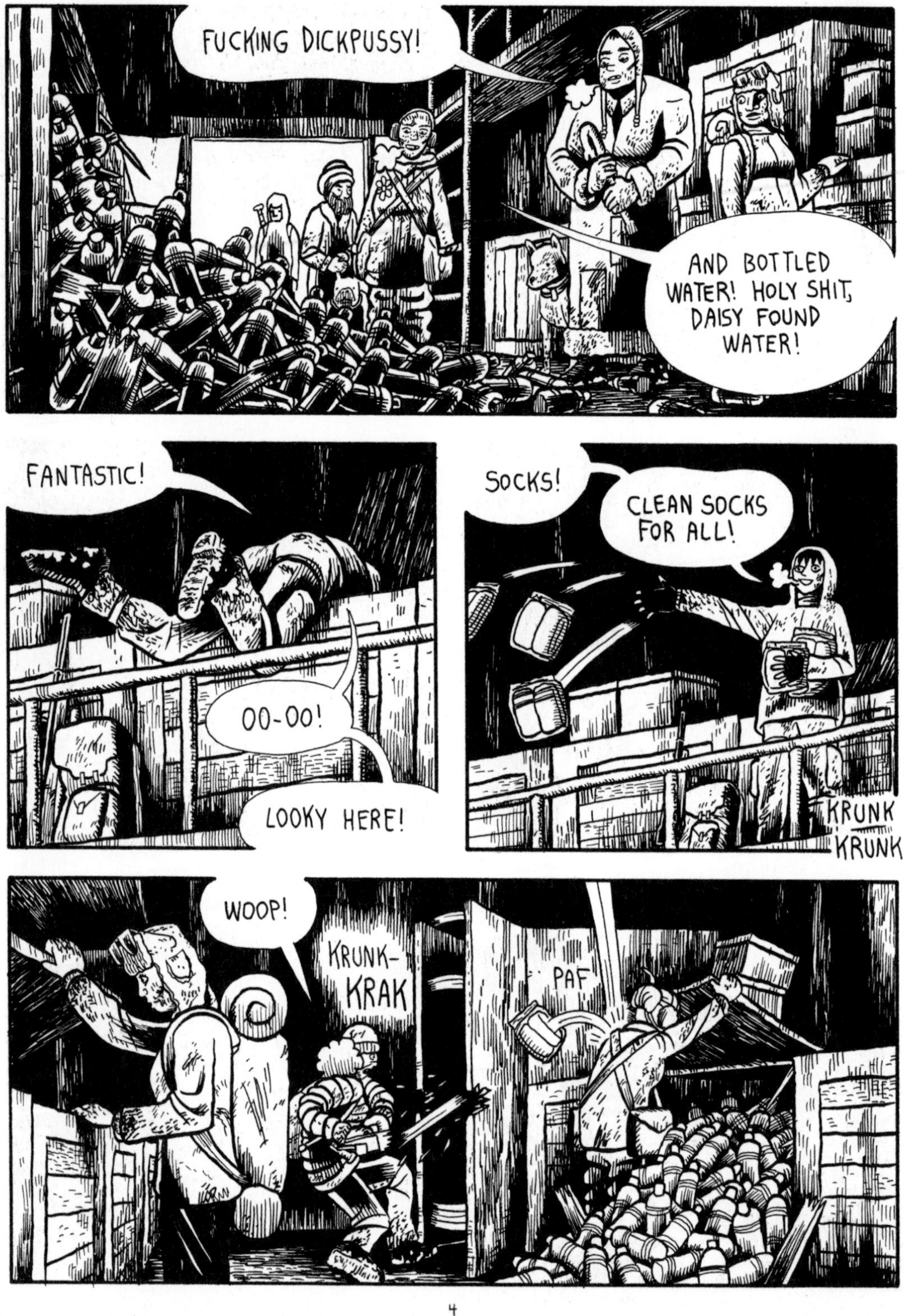
FUCKING DICKPUSSY!
AND BOTTLED WATER! HOLY SHIT, DAISY FOUND WATER!
FANTASTIC!
OO-OO!
LOOKY HERE!
SOCKS!
CLEAN SOCKS FOR ALL!
KRUNK
KRUNK
WOOP!
KRUNK-KRAK
PAF

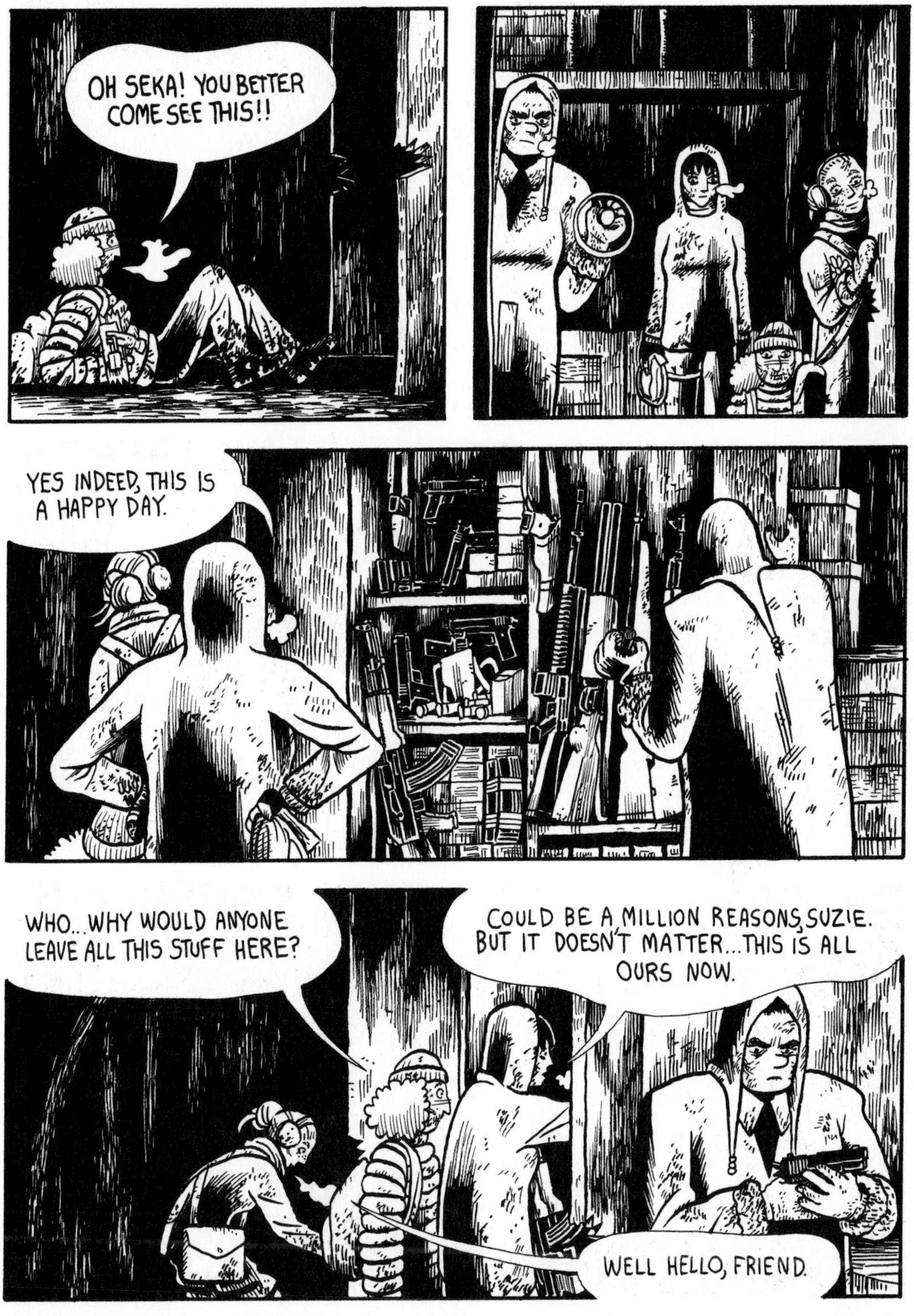
OH SEKA! YOU BETTER COME SEE THIS!!
YES INDEED, THIS IS A HAPPY DAY.
WHO...WHY WOULD ANYONE LEAVE ALL THIS STUFF HERE?
COULD BE A MILLION REASONS, SUZIE. BUT IT DOESN'T MATTER...THIS IS ALL OURS NOW.
WELL HELLO, FRIEND.

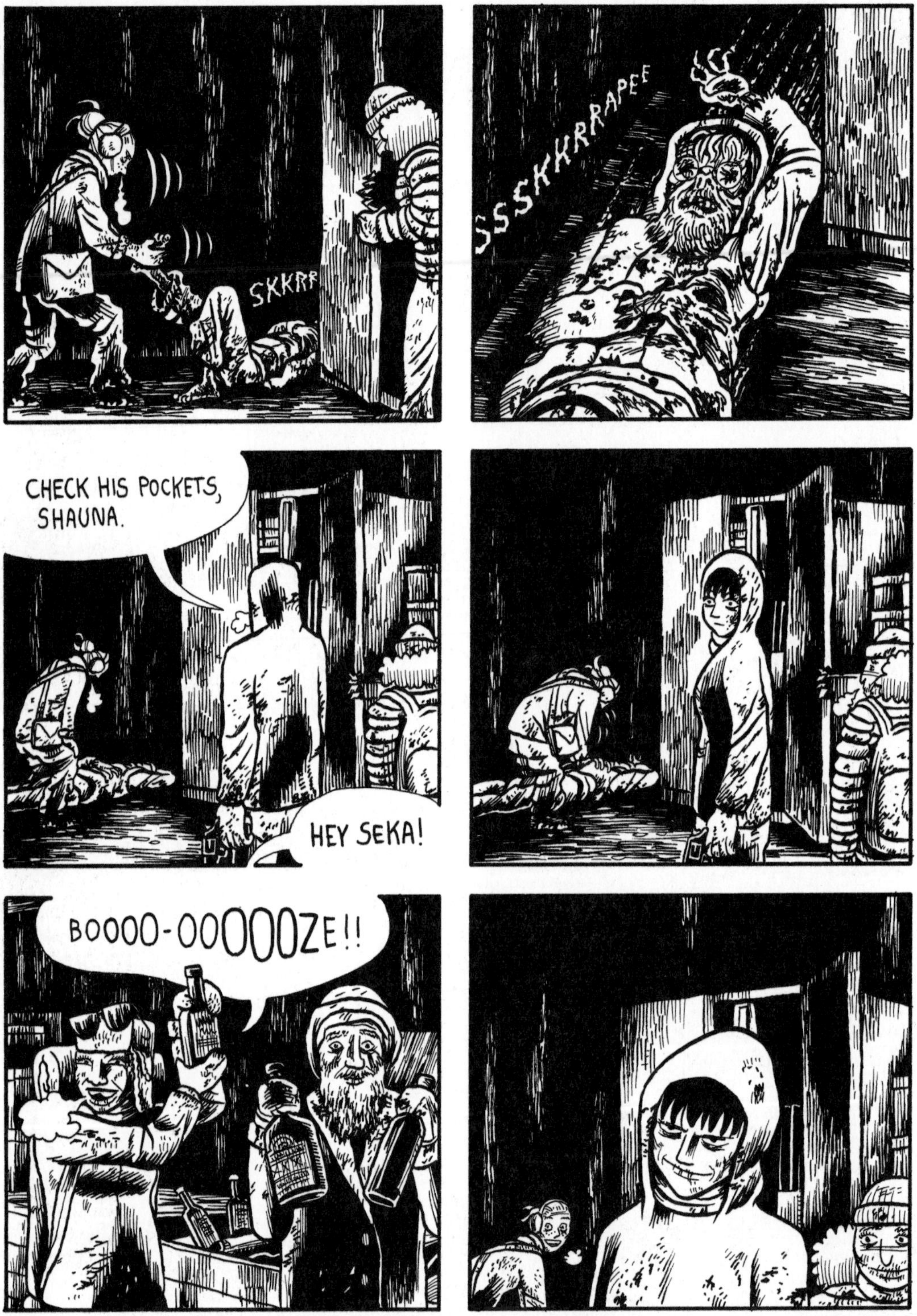
SKKRR
SSSKKRRAPEE
CHECK HIS POCKETS, SHAUNA.
HEY SEKA!
BOOOO-OOOOOZE!!

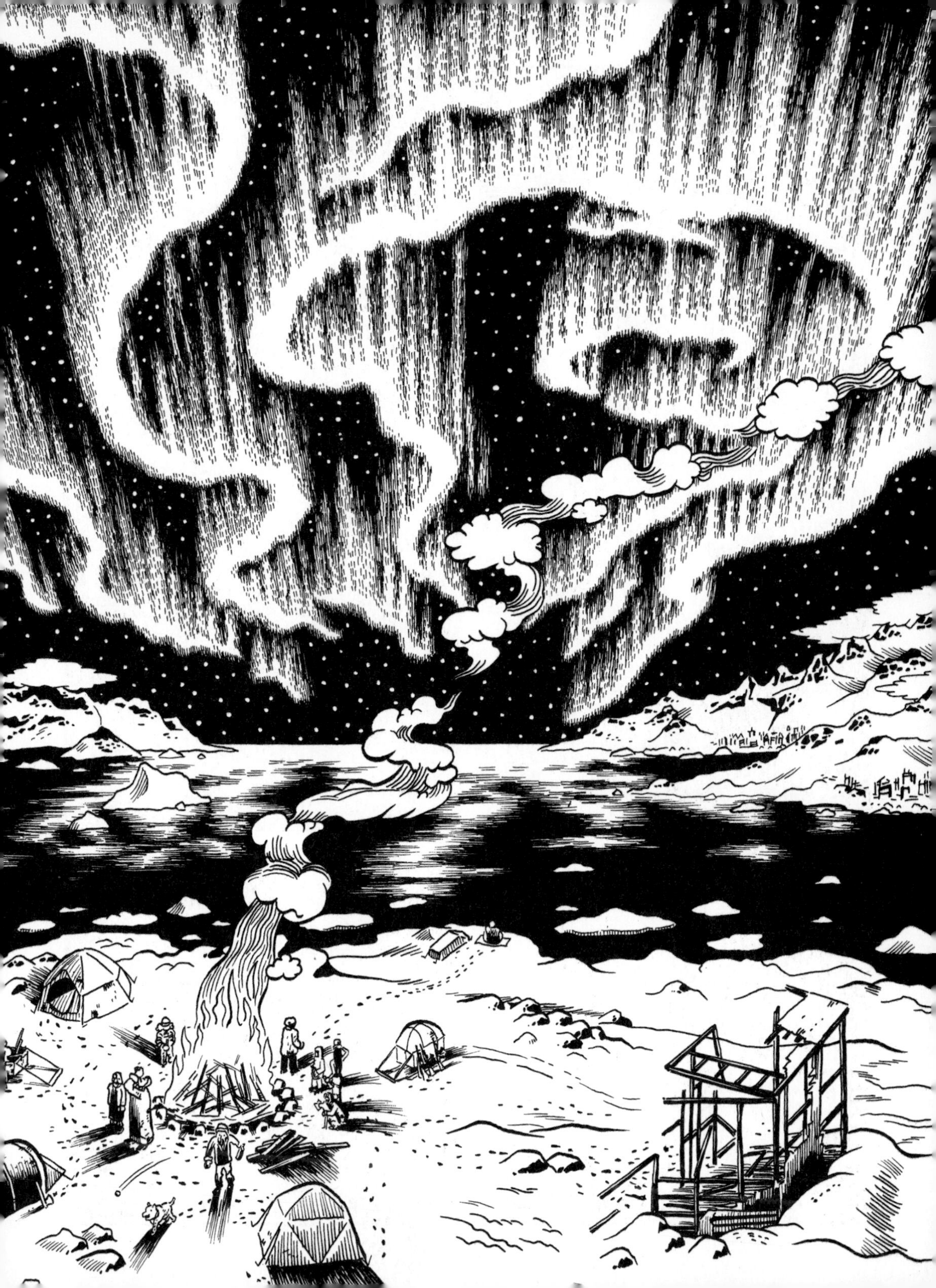

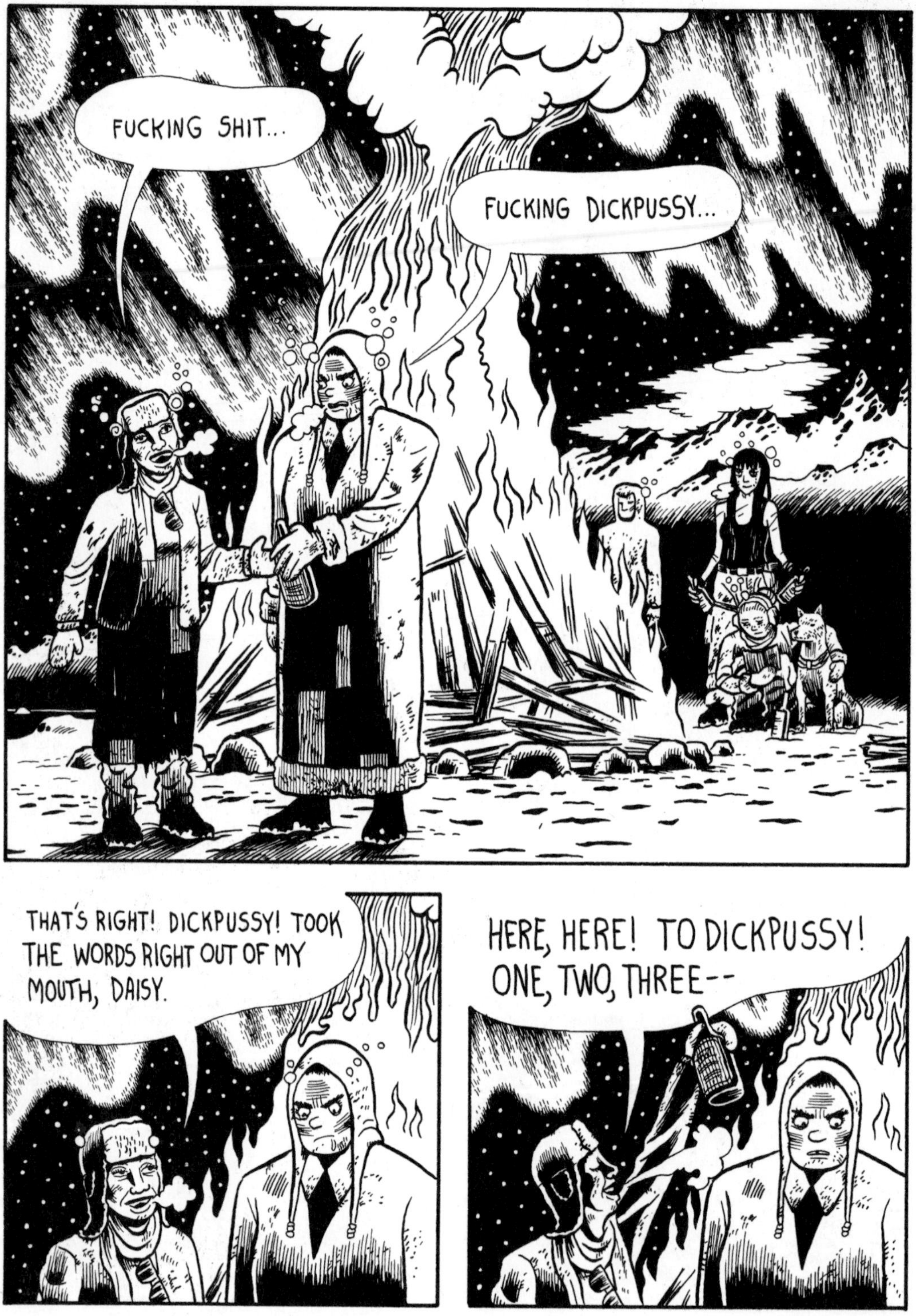
FUCKING SHIT...
FUCKING DICKPUSSY...
THAT'S RIGHT! DICKPUSSY! TOOK THE WORDS RIGHT OUT OF MY MOUTH, DAISY.
HERE, HERE! TO DICKPUSSY! ONE, TWO, THREE--

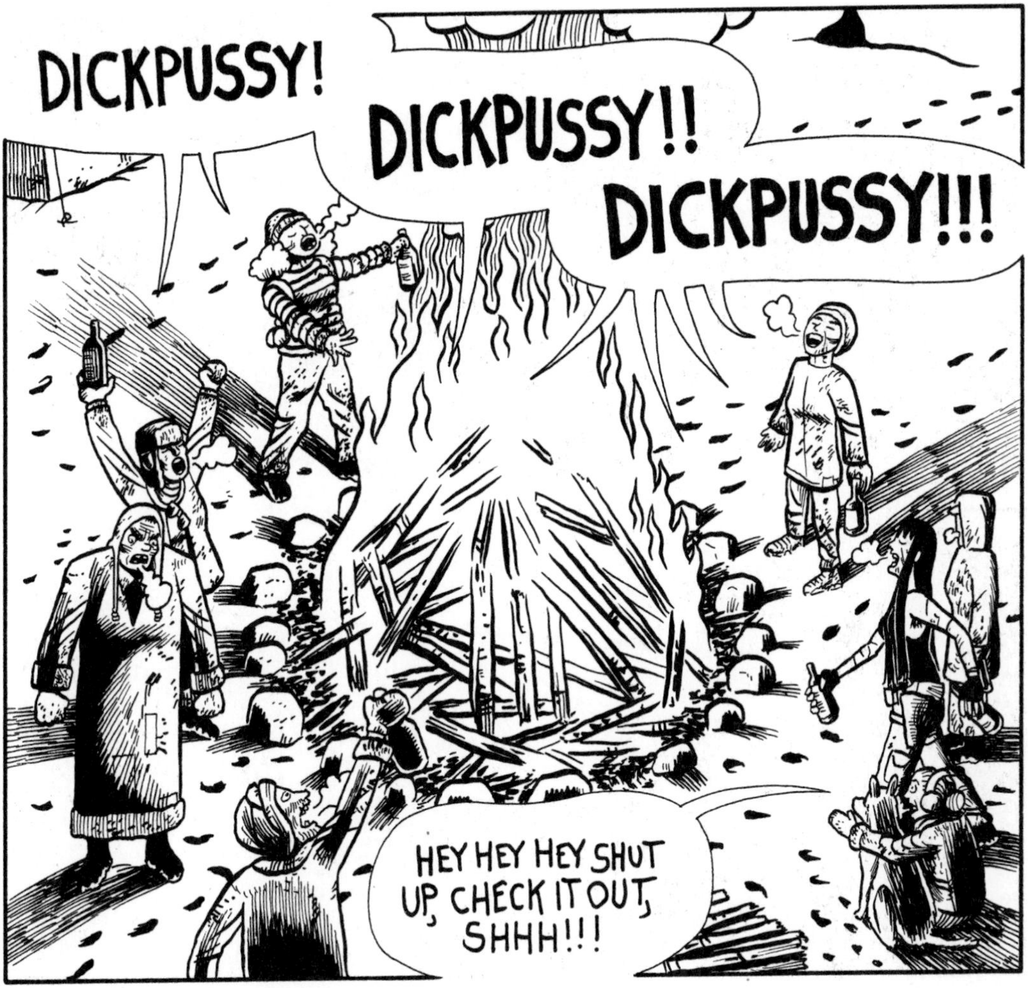
DICKPUSSY!
DICKPUSSY!!
DICKPUSSY!!!
HEY HEY HEY SHUT UP, CHECK IT OUT, SHHH!!!

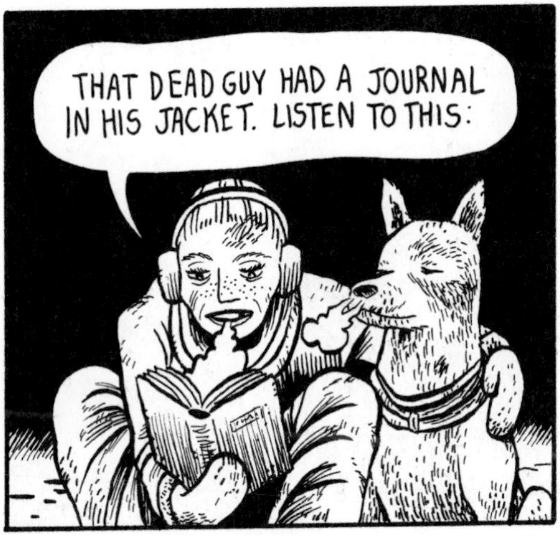
THAT DEAD GUY HAD A JOURNAL IN HIS JACKET. LISTEN TO THIS:

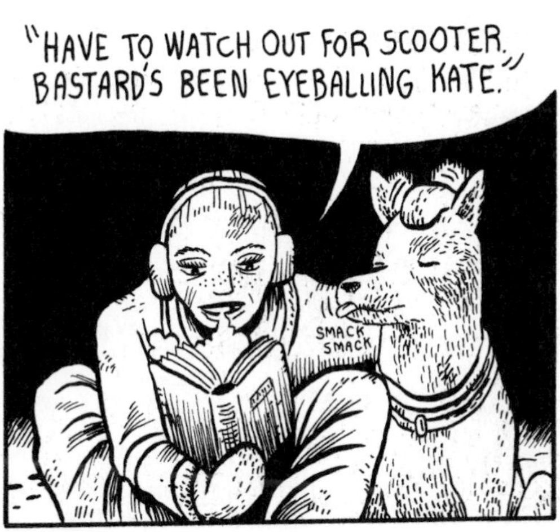
"HAVE TO WATCH OUT FOR SCOOTER. BASTARD'S BEEN EYEBALLING KATE."
SMACK SMACK

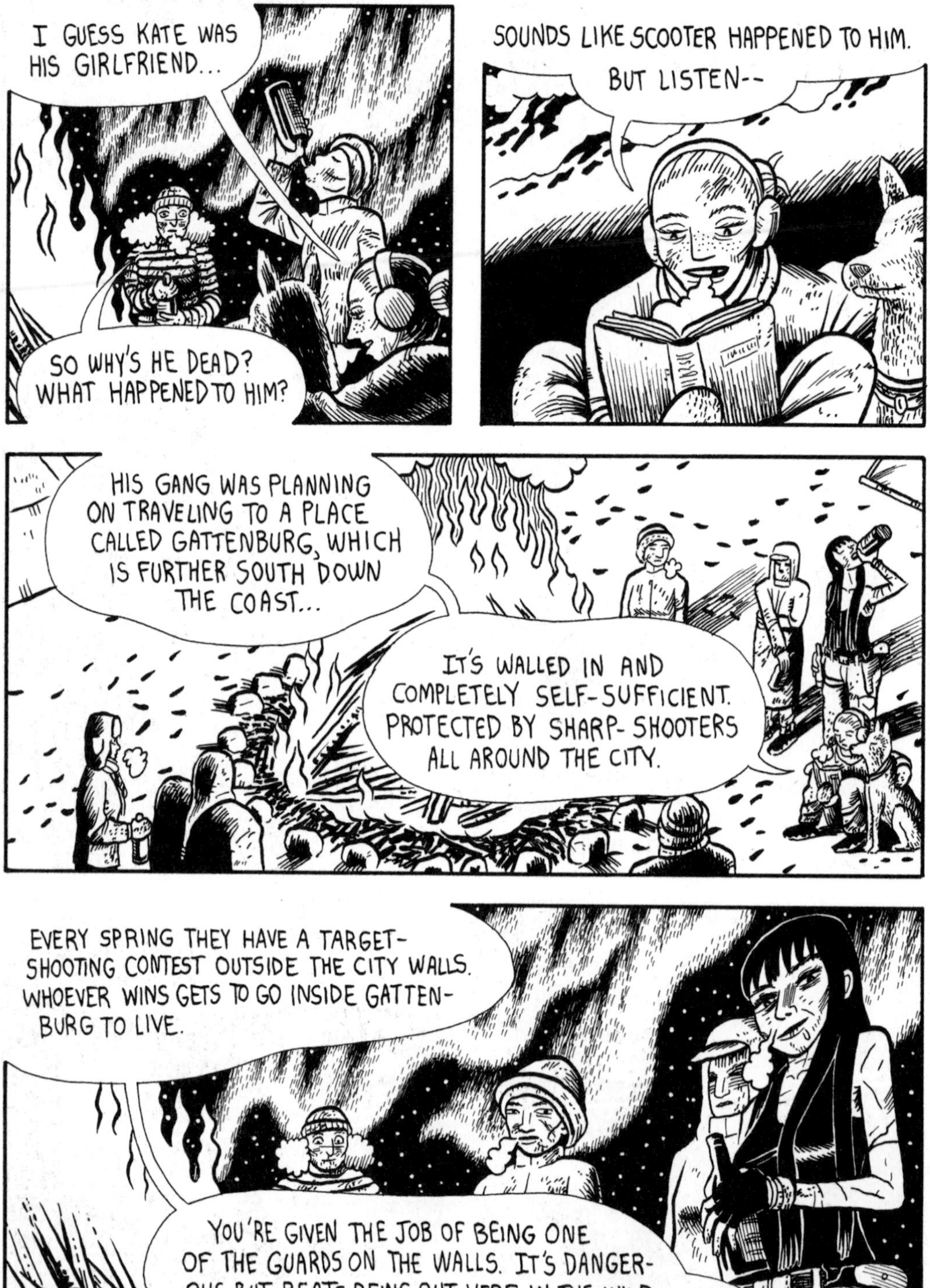
I GUESS KATE WAS HIS GIRLFRIEND...
SO WHY'S HE DEAD? WHAT HAPPENED TO HIM?
SOUNDS LIKE SCOOTER HAPPENED TO HIM.
BUT LISTEN--
HIS GANG WAS PLANNING ON TRAVELING TO A PLACE CALLED GATTENBURG, WHICH IS FURTHER SOUTH DOWN THE COAST...
IT'S WALLED IN AND COMPLETELY SELF-SUFFICIENT. PROTECTED BY SHARP-SHOOTERS ALL AROUND THE CITY.
EVERY SPRING THEY HAVE A TARGET-SHOOTING CONTEST OUTSIDE THE CITY WALLS. WHOEVER WINS GETS TO GO INSIDE GATTEN-BURG TO LIVE.
YOU'RE GIVEN THE JOB OF BEING ONE OF THE GUARDS ON THE WALLS. IT'S DANGER-OUS, BUT BEATS BEING OUT HERE IN THE WILD.

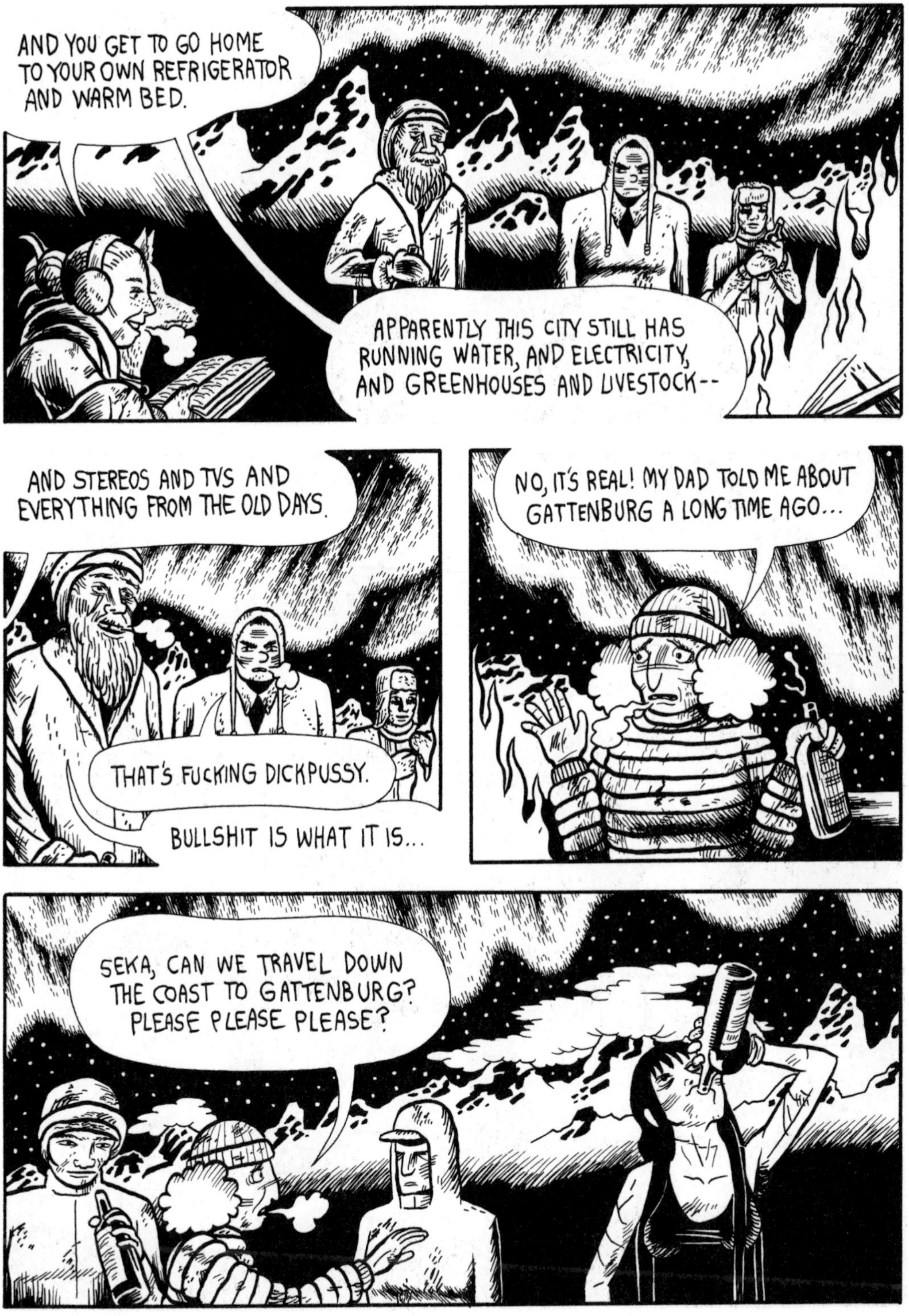

AND YOU GET TO GO HOME TO YOUR OWN REFRIGERATOR AND WARM BED.
APPARENTLY THIS CITY STILL HAS RUNNING WATER, AND ELECTRICITY, AND GREENHOUSES AND LIVESTOCK--
AND STEREOS AND TVS AND EVERYTHING FROM THE OLD DAYS.
THAT'S FUCKING DICKPUSSY.
BULLSHIT IS WHAT IT IS...
NO, IT'S REAL! MY DAD TOLD ME ABOUT GATTENBURG A LONG TIME AGO...
SEKA, CAN WE TRAVEL DOWN THE COAST TO GATTENBURG? PLEASE PLEASE PLEASE?

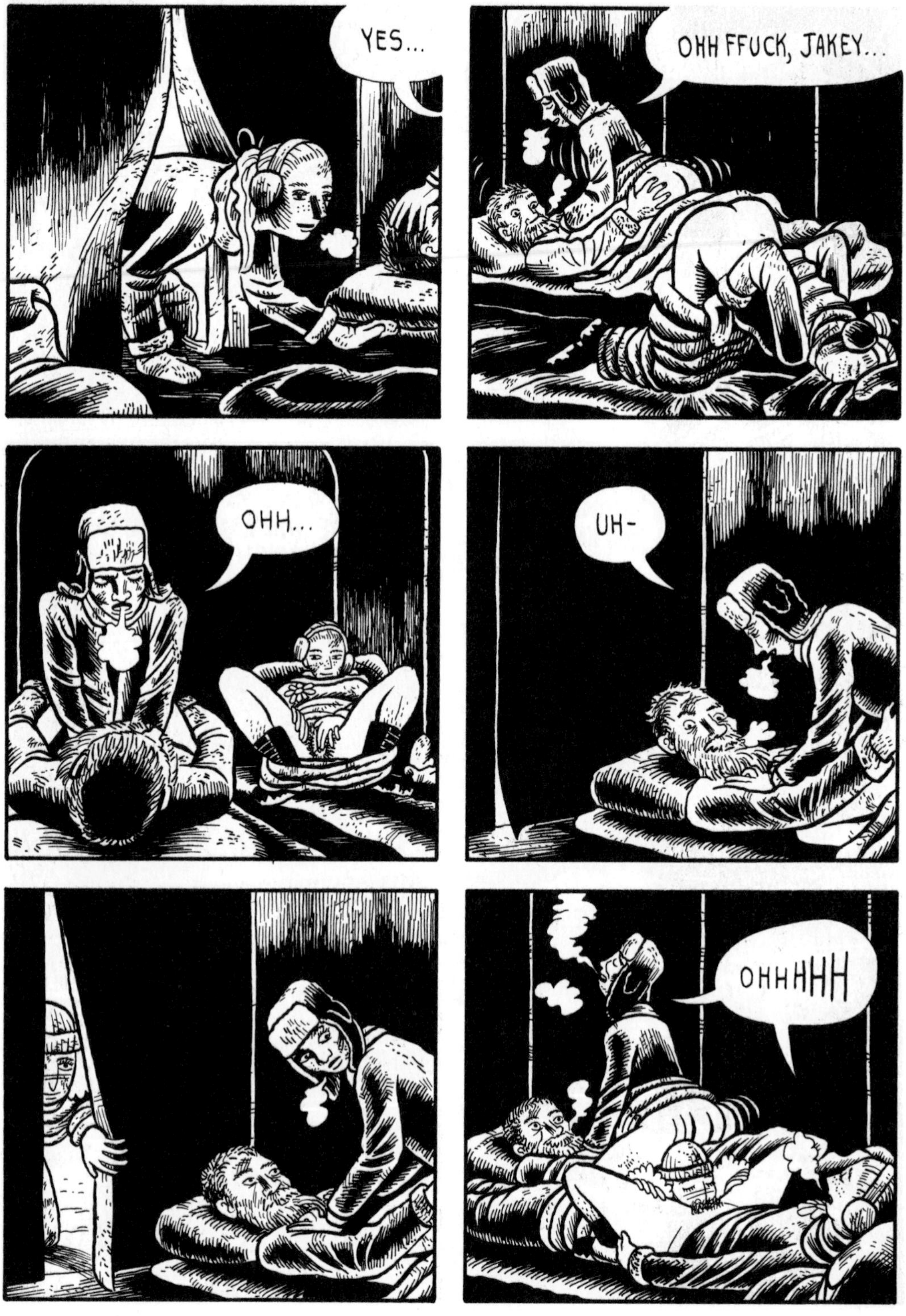
YES...
OHH FFUCK, JAKEY...
OHH...
UH-
OHHHHH

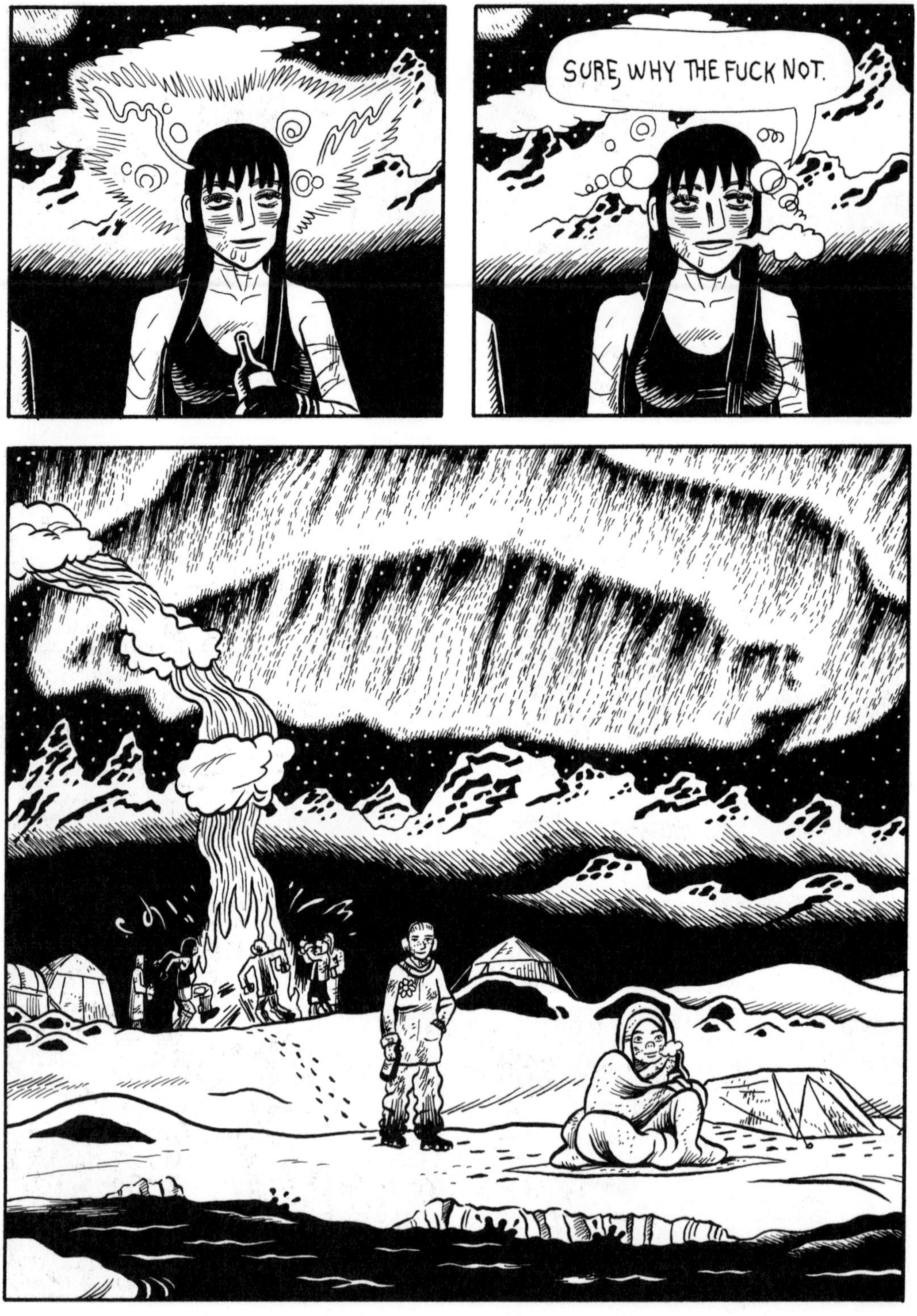
SURE, WHY THE FUCK NOT.

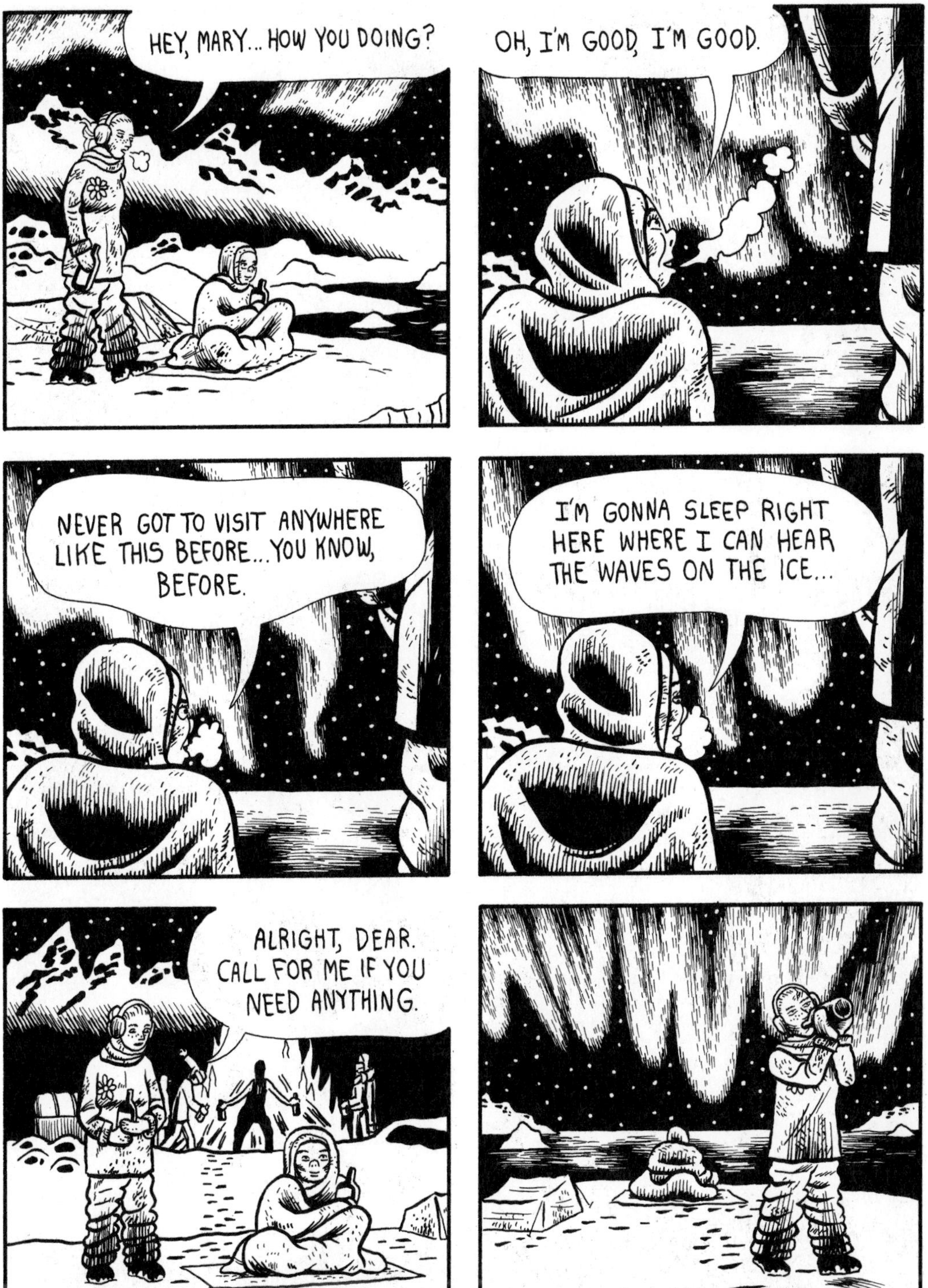
HEY, MARY... HOW YOU DOING?
OH, I'M GOOD, I'M GOOD.
NEVER GOT TO VISIT ANYWHERE LIKE THIS BEFORE... YOU KNOW, BEFORE.
I'M GONNA SLEEP RIGHT HERE WHERE I CAN HEAR THE WAVES ON THE ICE...
ALRIGHT, DEAR. CALL FOR ME IF YOU NEED ANYTHING.

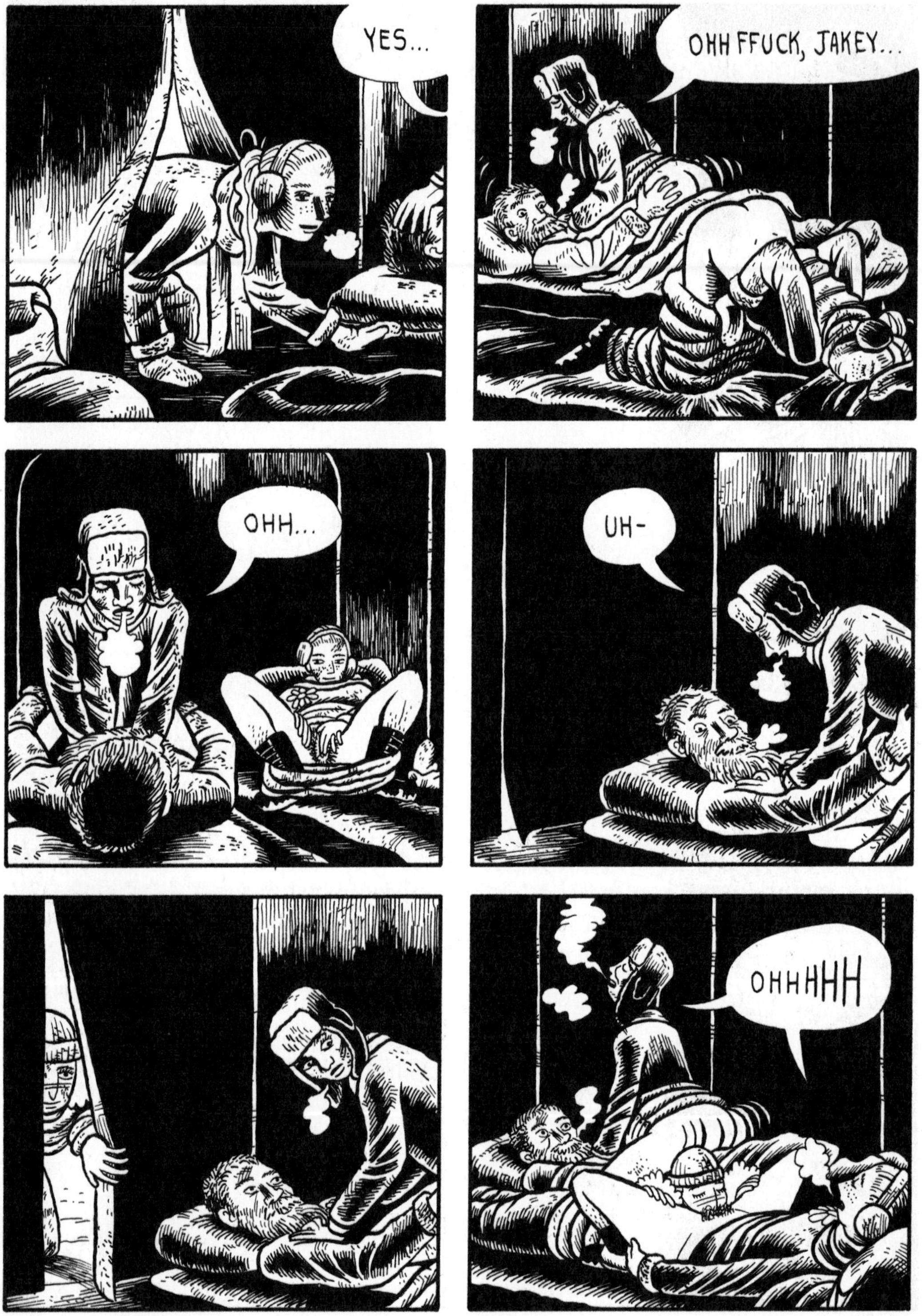
YES...
OHH FFUCK, JAKEY...
OHH...
UH-
OHHHHH

CK-
CRK-
CUK-
CRAK
HUH? WUZZAT?
JUS' ICE SETTLIN'... DON' WORRY, SUZIE...

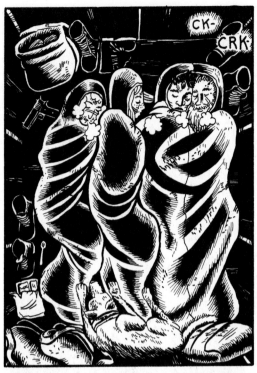

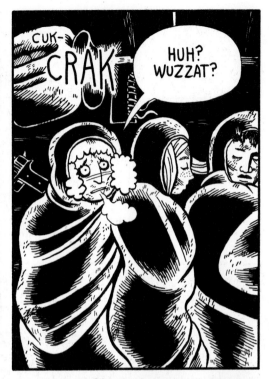

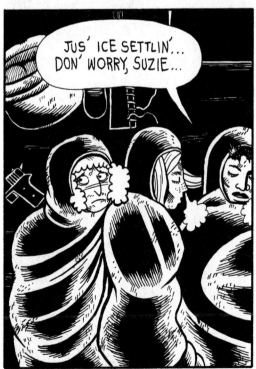

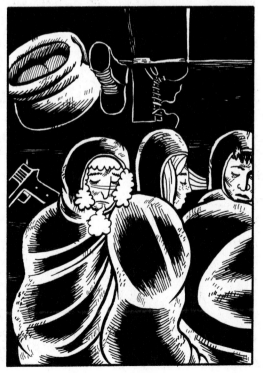

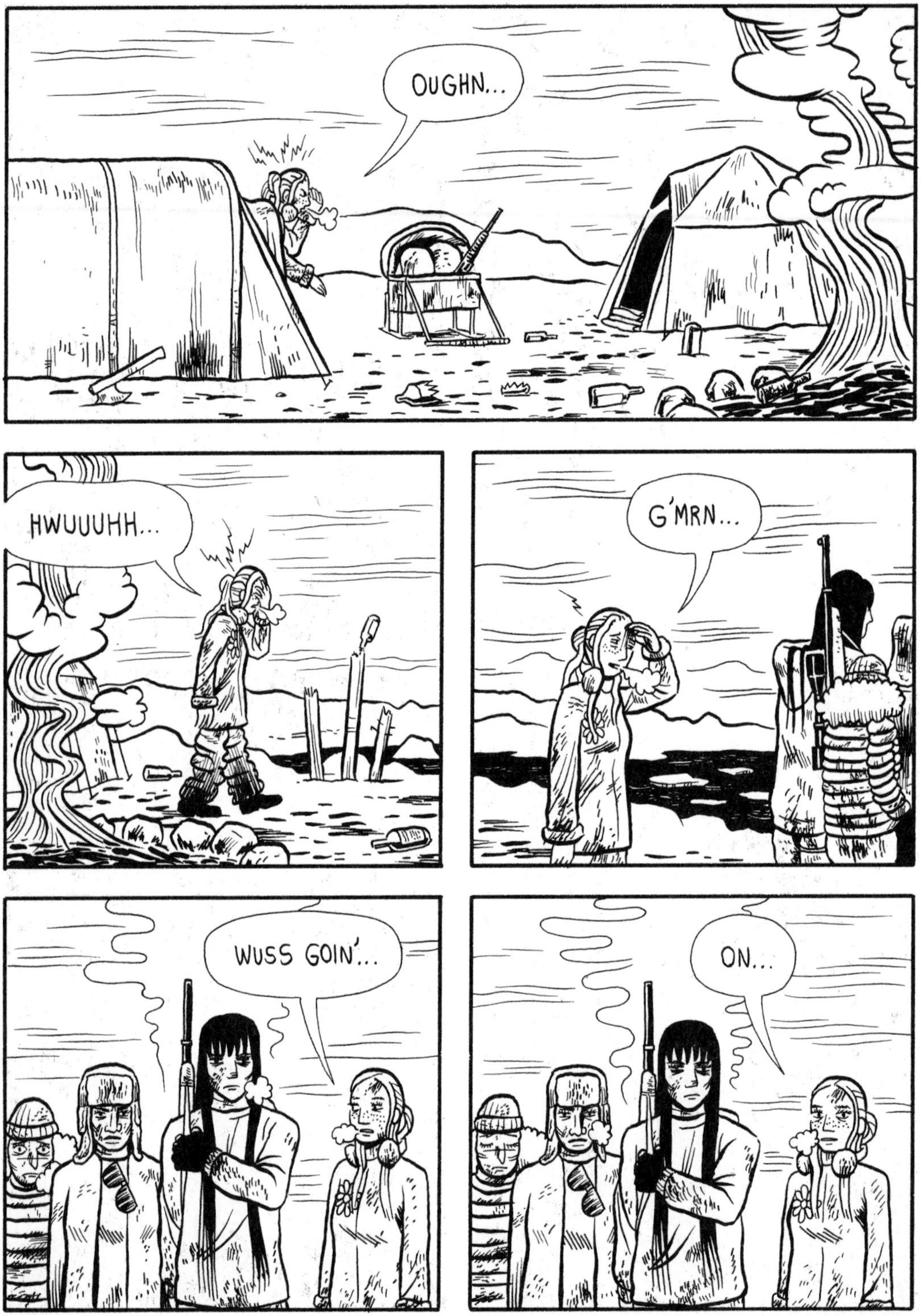
OUGHN...
HWUUUHH...
G'MRN...
WUSS GOIN'...
ON...

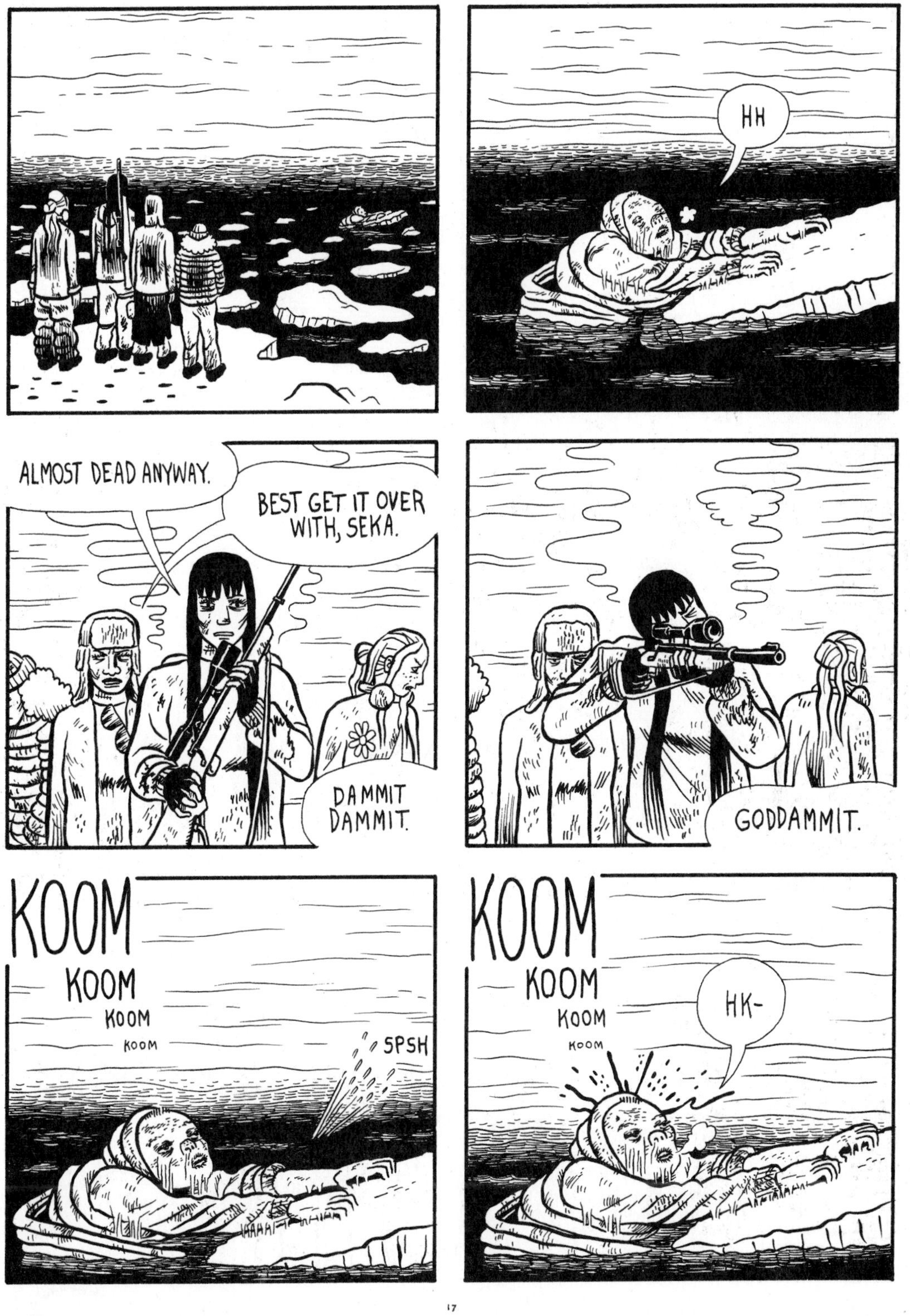
HH
ALMOST DEAD ANYWAY.
BEST GET IT OVER WITH, SEKA.
DAMMIT DAMMIT.
GODDAMMIT.
KOOM
KOOM
KOOM
KOOM
SPSH
KOOM
KOOM
KOOM
KOOM
HK-

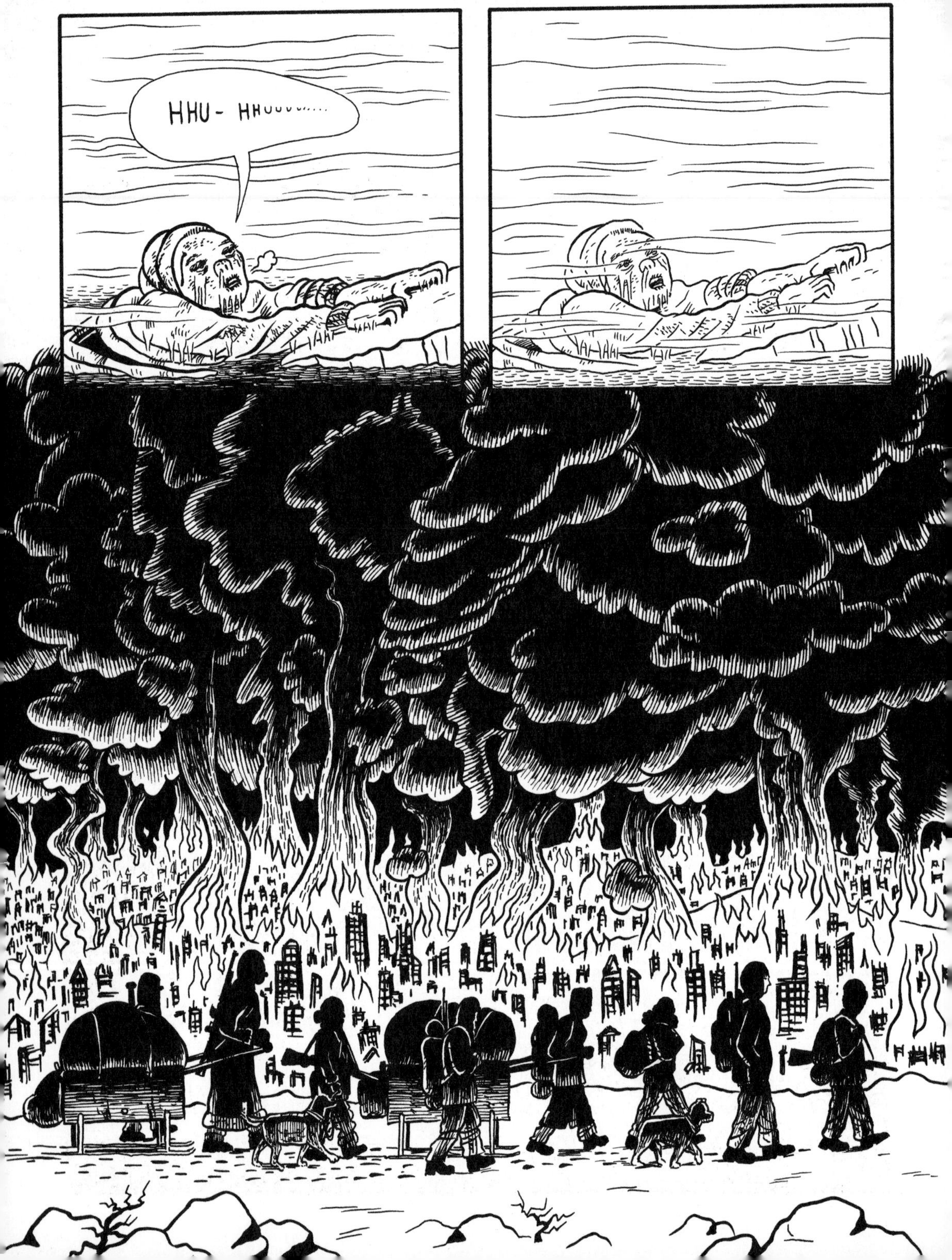
HHU- HHUUUU.....

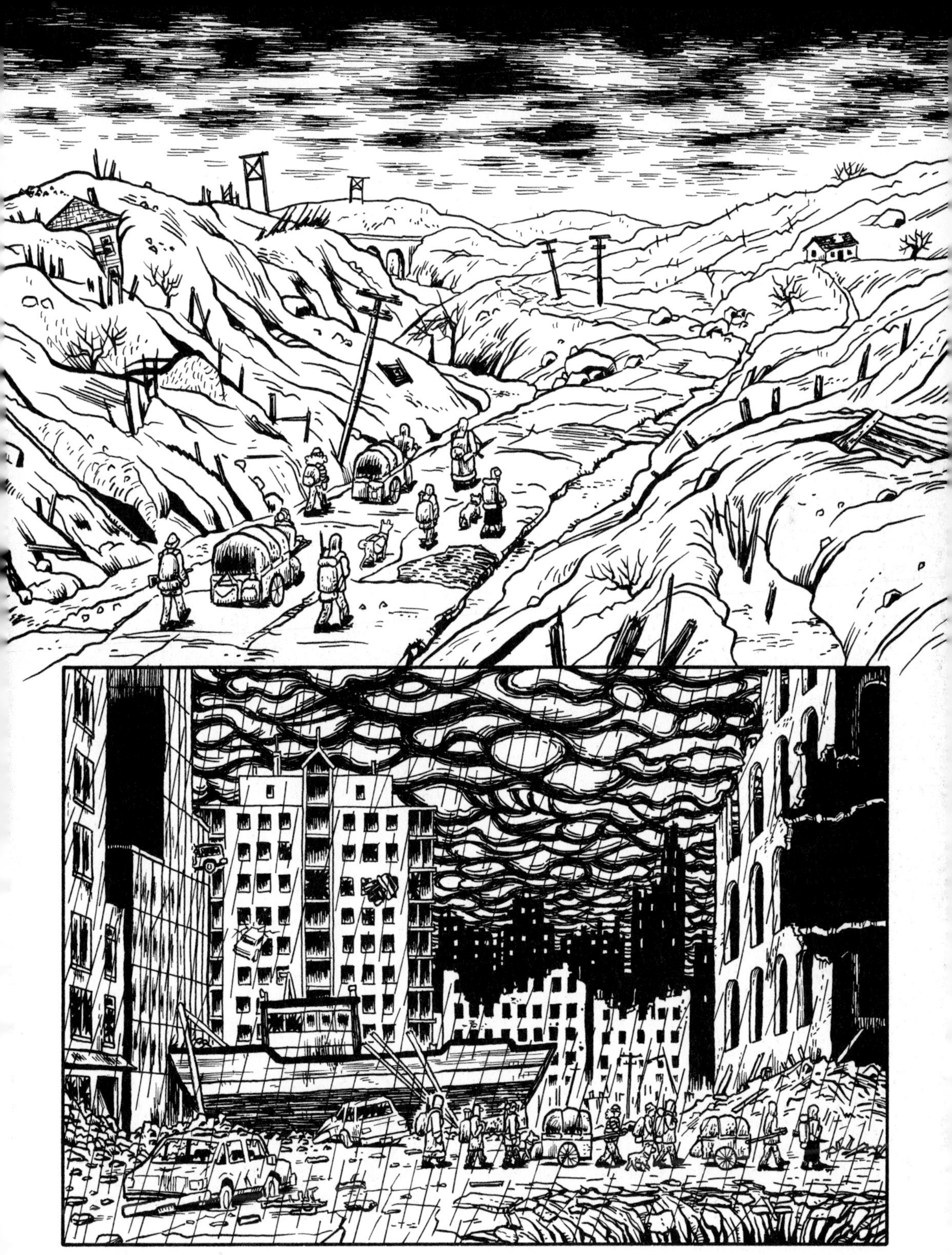

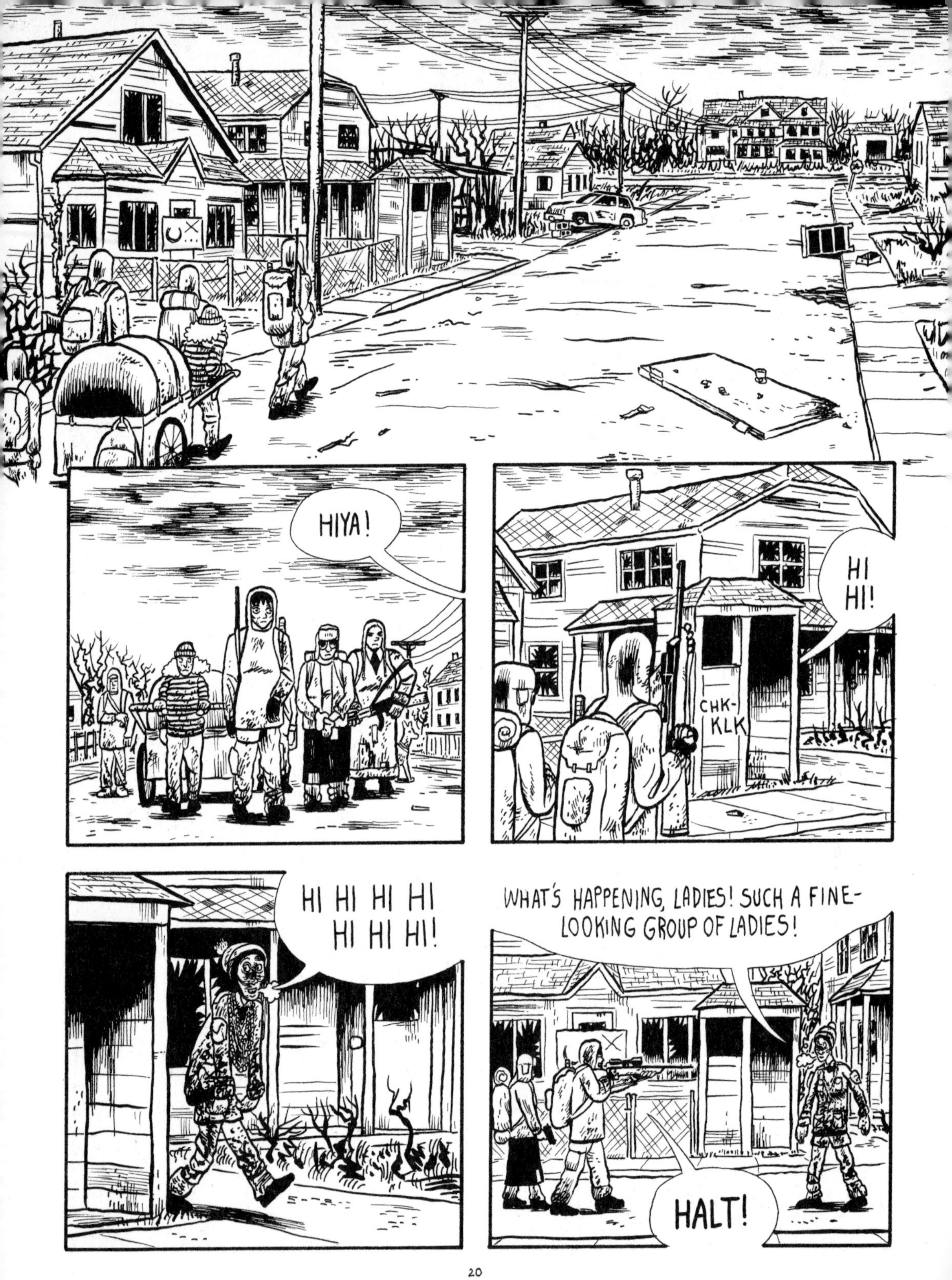
HIYA!
HI HI!
CHK-KLK
HI HI HI HI HI HI HI!
WHAT'S HAPPENING, LADIES! SUCH A FINE-LOOKING GROUP OF LADIES!
HALT!

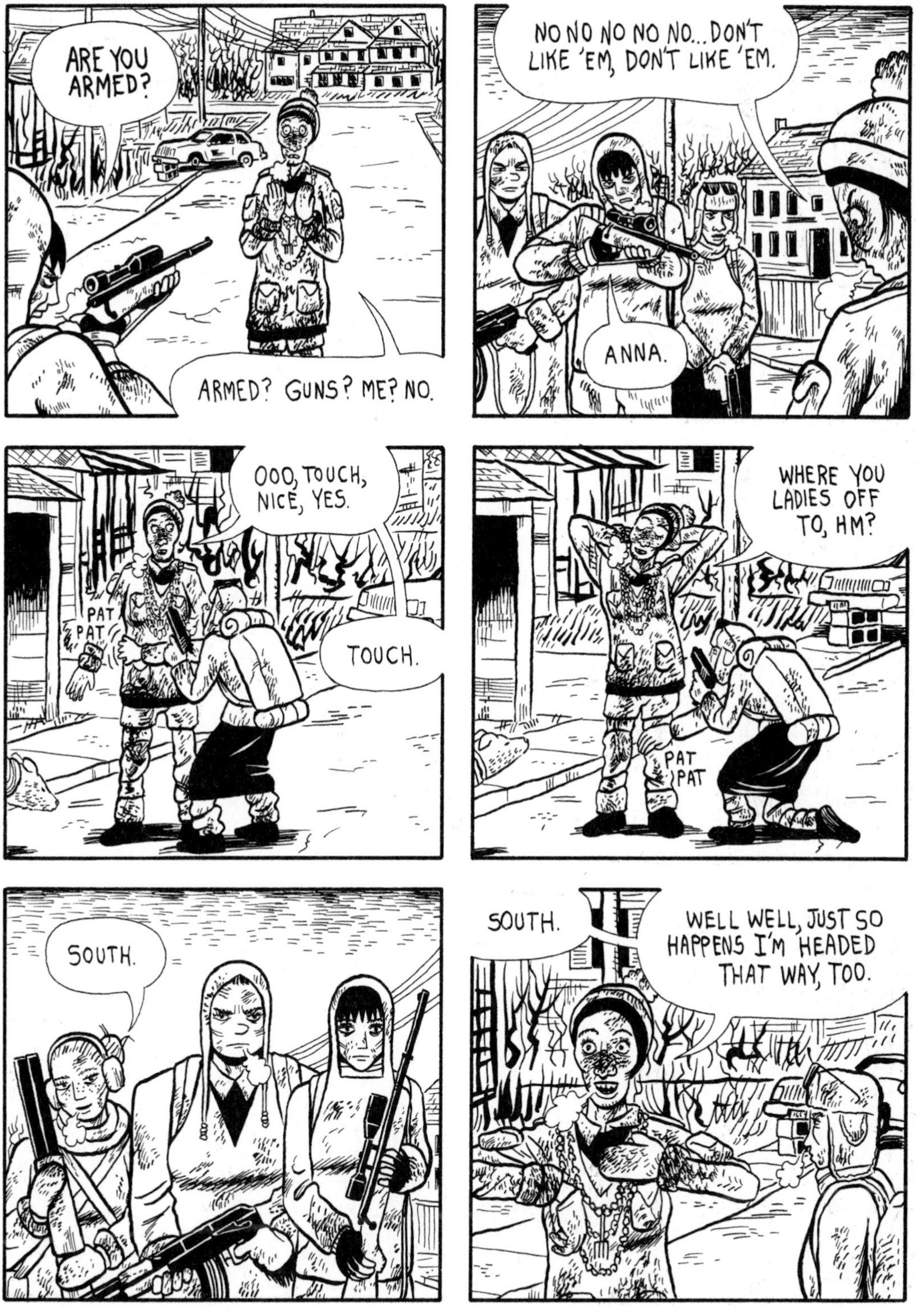
ARE YOU ARMED?
ARMED? GUNS? ME? NO.
NO NO NO NO NO... DON'T LIKE 'EM, DON'T LIKE 'EM.
ANNA.
OOO, TOUCH, NICE, YES.
PAT PAT
TOUCH.
WHERE YOU LADIES OFF TO, HM?
PAT PAT
SOUTH.
SOUTH.
WELL WELL, JUST SO HAPPENS I'M HEADED THAT WAY, TOO.

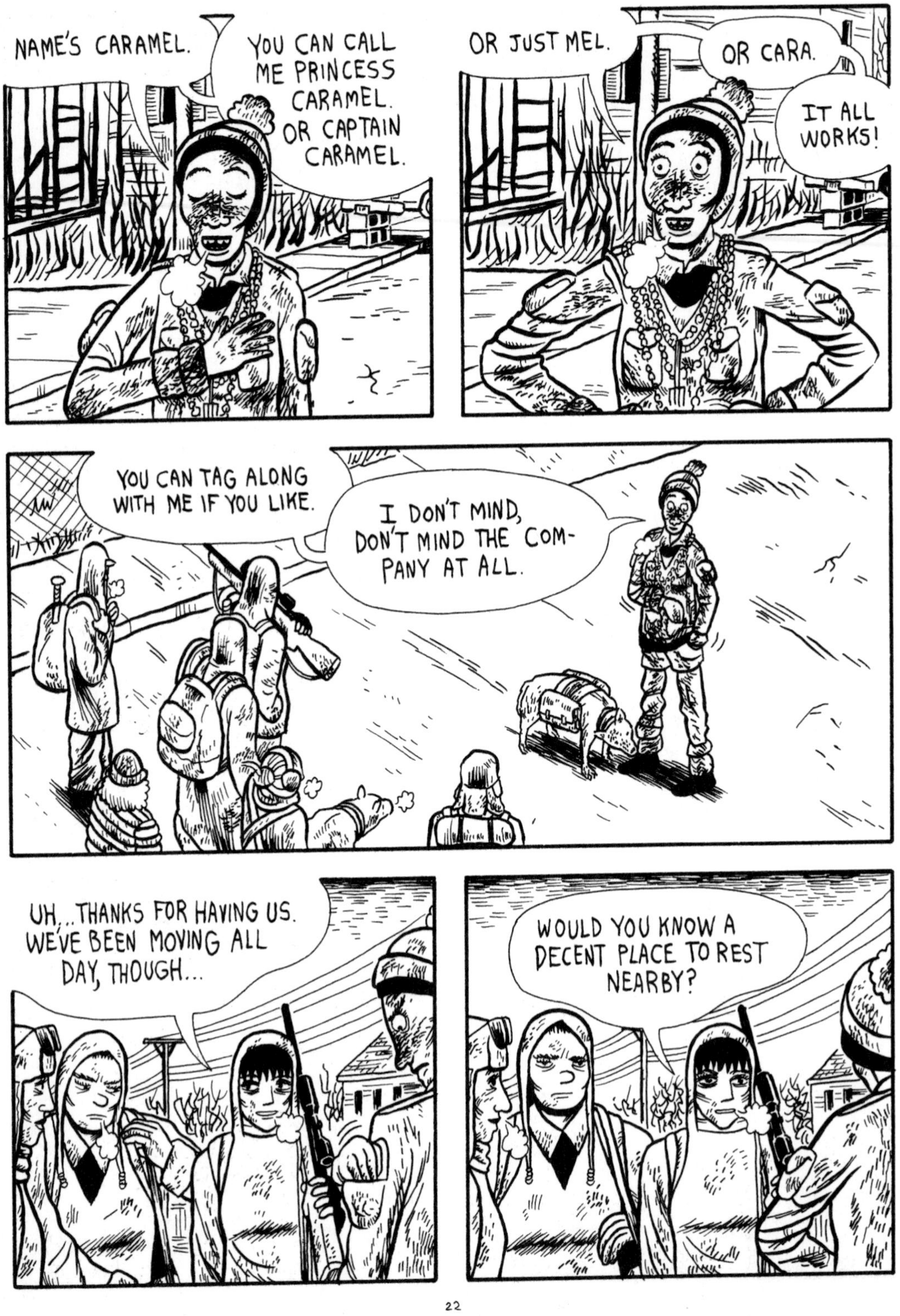
NAME'S CARAMEL.
YOU CAN CALL ME PRINCESS CARAMEL. OR CAPTAIN CARAMEL.
OR JUST MEL.
OR CARA.
IT ALL WORKS!
YOU CAN TAG ALONG WITH ME IF YOU LIKE.
I DON'T MIND, DON'T MIND THE COMPANY AT ALL.
UH...THANKS FOR HAVING US. WE'VE BEEN MOVING ALL DAY, THOUGH...
WOULD YOU KNOW A DECENT PLACE TO REST NEARBY?

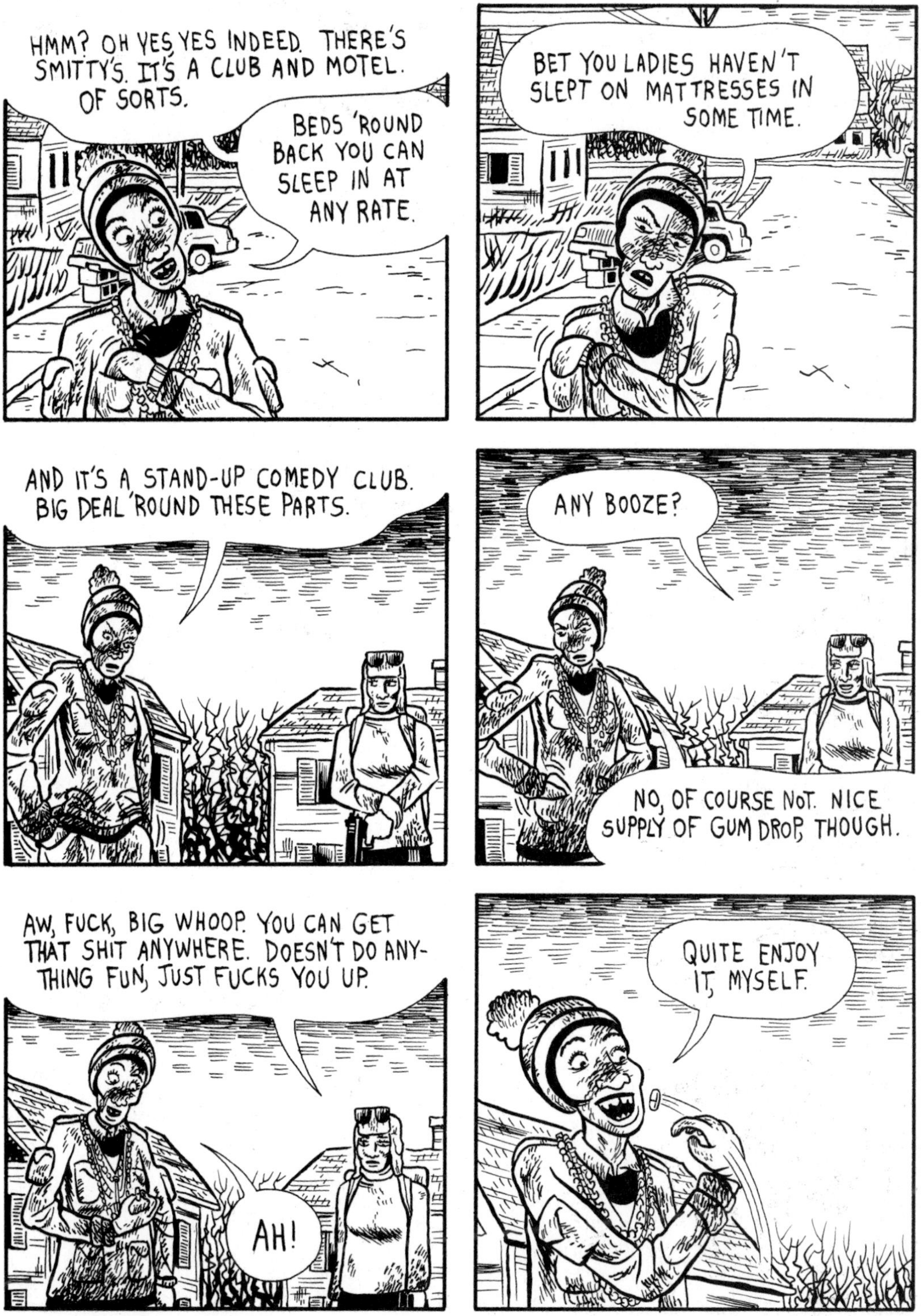
HMM? OH YES, YES INDEED. THERE'S SMITTY'S. IT'S A CLUB AND MOTEL. OF SORTS.
BEDS 'ROUND BACK YOU CAN SLEEP IN AT ANY RATE.
BET YOU LADIES HAVEN'T SLEPT ON MATTRESSES IN SOME TIME.
AND IT'S A STAND-UP COMEDY CLUB. BIG DEAL 'ROUND THESE PARTS.
ANY BOOZE?
NO, OF COURSE NOT. NICE SUPPLY OF GUM DROP, THOUGH.
AW, FUCK, BIG WHOOP. YOU CAN GET THAT SHIT ANYWHERE. DOESN'T DO ANY-THING FUN, JUST FUCKS YOU UP.
AH!
QUITE ENJOY IT, MYSELF.

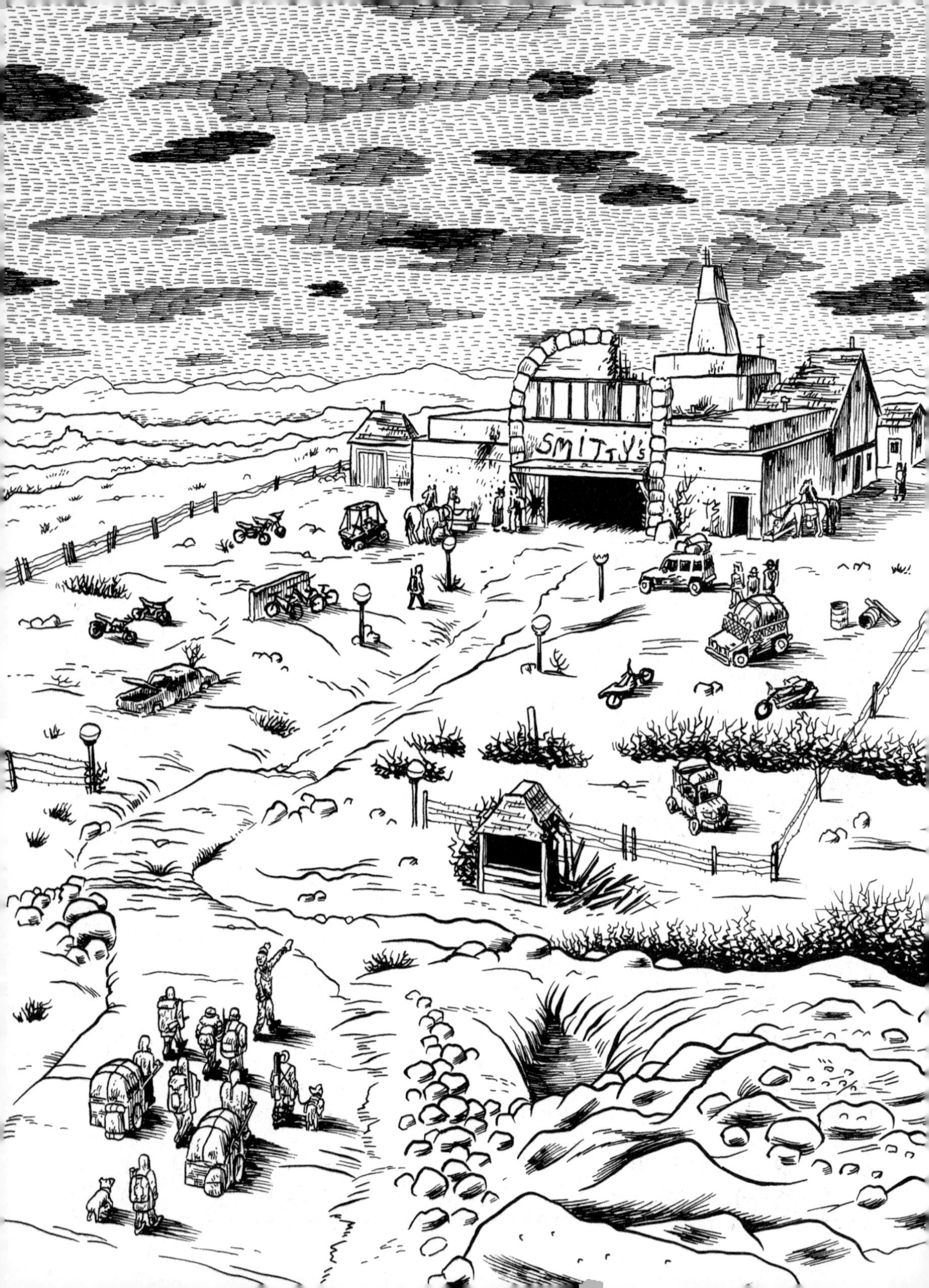
SMITTY'S

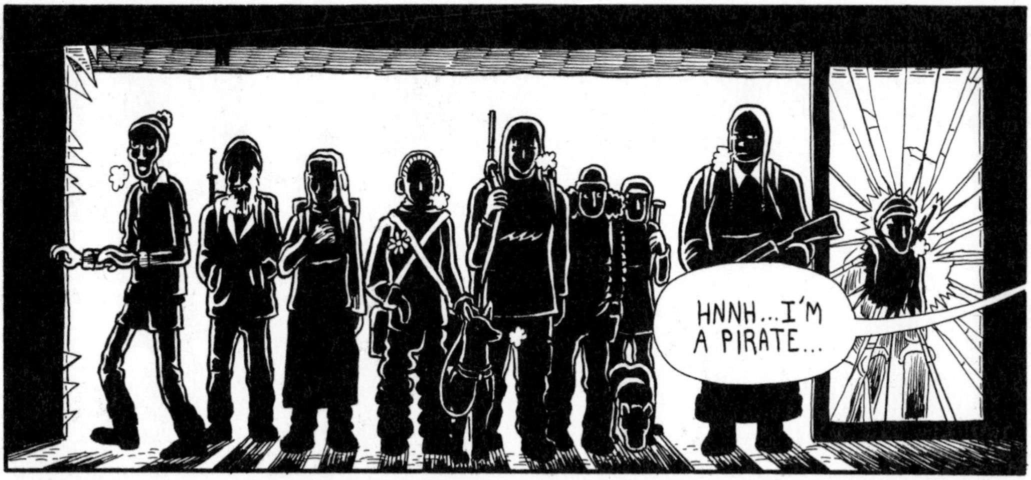
HNNH...I'M A PIRATE...

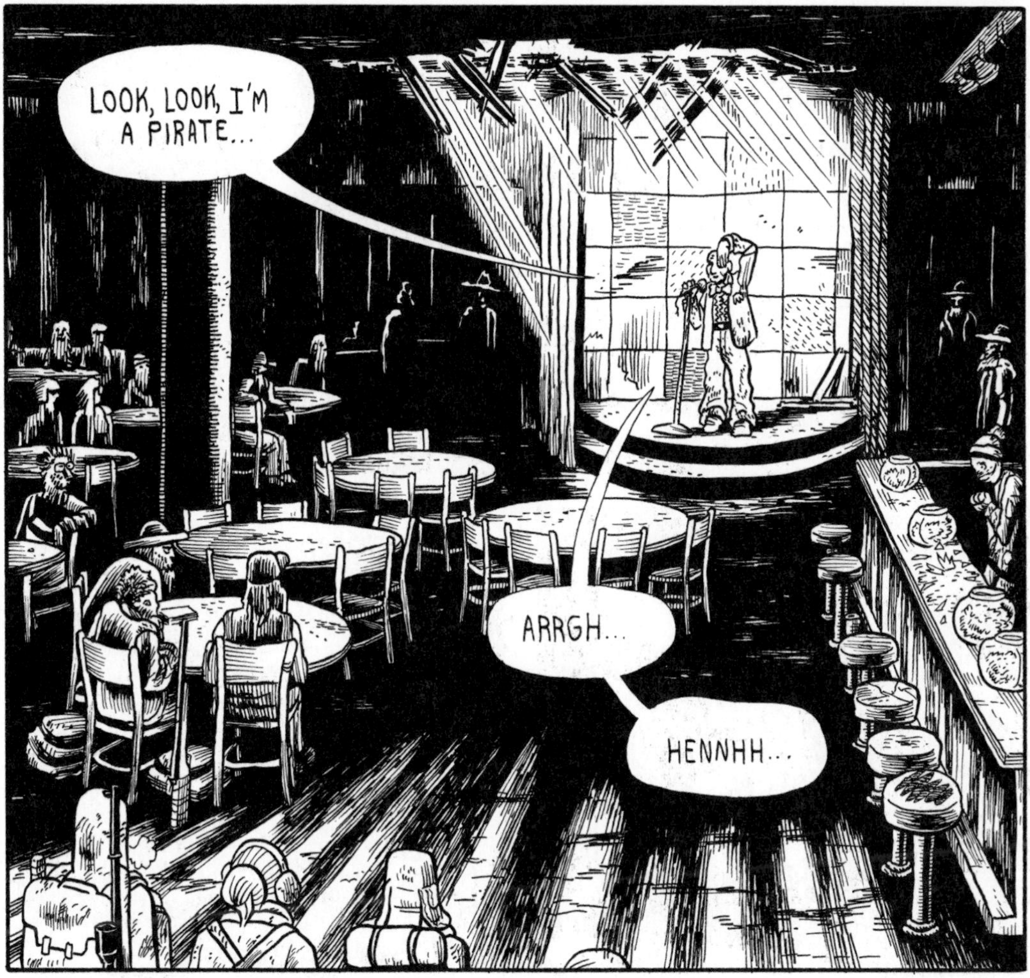
LOOK, LOOK, I'M A PIRATE...
ARRGH...
HENNHH...

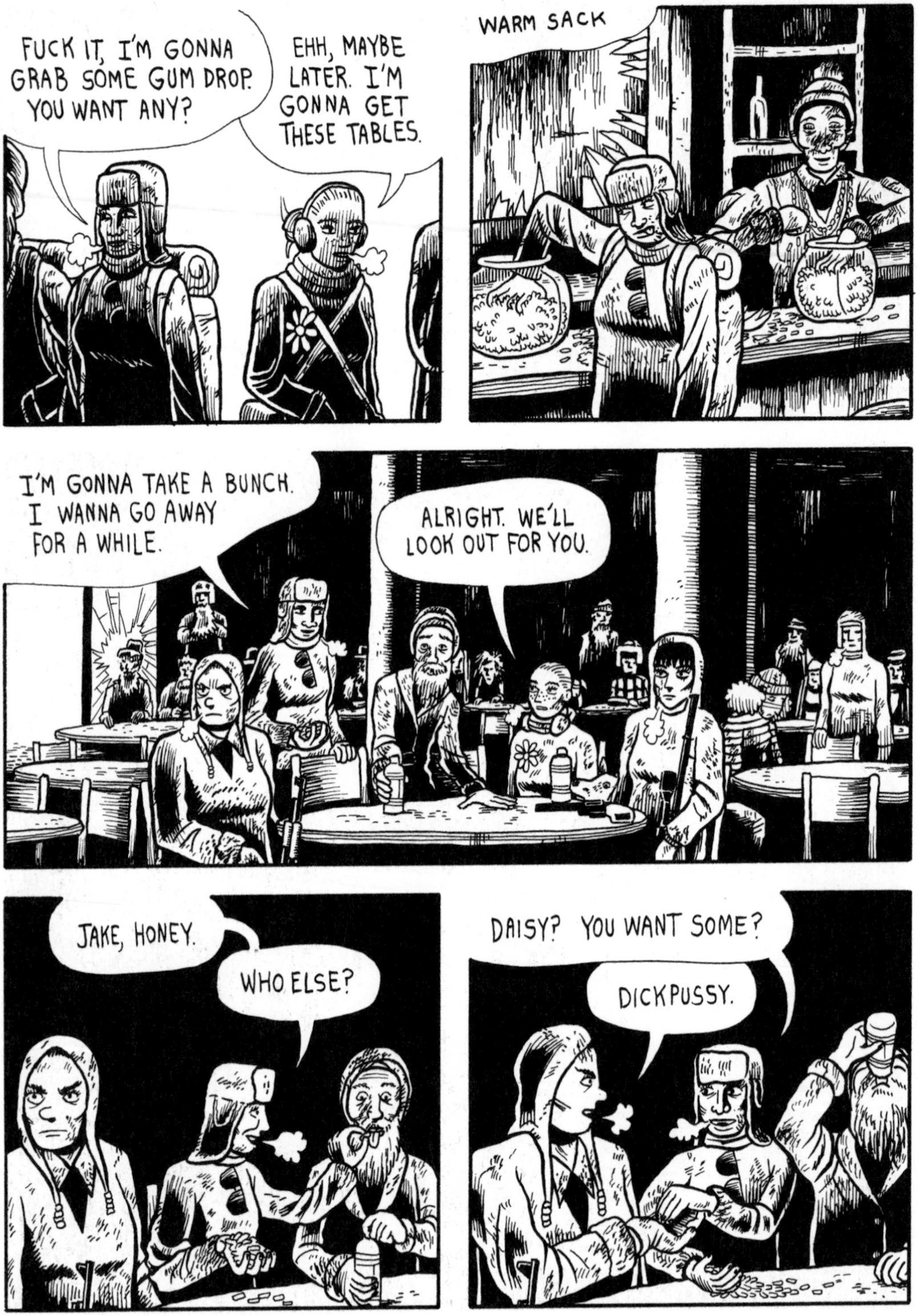
FUCK IT, I'M GONNA GRAB SOME GUM DROP. YOU WANT ANY?
EHH, MAYBE LATER. I'M GONNA GET THESE TABLES.
WARM SACK
I'M GONNA TAKE A BUNCH. I WANNA GO AWAY FOR A WHILE.
ALRIGHT. WE'LL LOOK OUT FOR YOU.
JAKE, HONEY.
WHO ELSE?
DAISY? YOU WANT SOME?
DICKPUSSY.

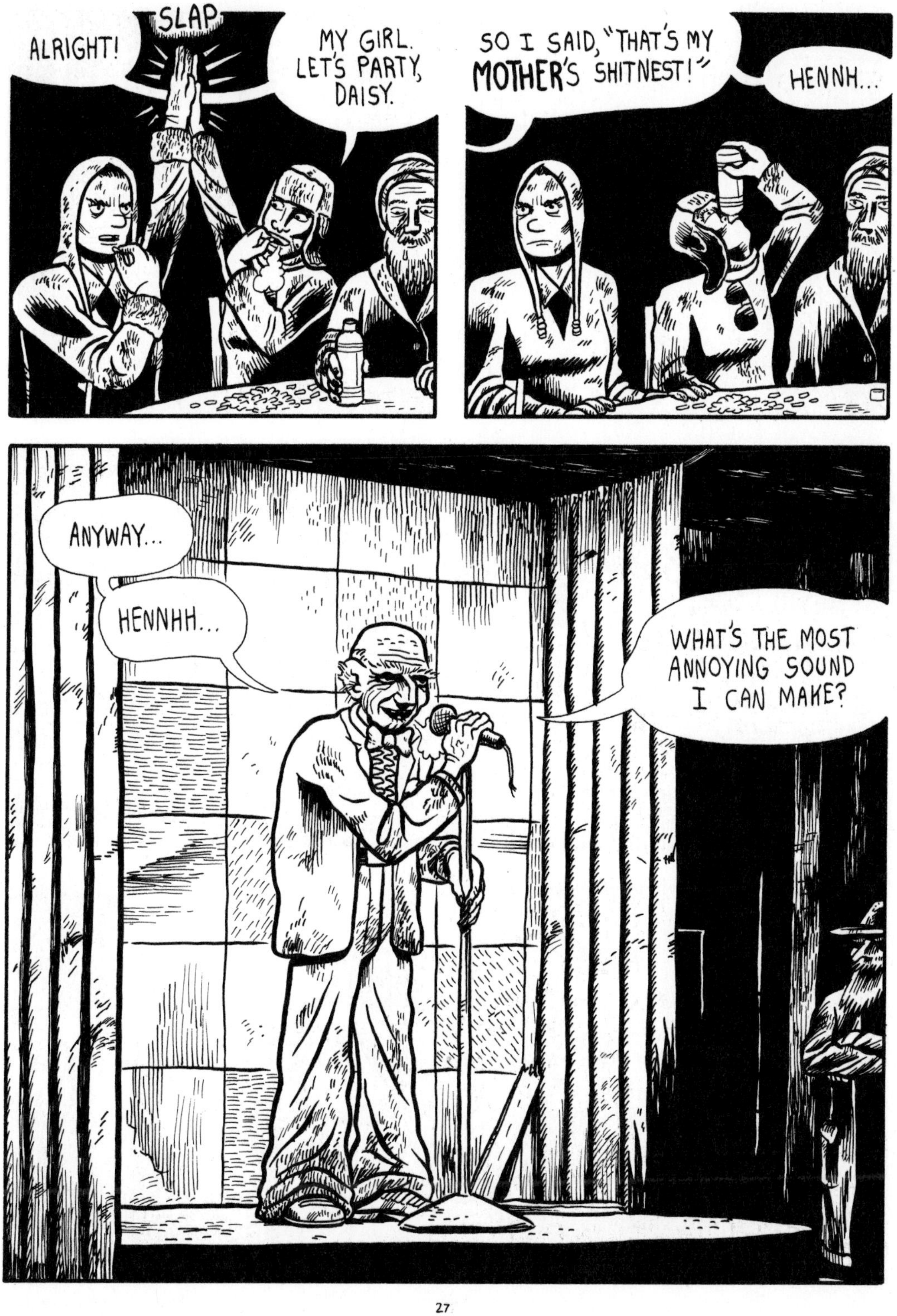
ALRIGHT!
SLAP
MY GIRL. LET'S PARTY, DAISY.
SO I SAID, "THAT'S MY MOTHER'S SHITNEST!"
HENNH...
ANYWAY...
HENNHH...
WHAT'S THE MOST ANNOYING SOUND I CAN MAKE?

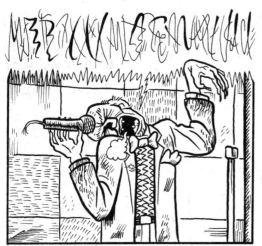

OH OH OH LOOKIT THAT, EH KREBS? A SHOW A SHOW A SHOW. HOW YOU LIKE THAT, HUH?

JINGLE JINGLE

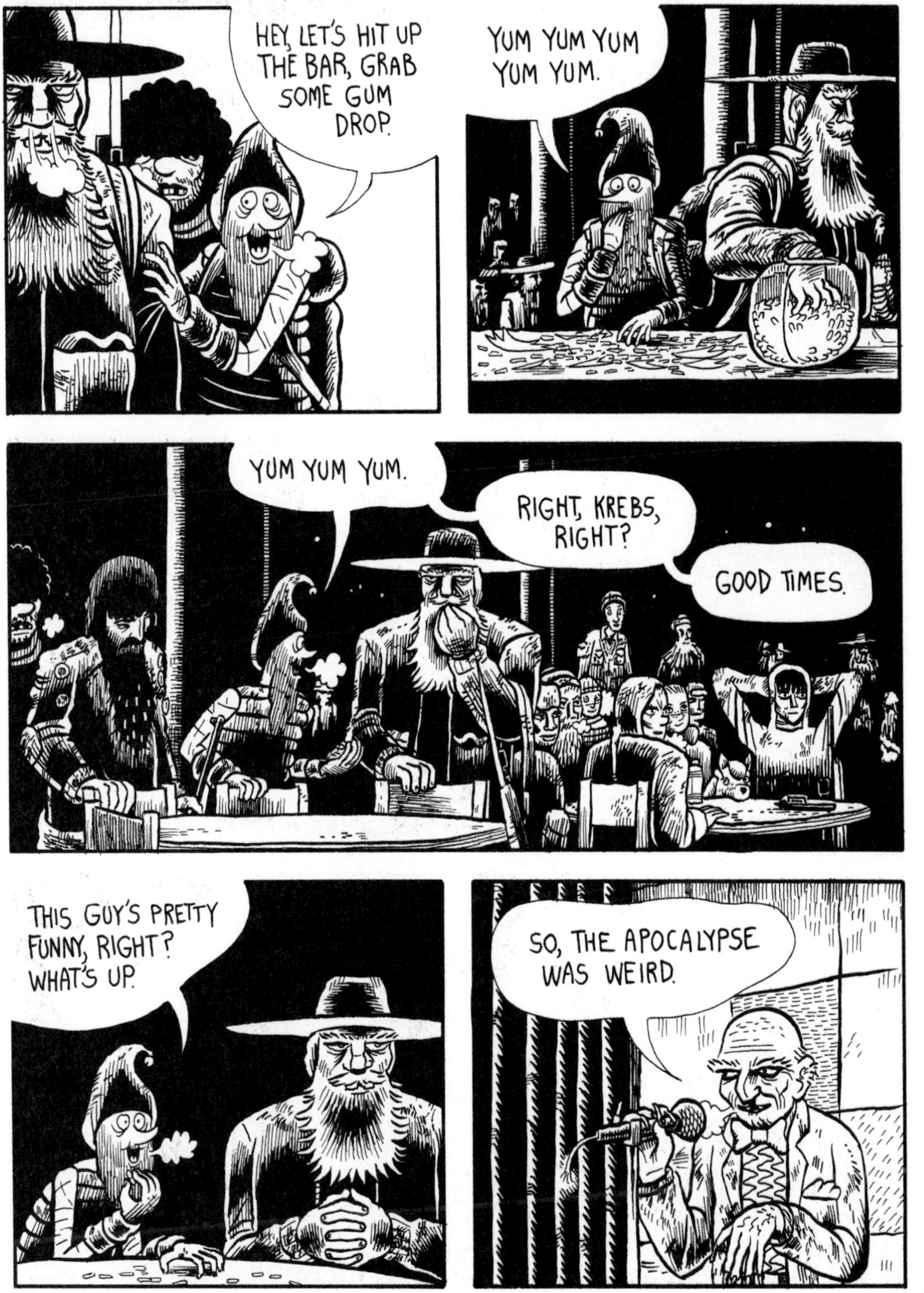

HEY, LET'S HIT UP THE BAR, GRAB SOME GUM DROP.
YUM YUM YUM YUM YUM.
YUM YUM YUM.
RIGHT, KREBS, RIGHT?
GOOD TIMES.
THIS GUY'S PRETTY FUNNY, RIGHT? WHAT'S UP.
SO, THE APOCALYPSE WAS WEIRD.

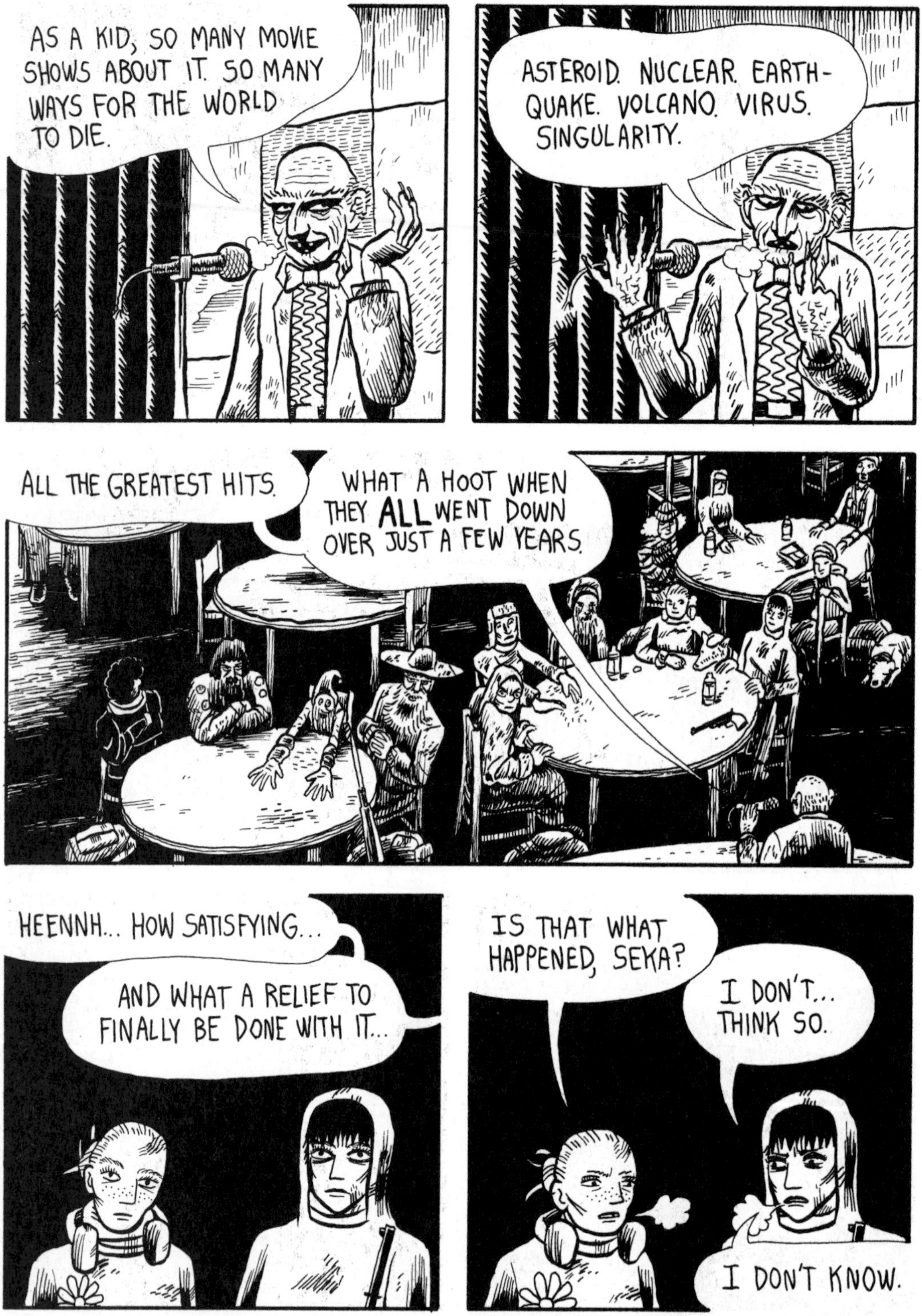

AS A KID, SO MANY MOVIE SHOWS ABOUT IT. SO MANY WAYS FOR THE WORLD TO DIE.
ASTEROID. NUCLEAR. EARTH-QUAKE. VOLCANO. VIRUS. SINGULARITY.
ALL THE GREATEST HITS.
WHAT A HOOT WHEN THEY ALL WENT DOWN OVER JUST A FEW YEARS.
HEENNH... HOW SATISFYING...
AND WHAT A RELIEF TO FINALLY BE DONE WITH IT...
IS THAT WHAT HAPPENED, SEKA?
I DON'T... THINK SO.
I DON'T KNOW.

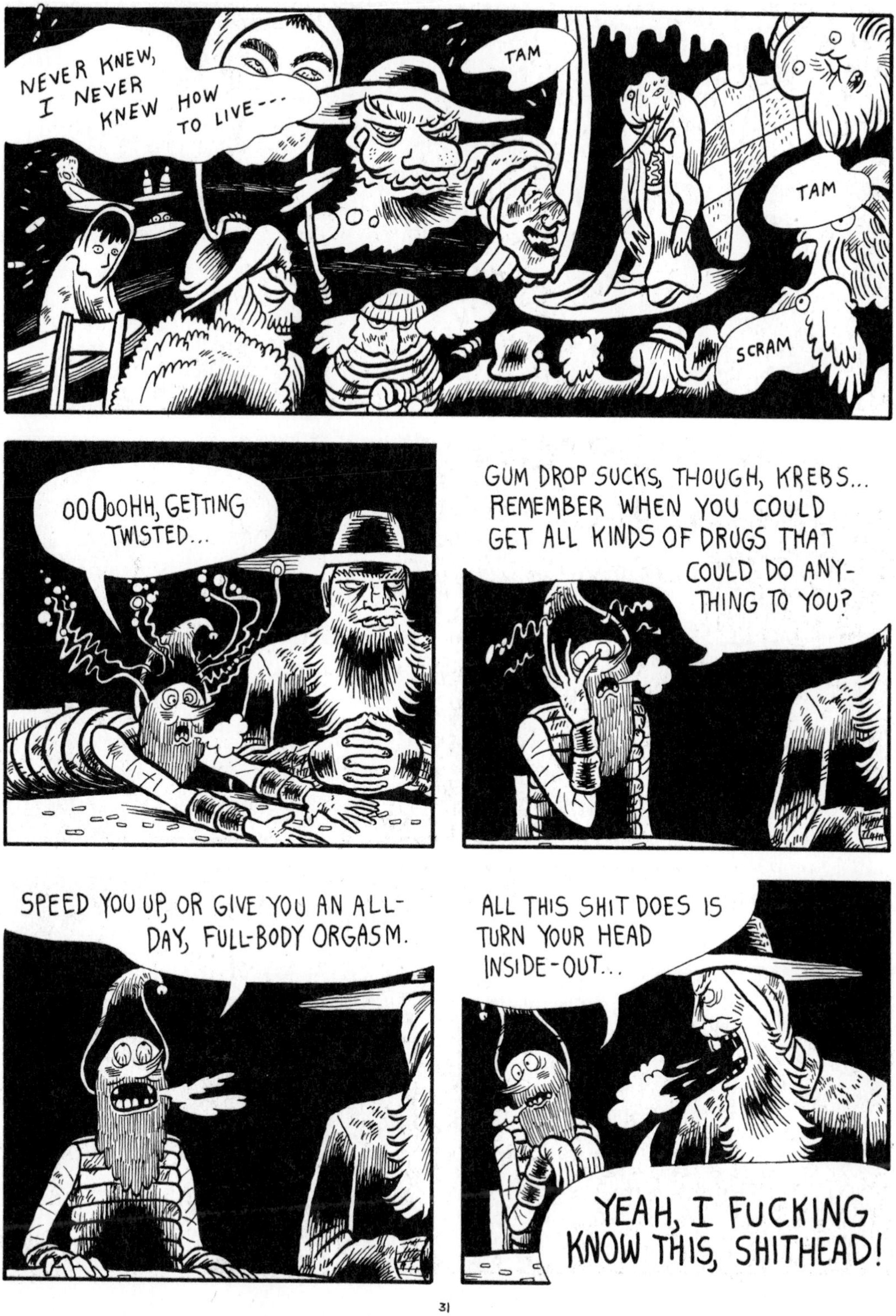
NEVER KNEW, I NEVER KNEW HOW TO LIVE---
TAM
TAM
SCRAM
OOOOOHH, GETTING TWISTED...
GUM DROP SUCKS, THOUGH, KREBS... REMEMBER WHEN YOU COULD GET ALL KINDS OF DRUGS THAT COULD DO ANYTHING TO YOU?
SPEED YOU UP, OR GIVE YOU AN ALL-DAY, FULL-BODY ORGASM.
ALL THIS SHIT DOES IS TURN YOUR HEAD INSIDE-OUT...
YEAH, I FUCKING KNOW THIS, SHITHEAD!

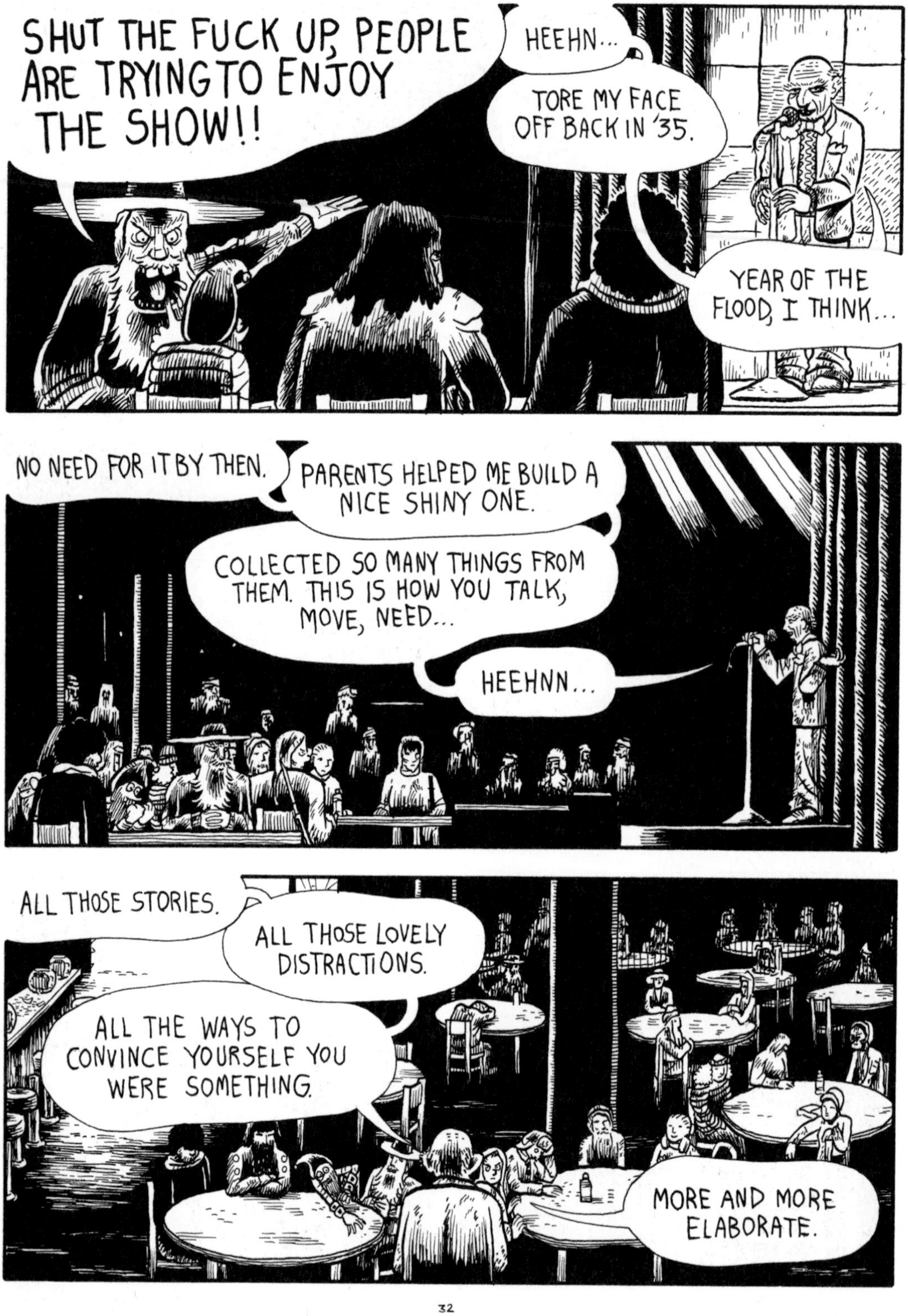
SHUT THE FUCK UP, PEOPLE ARE TRYING TO ENJOY THE SHOW!!
HEEHN...
TORE MY FACE OFF BACK IN '35.
YEAR OF THE FLOOD, I THINK...
NO NEED FOR IT BY THEN.
PARENTS HELPED ME BUILD A NICE SHINY ONE.
COLLECTED SO MANY THINGS FROM THEM. THIS IS HOW YOU TALK, MOVE, NEED...
HEEHNN...
ALL THOSE STORIES.
ALL THOSE LOVELY DISTRACTIONS.
ALL THE WAYS TO CONVINCE YOURSELF YOU WERE SOMETHING.
MORE AND MORE ELABORATE.

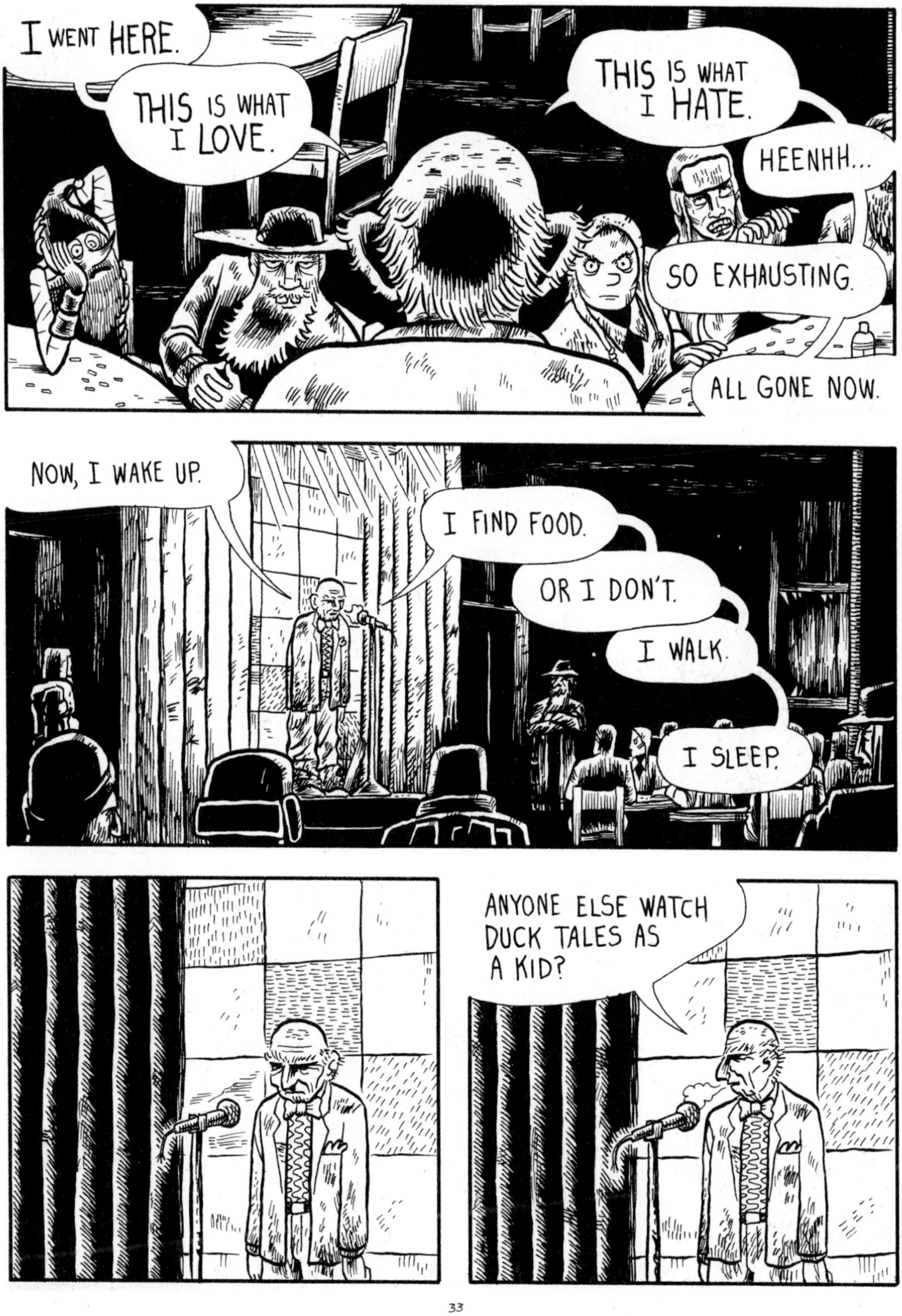
I WENT HERE.
THIS IS WHAT I LOVE.
THIS IS WHAT I HATE.
HEENHH...
SO EXHAUSTING.
ALL GONE NOW.
NOW, I WAKE UP.
I FIND FOOD.
OR I DON'T.
I WALK.
I SLEEP.
ANYONE ELSE WATCH DUCK TALES AS A KID?

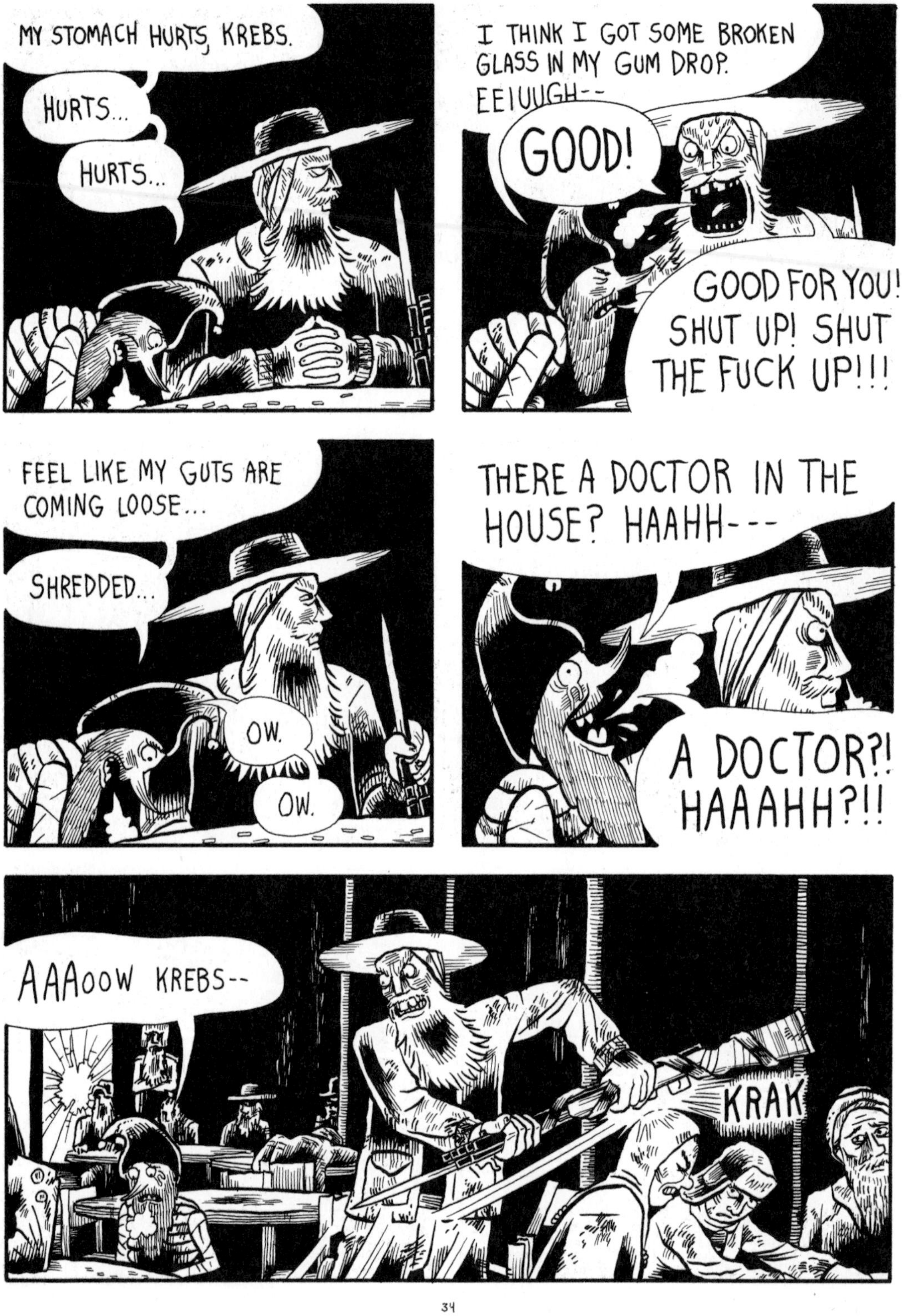
MY STOMACH HURTS, KREBS.
HURTS...
HURTS...
I THINK I GOT SOME BROKEN GLASS IN MY GUM DROP. EEIUUGH--
GOOD!
GOOD FOR YOU! SHUT UP! SHUT THE FUCK UP!!!
FEEL LIKE MY GUTS ARE COMING LOOSE...
SHREDDED...
OW.
OW.
THERE A DOCTOR IN THE HOUSE? HAAHH---
A DOCTOR?! HAAAHH?!!
AAAoow KREBS--
KRAK

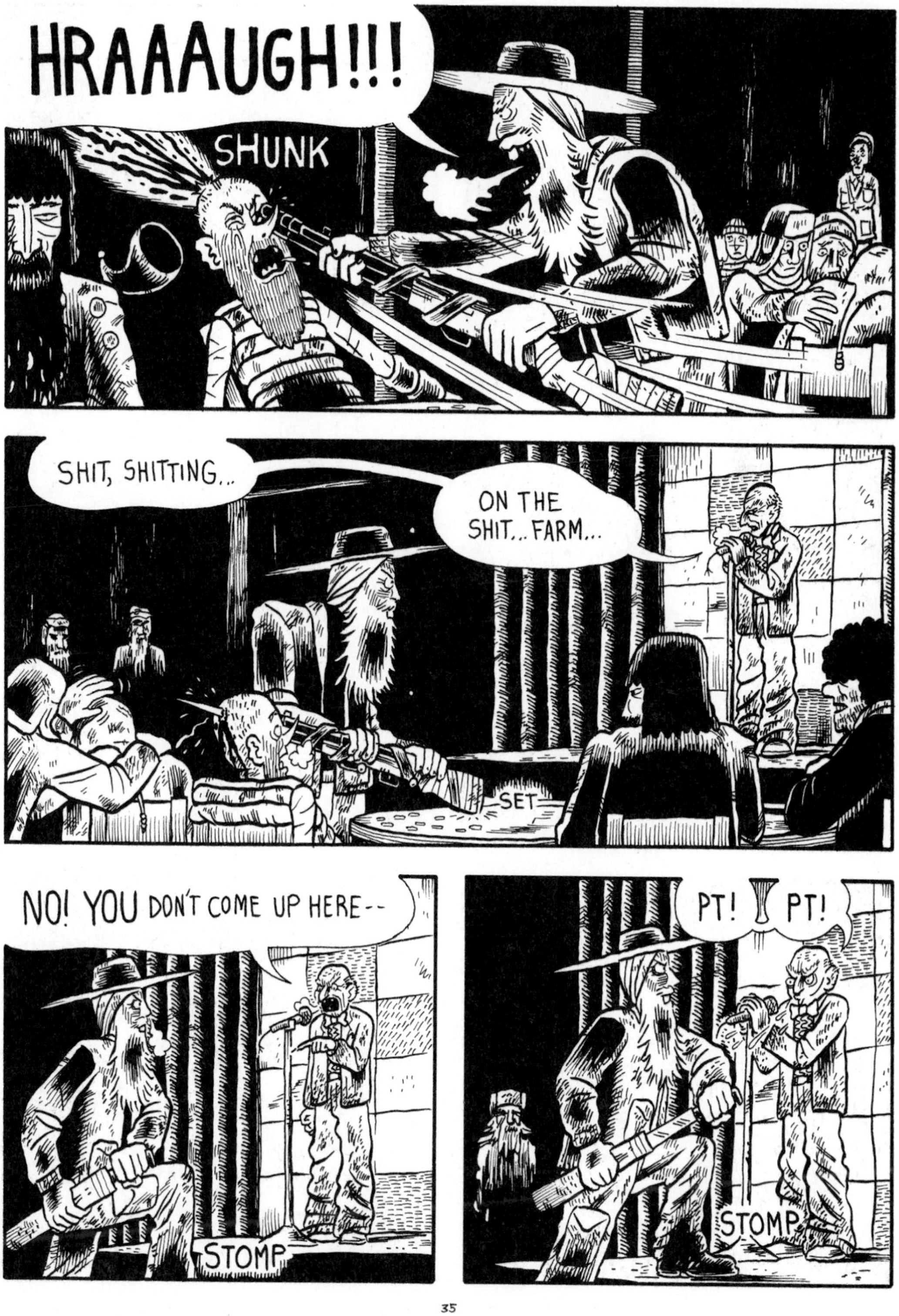

HRAAAUGH!!!
SHUNK
SHIT, SHITTING...
ON THE SHIT... FARM...
SET
NO! YOU DON'T COME UP HERE--
STOMP
PT! PT!
STOMP

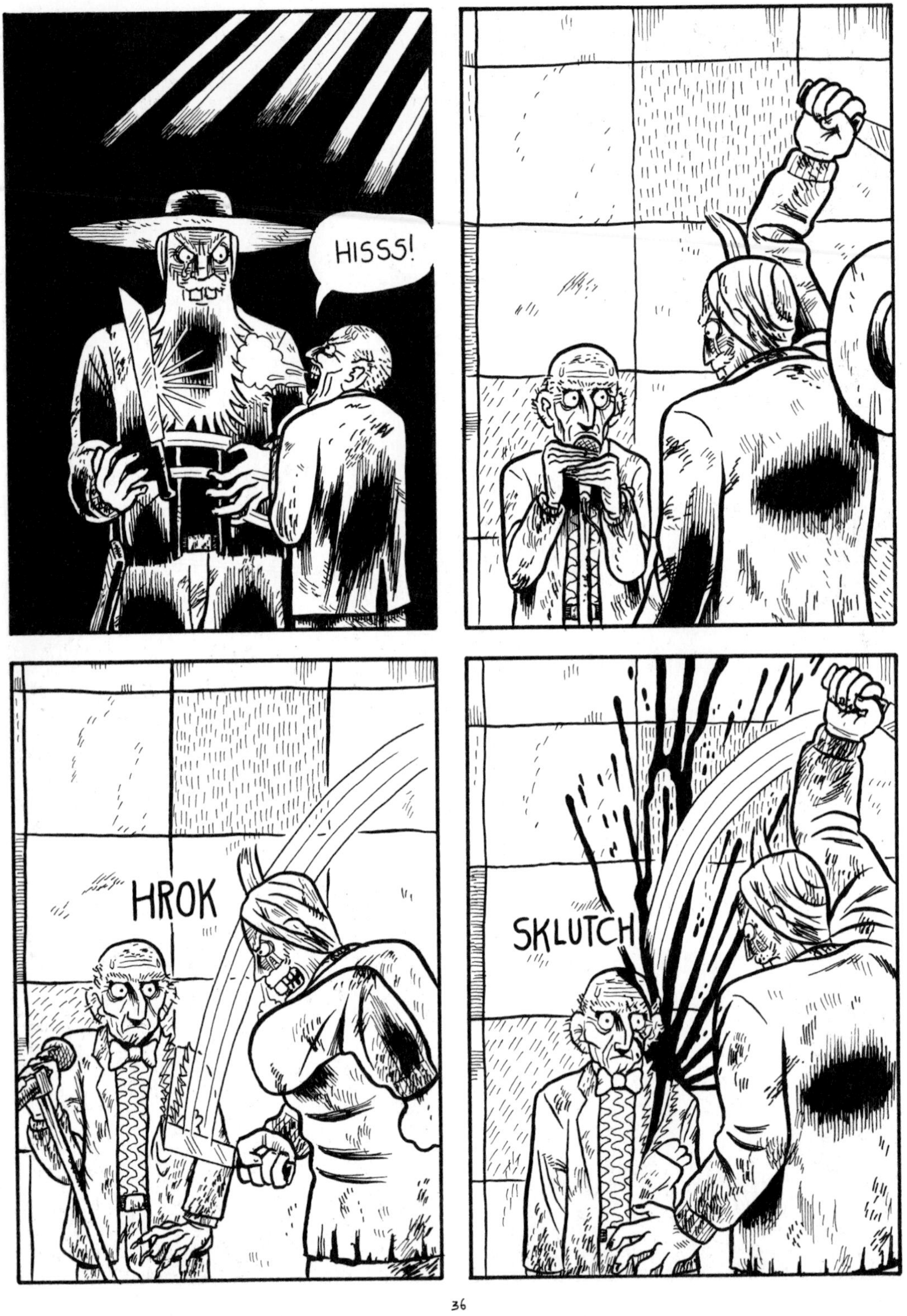
HISSS!
HROK
SKLUTCH

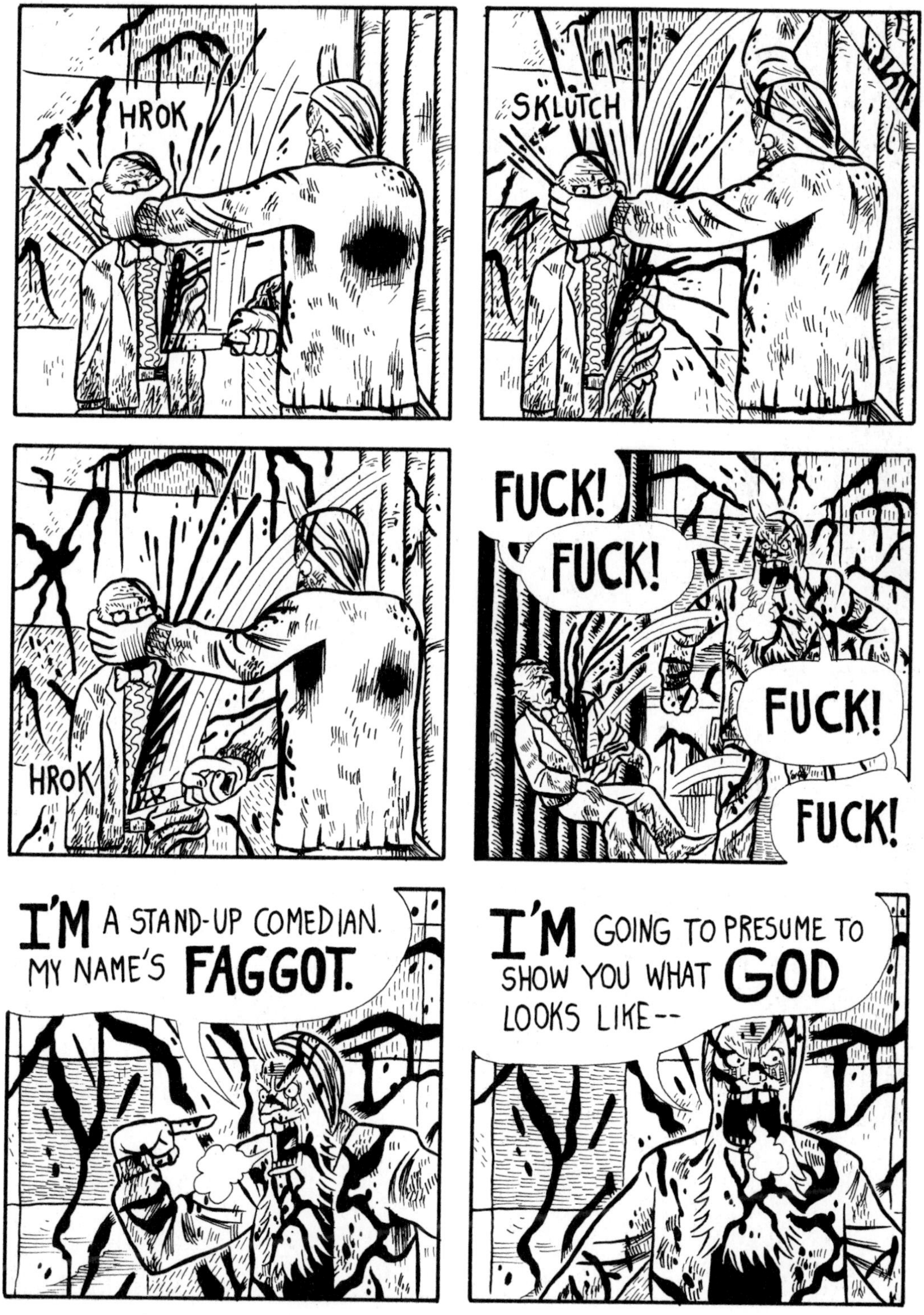
HROK
SKLUTCH
HROK
FUCK!
FUCK!
FUCK!
FUCK!
I'M A STAND-UP COMEDIAN. MY NAME'S FAGGOT.
I'M GOING TO PRESUME TO SHOW YOU WHAT GOD LOOKS LIKE--

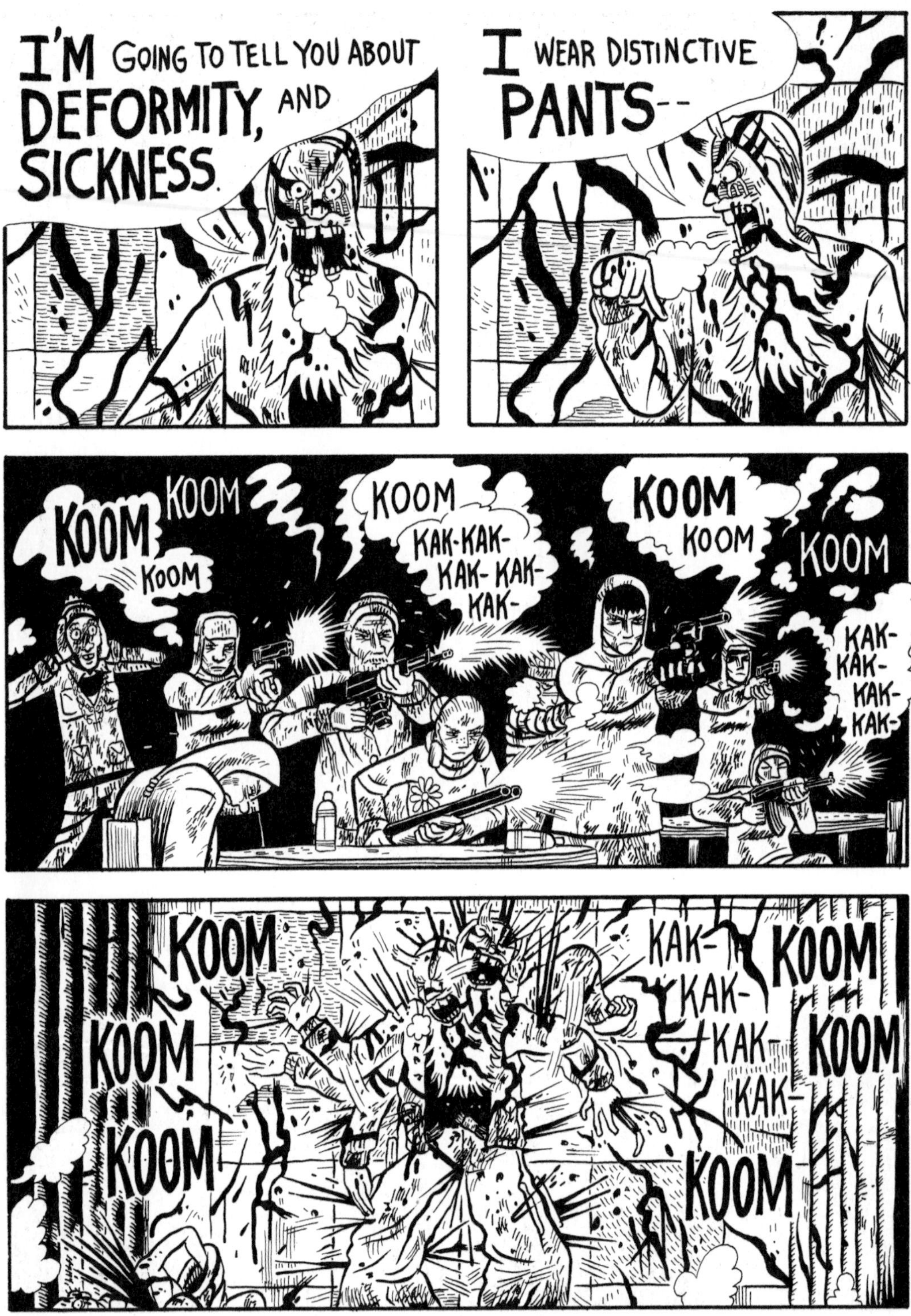
I'M GOING TO TELL YOU ABOUT DEFORMITY, AND SICKNESS.
I WEAR DISTINCTIVE PANTS--
KOOM KOOM
KOOM
KOOM
KOOM
KAK-KAK-KAK-KAK-KAK-
KOOM
KOOM
KOOM
KAK-KAK-KAK-KAK-
KOOM
KOOM
KOOM
KAK-KAK-KAK-KAK-
KOOM
KOOM
KOOM

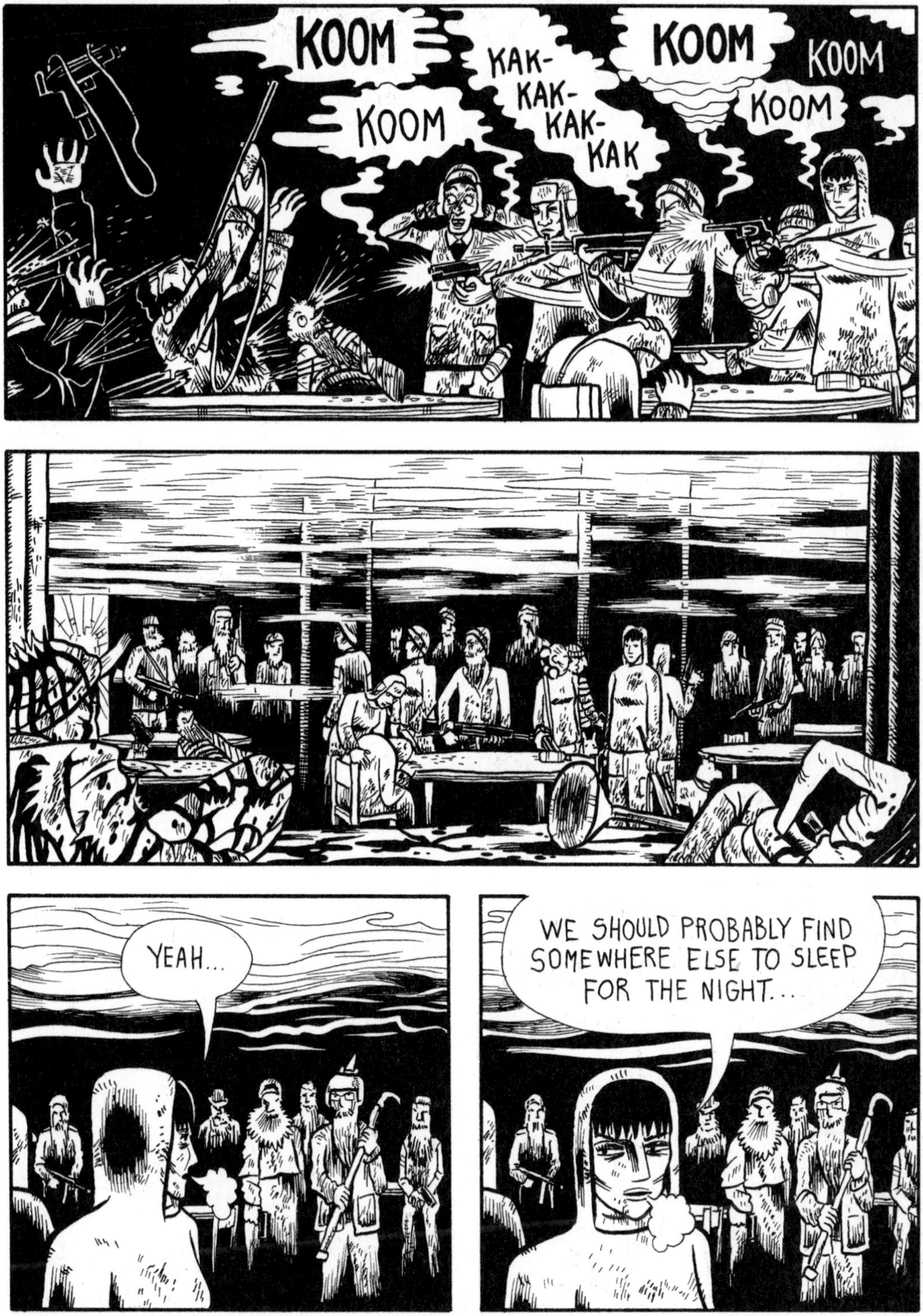
KOOM
KAK-KAK-KAK-KAK
KOOM
KOOM
KOOM
KOOM
YEAH...
WE SHOULD PROBABLY FIND SOMEWHERE ELSE TO SLEEP FOR THE NIGHT...

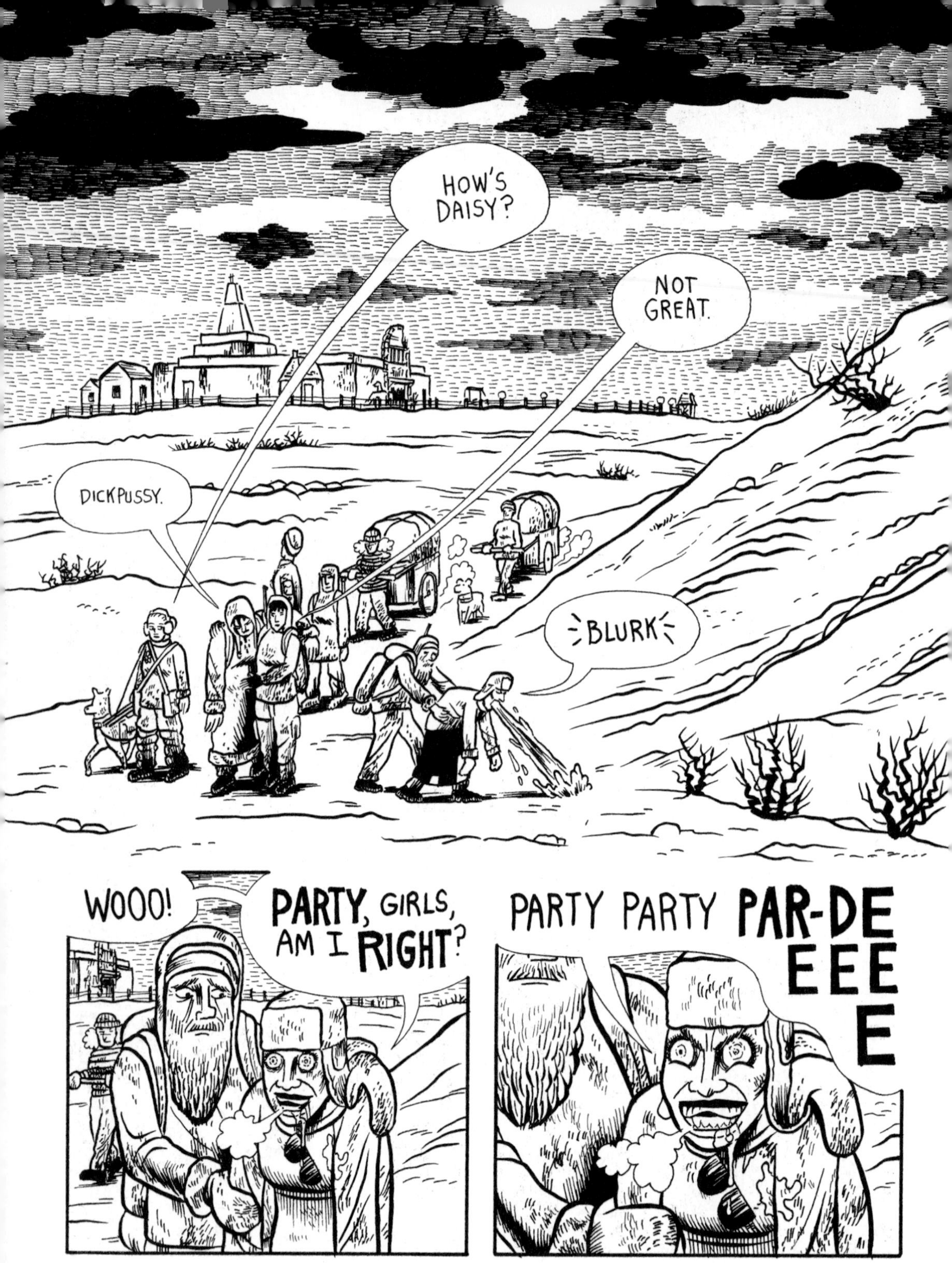
HOW'S DAISY?
NOT GREAT.
DICKPUSSY.
BLURK
WOOO!
PARTY, GIRLS, AM I RIGHT?
PARTY PARTY PAR-DEEEEE

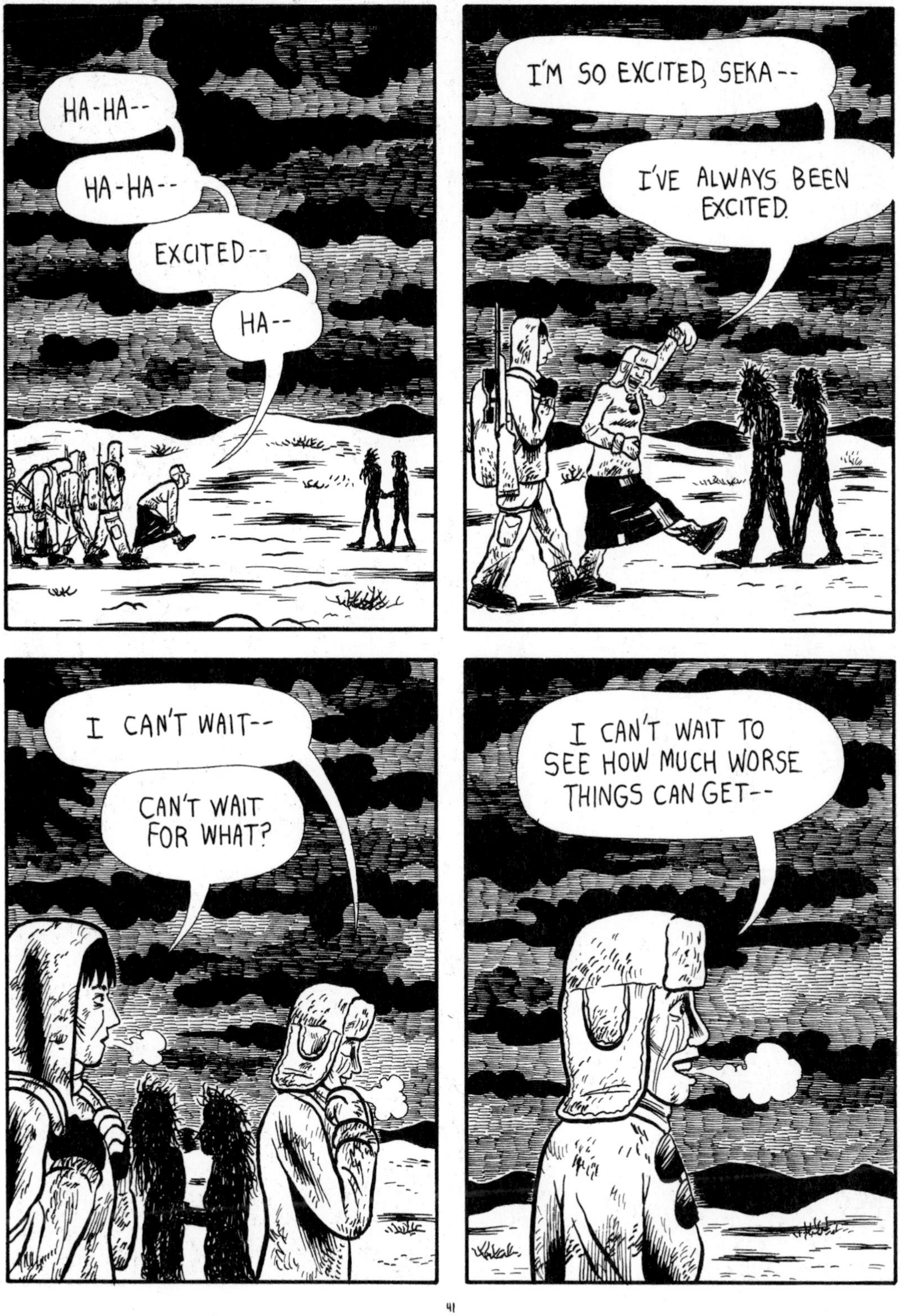
HA-HA--
HA-HA--
EXCITED--
HA--
I'M SO EXCITED, SEKA--
I'VE ALWAYS BEEN EXCITED.
I CAN'T WAIT--
CAN'T WAIT FOR WHAT?
I CAN'T WAIT TO SEE HOW MUCH WORSE THINGS CAN GET--

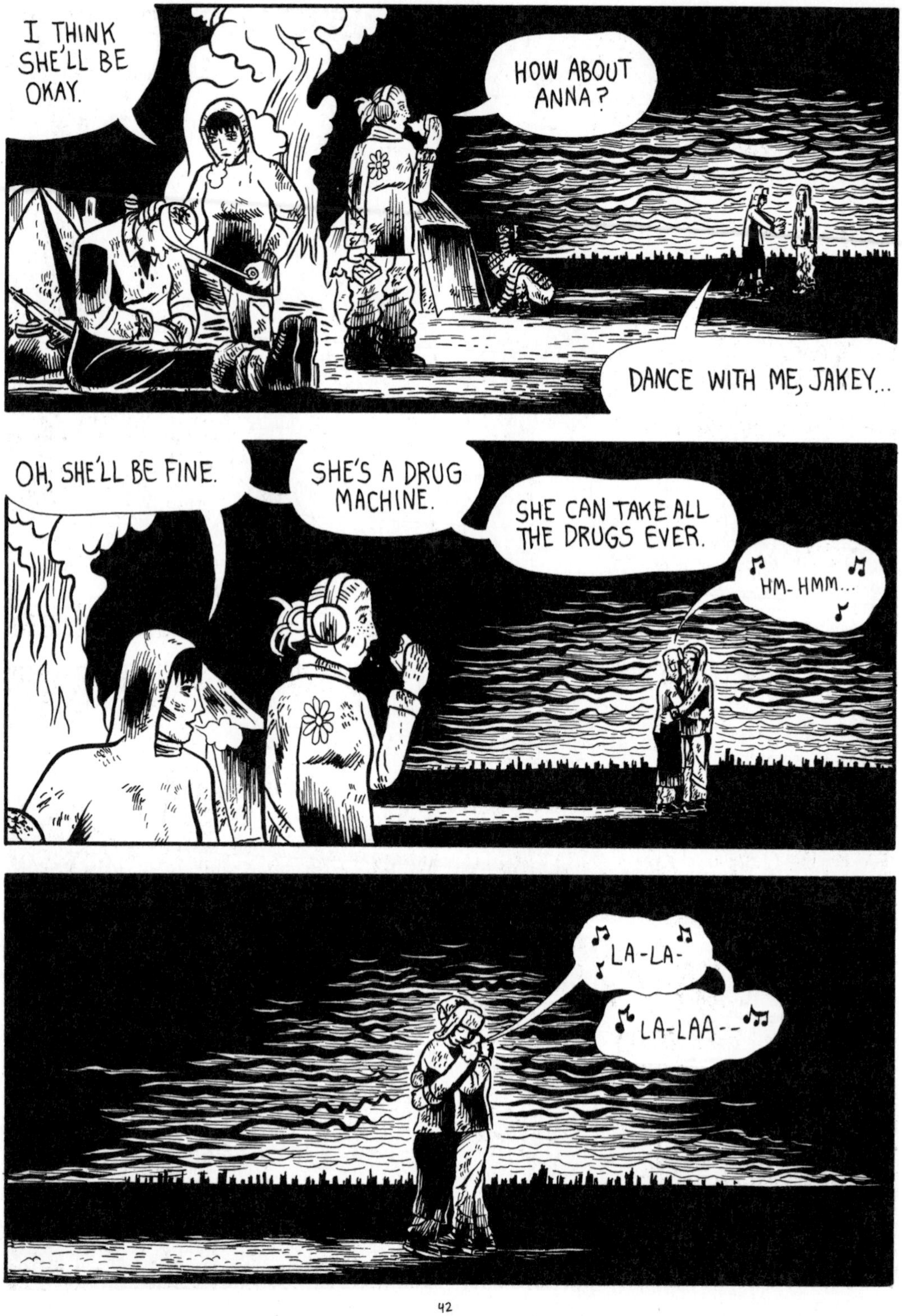
I THINK SHE'LL BE OKAY.
HOW ABOUT ANNA?
DANCE WITH ME, JAKEY...
OH, SHE'LL BE FINE.
SHE'S A DRUG MACHINE.
SHE CAN TAKE ALL THE DRUGS EVER.
HM-HMM...
LA-LA-
LA-LAA--

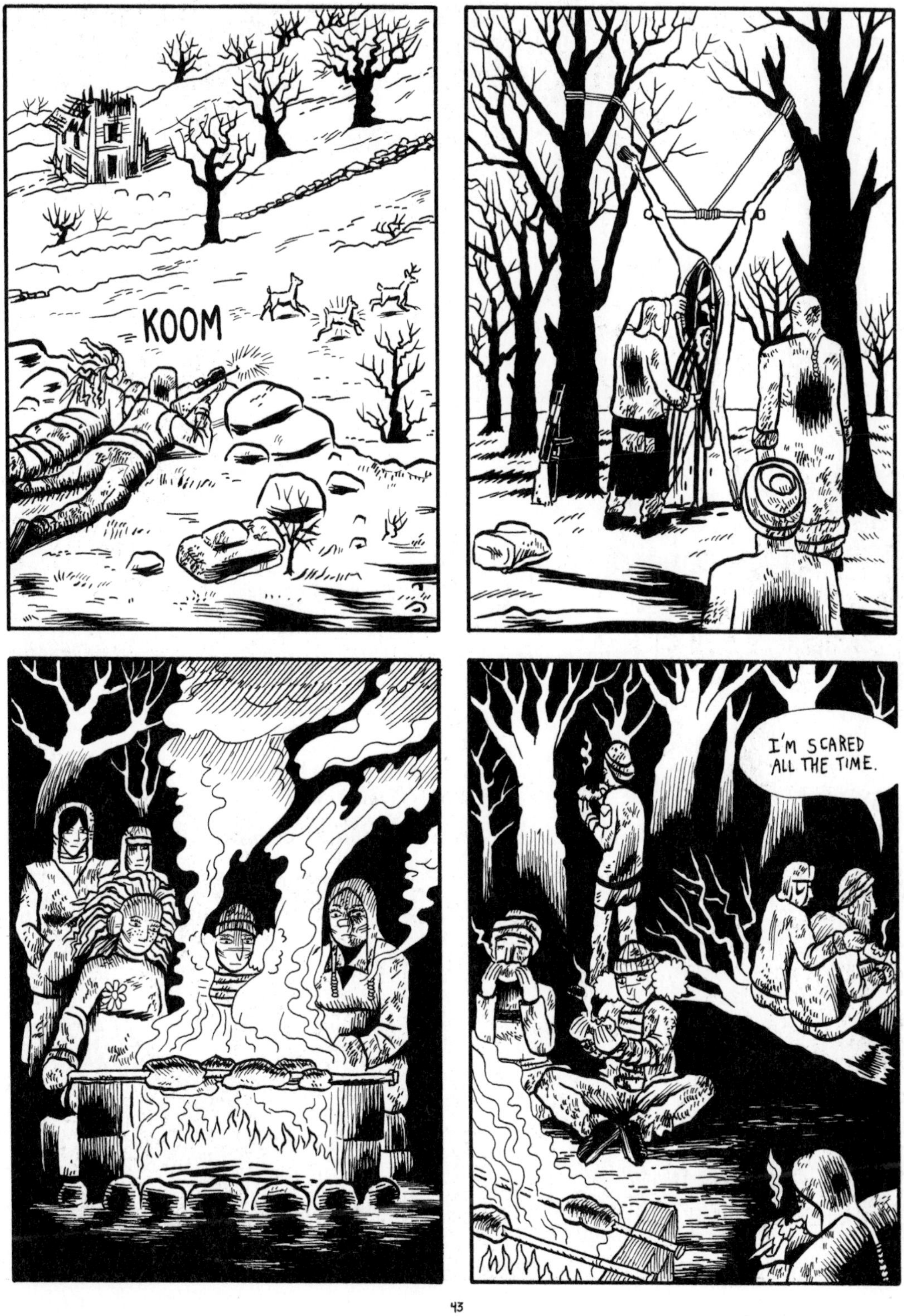
KOOM
I'M SCARED ALL THE TIME.

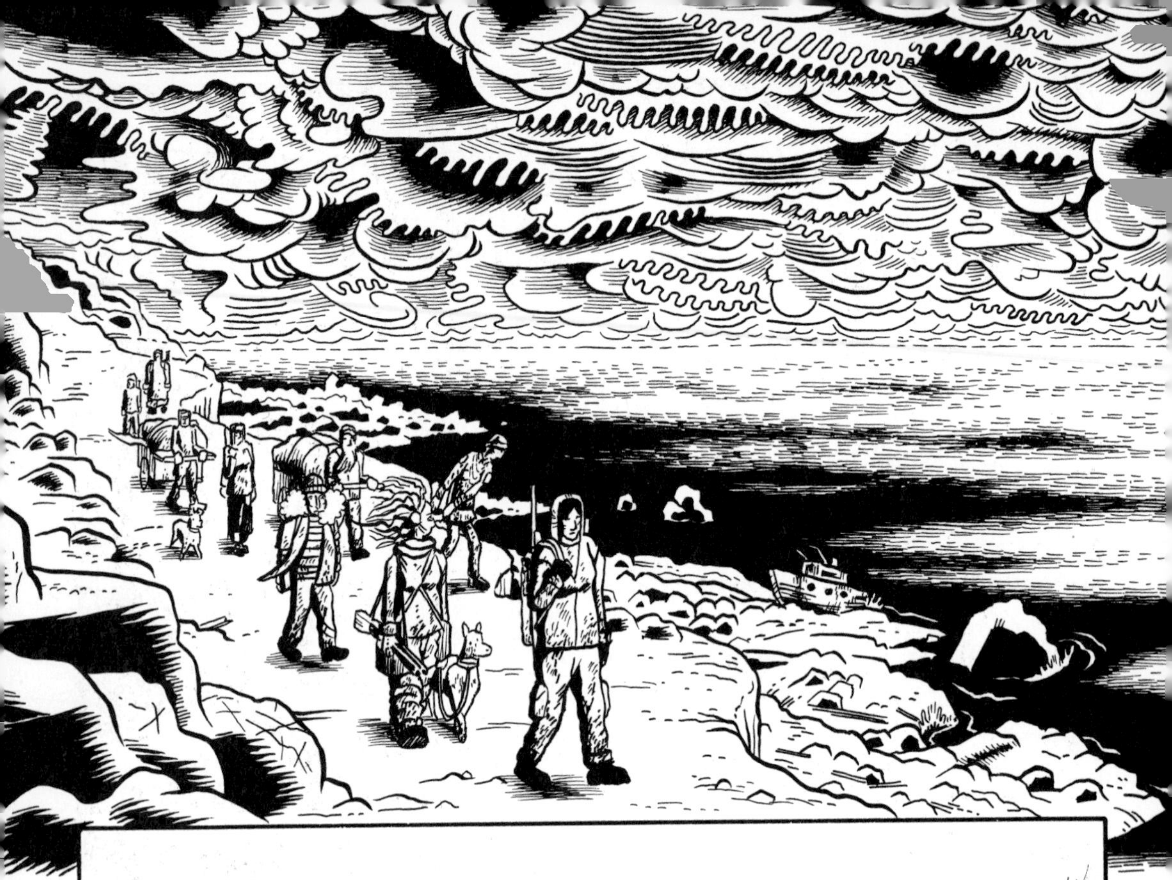

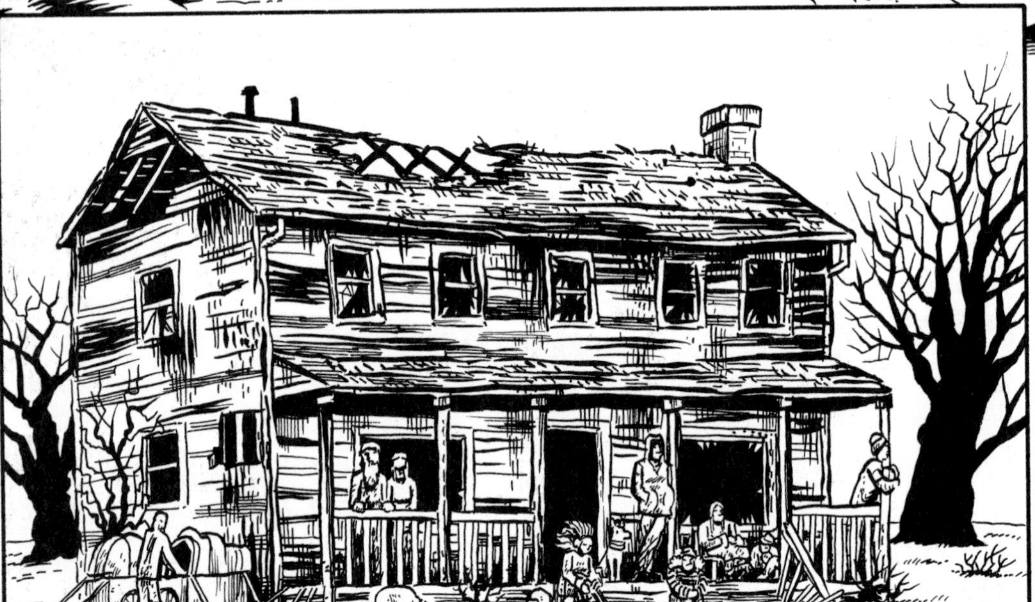

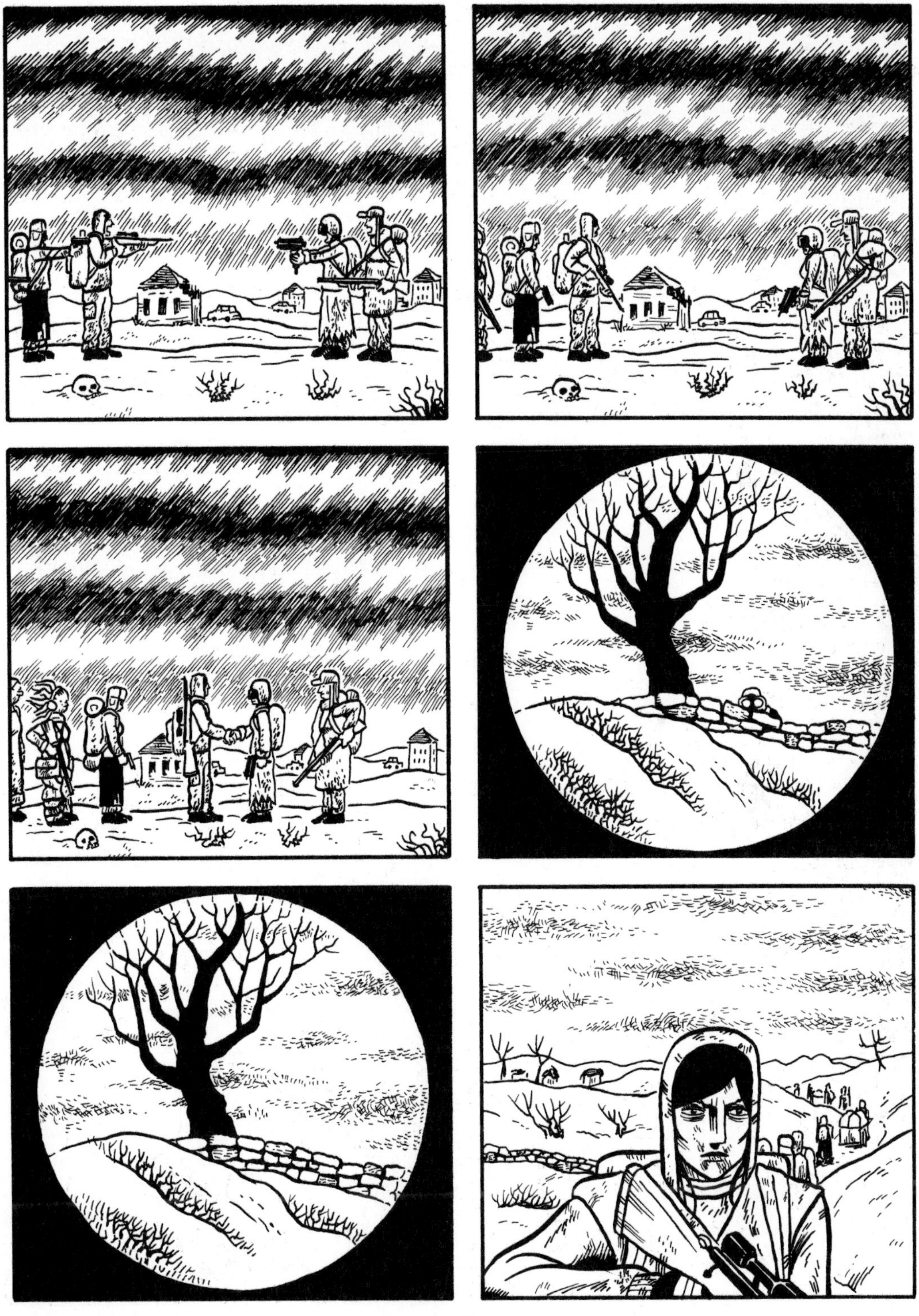

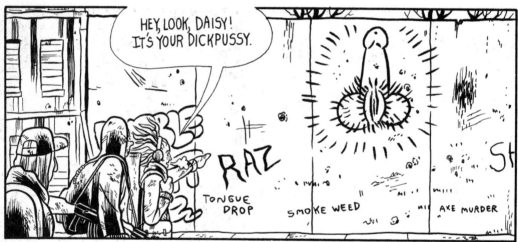

HEY, LOOK, DAISY!
IT'S YOUR DICKPUSSY.

RAZ

TONGUE
DROP

SMOKE WEED

AXE MURDER

SH

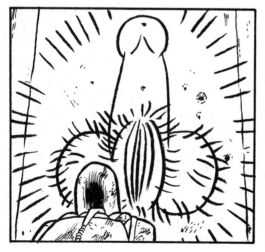

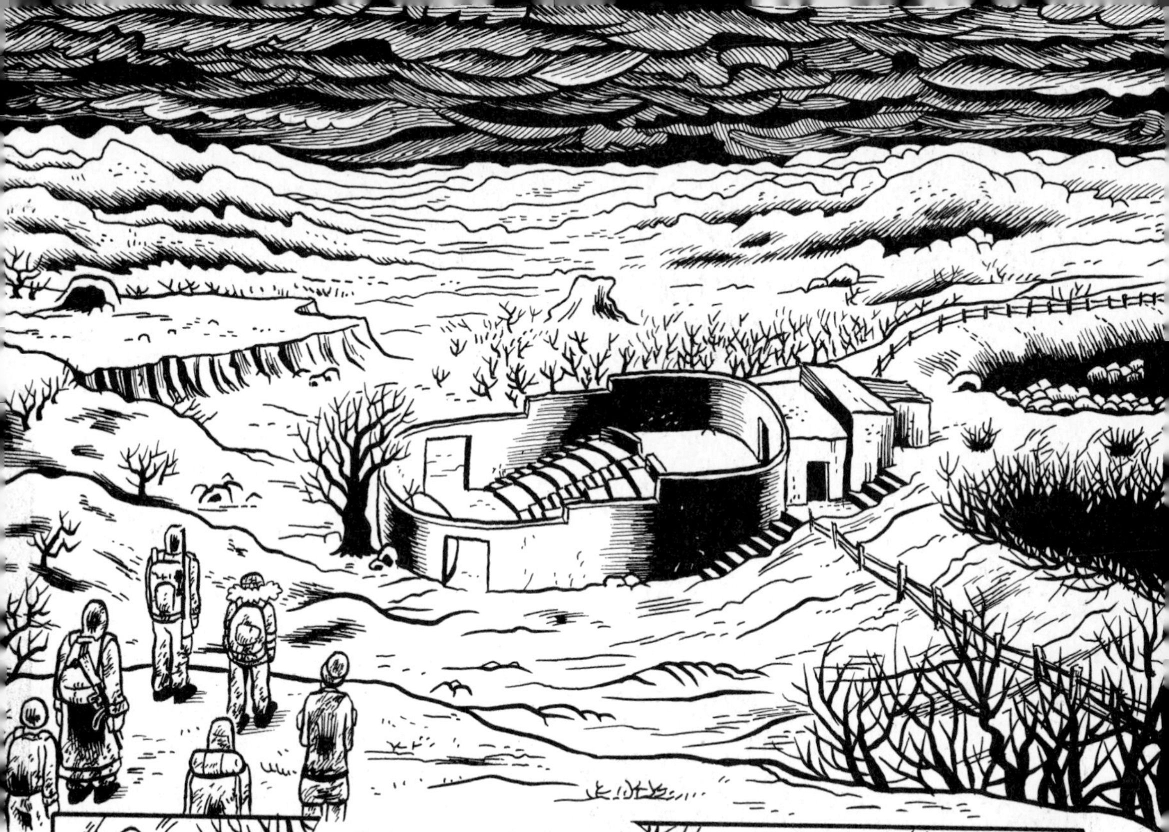

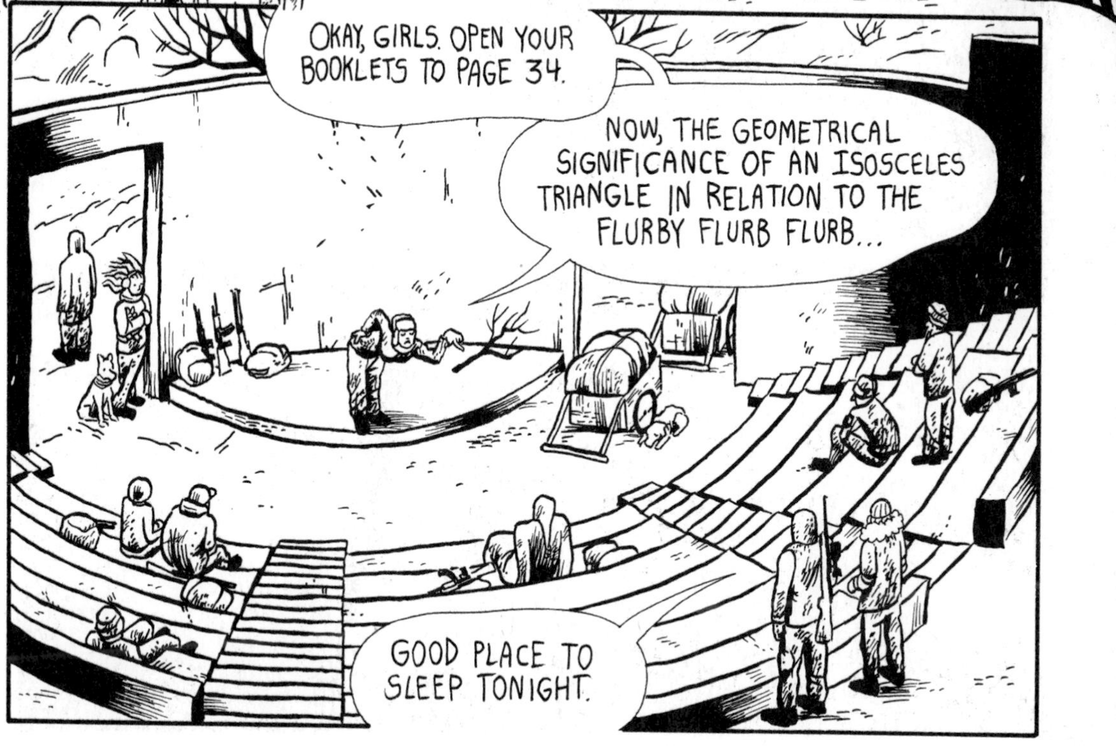
OKAY, GIRLS. OPEN YOUR BOOKLETS TO PAGE 34.
NOW, THE GEOMETRICAL SIGNIFICANCE OF AN ISOSCELES TRIANGLE IN RELATION TO THE FLURBY FLURB FLURB...
GOOD PLACE TO SLEEP TONIGHT.

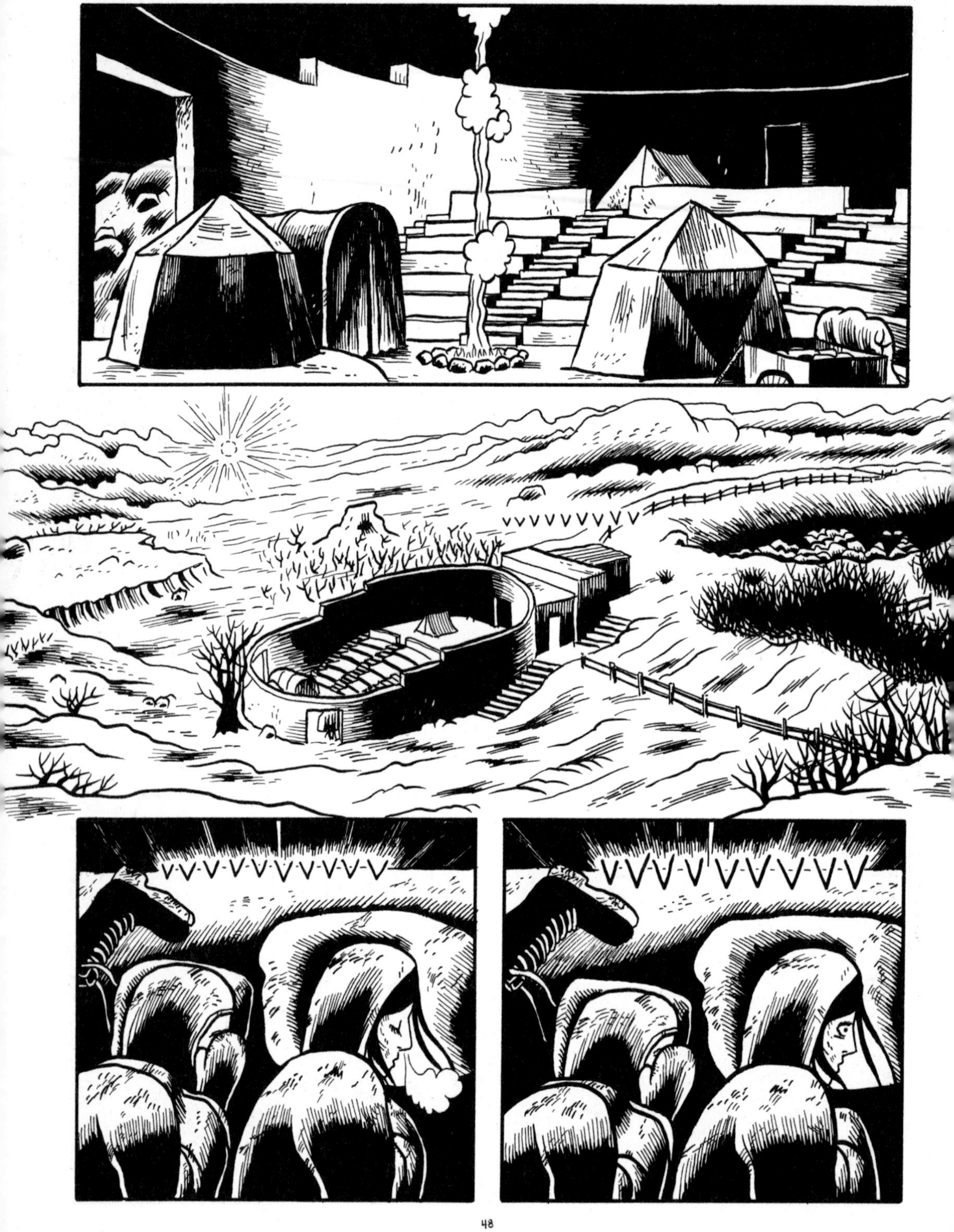

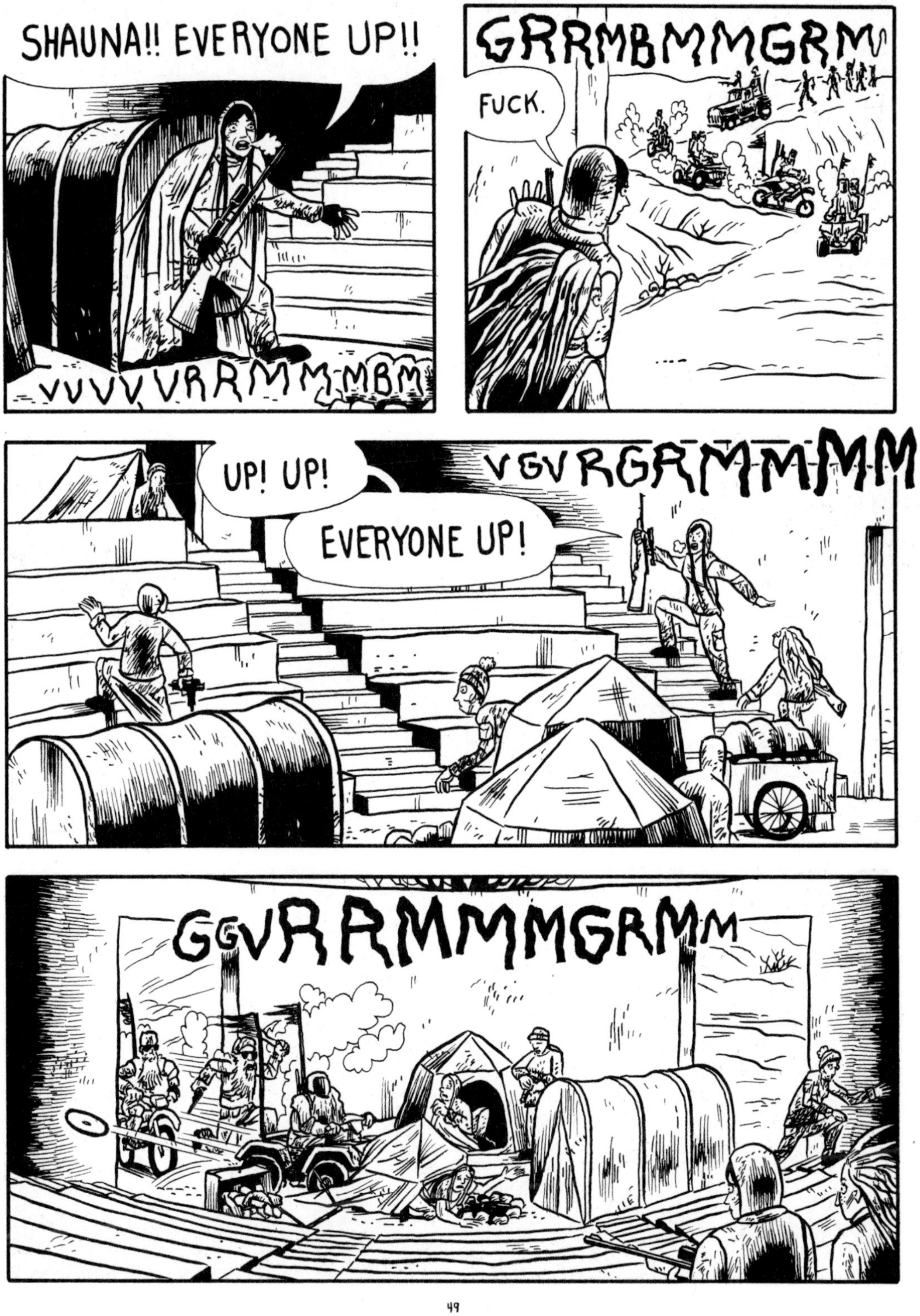
SHAUNA!! EVERYONE UP!!
VVVVVRRMMMBM
GRRMBMMGRM
FUCK.
UP! UP!
EVERYONE UP!
VGVRGRMMMM
GGVRRMMMGRMM

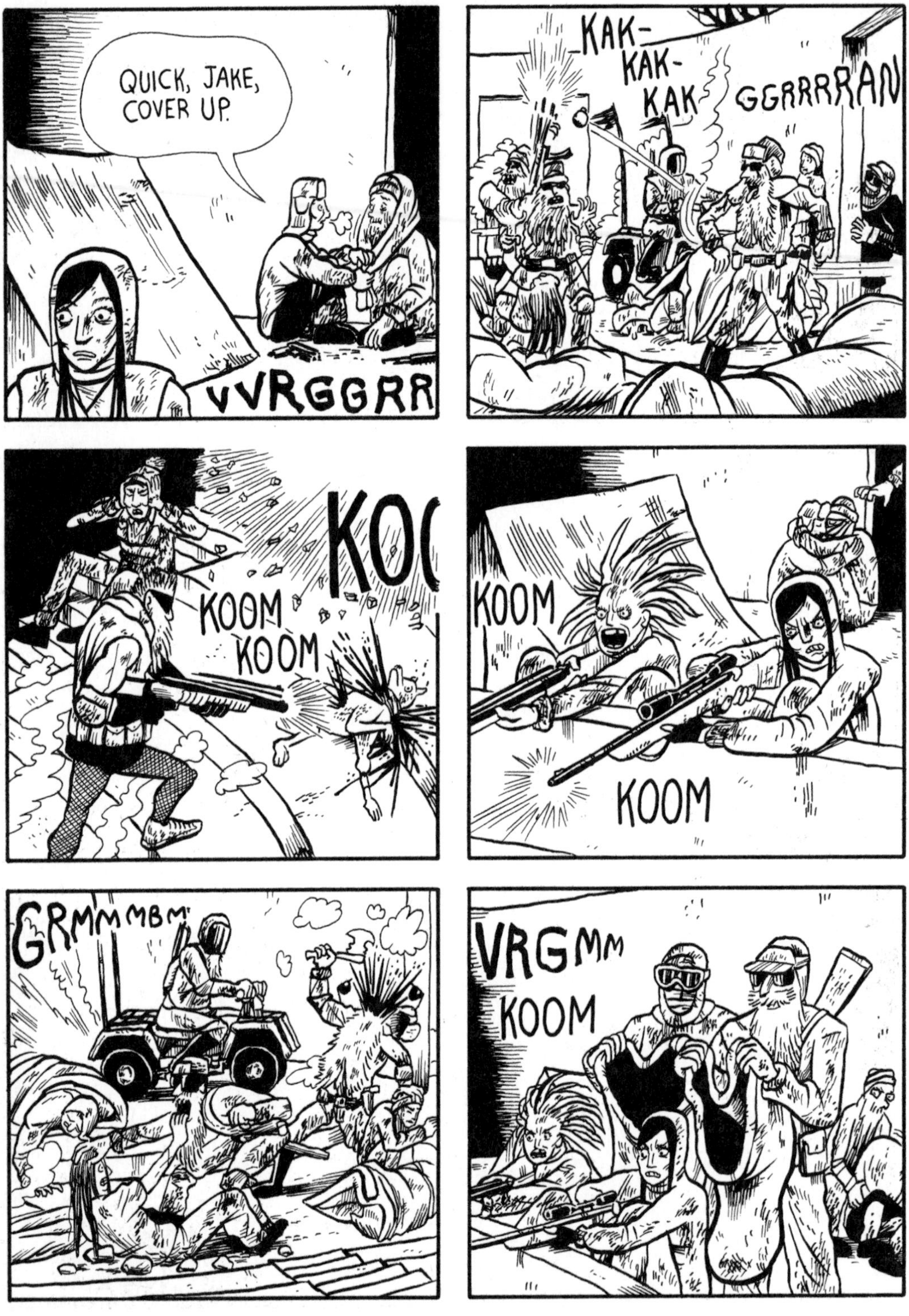
QUICK, JAKE, COVER UP.
VVRGGRR
KAK-
KAK-
KAK
GGRRRRAN
KOO
KOOM
KOOM
KOOM
KOOM
GRMMMBM
VRGMM
KOOM

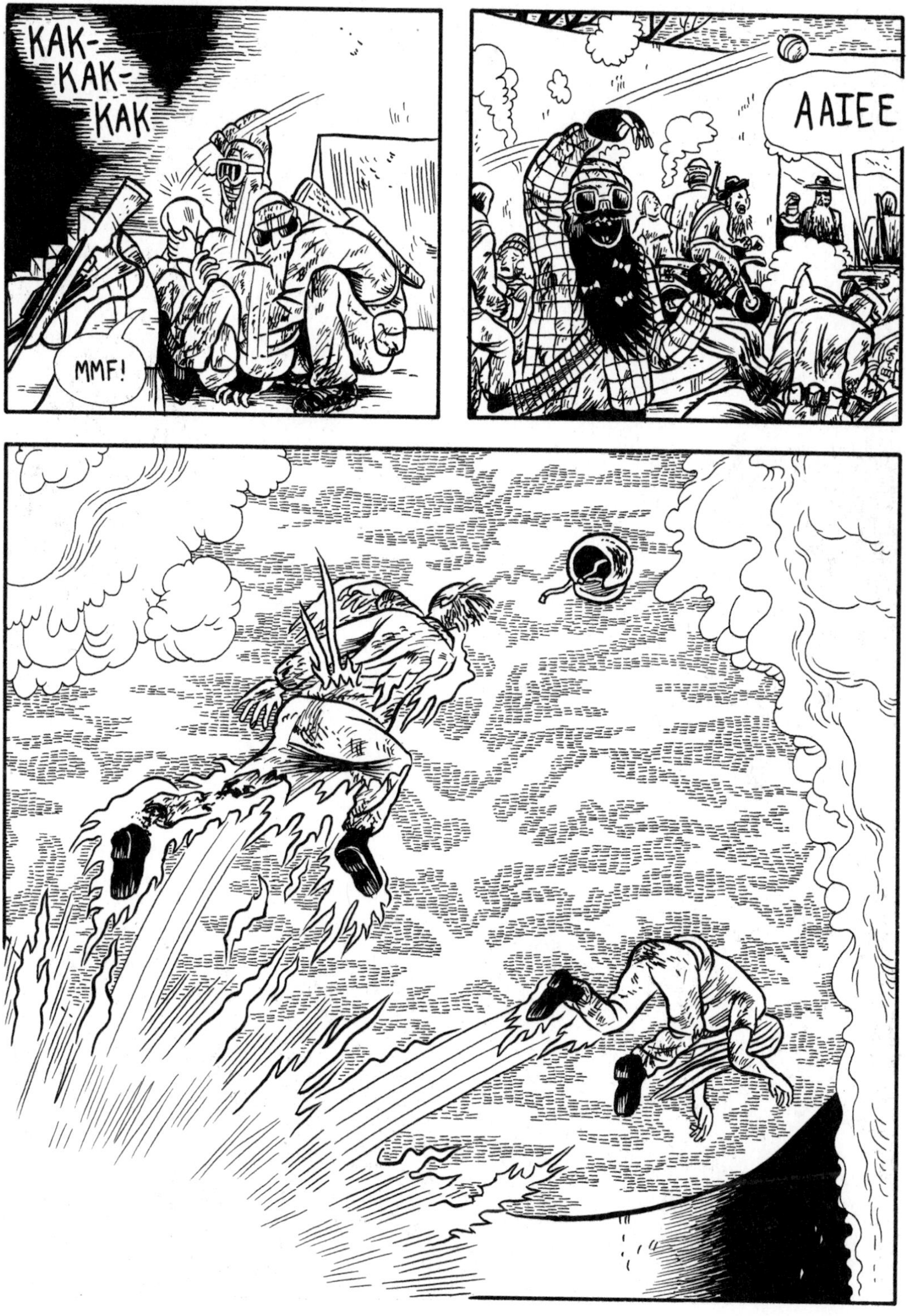
KAK-
KAK-
KAK
MMF!
AAIEE

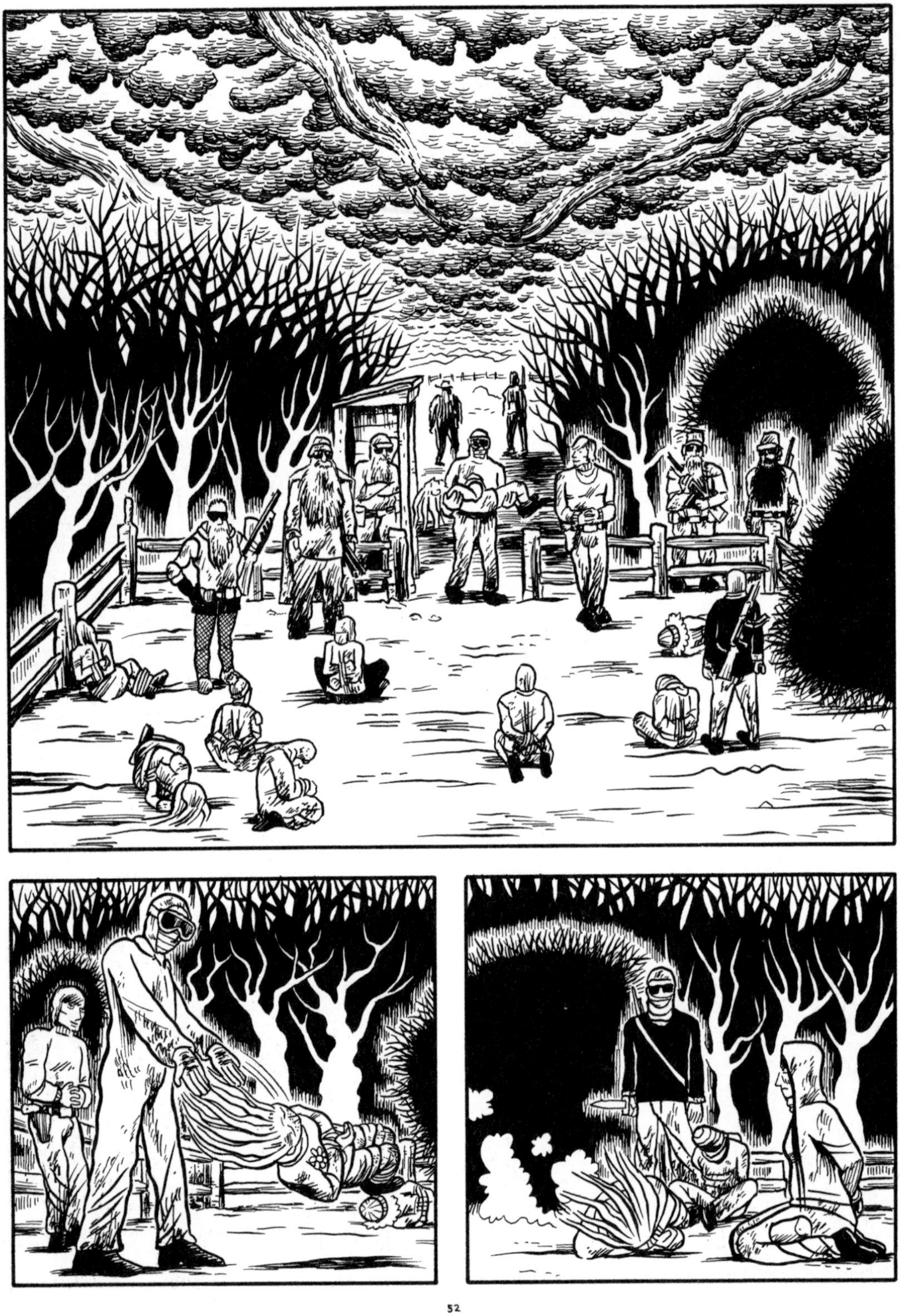

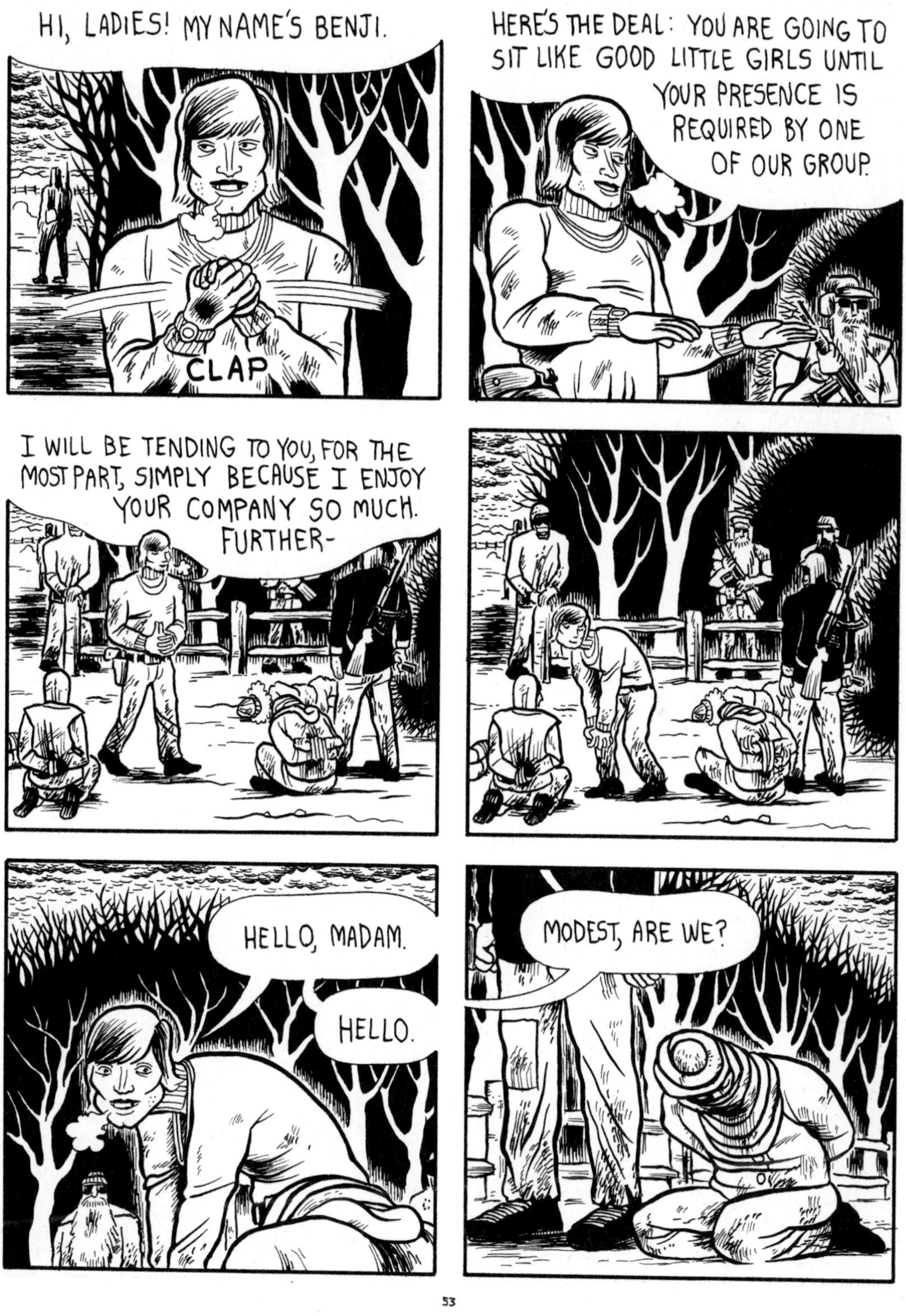
HI, LADIES! MY NAME'S BENJI.
CLAP
HERE'S THE DEAL: YOU ARE GOING TO SIT LIKE GOOD LITTLE GIRLS UNTIL YOUR PRESENCE IS REQUIRED BY ONE OF OUR GROUP.
I WILL BE TENDING TO YOU, FOR THE MOST PART, SIMPLY BECAUSE I ENJOY YOUR COMPANY SO MUCH. FURTHER-
HELLO, MADAM.
HELLO.
MODEST, ARE WE?

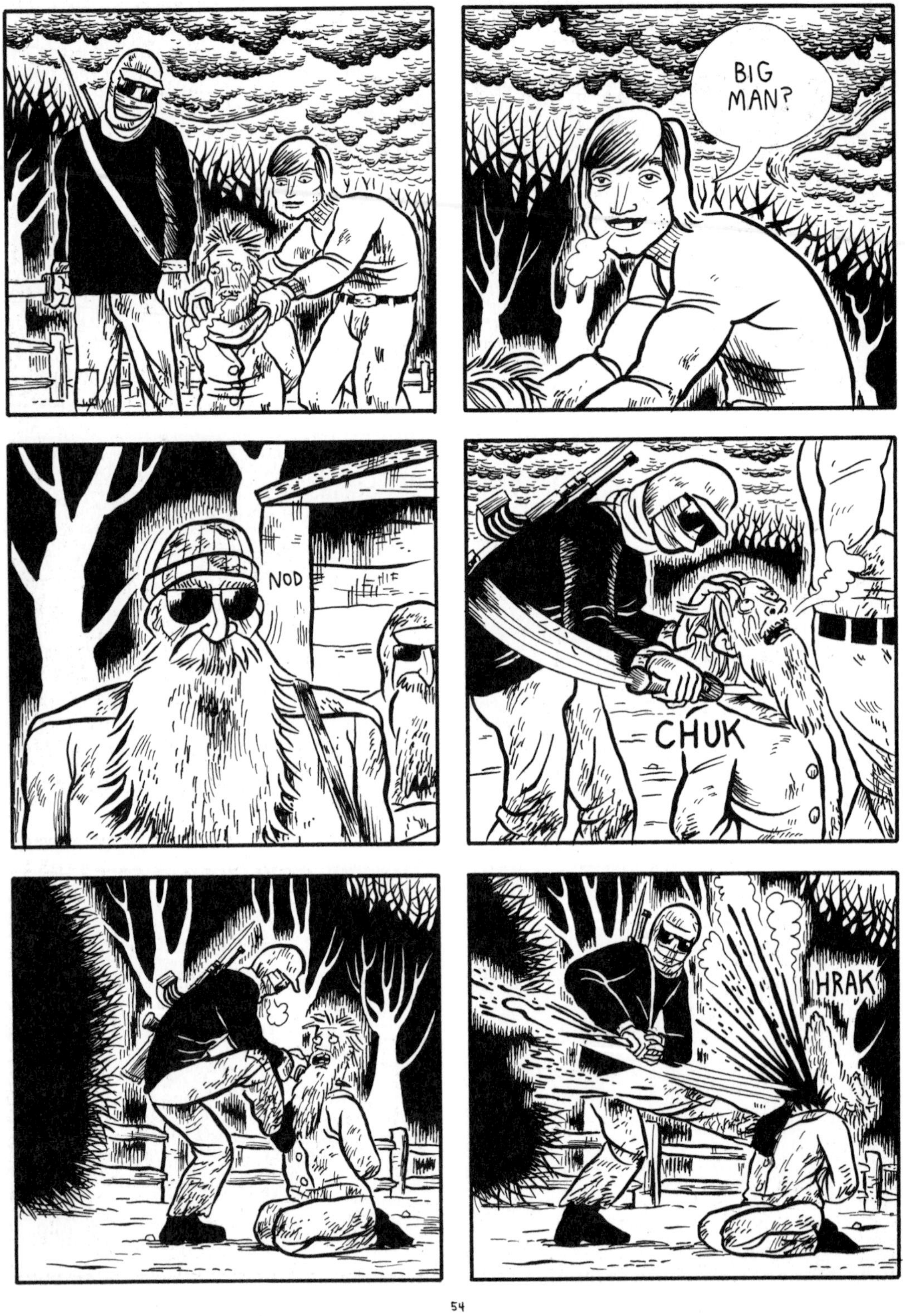
BIG MAN?
NOD
CHUK
HRAK

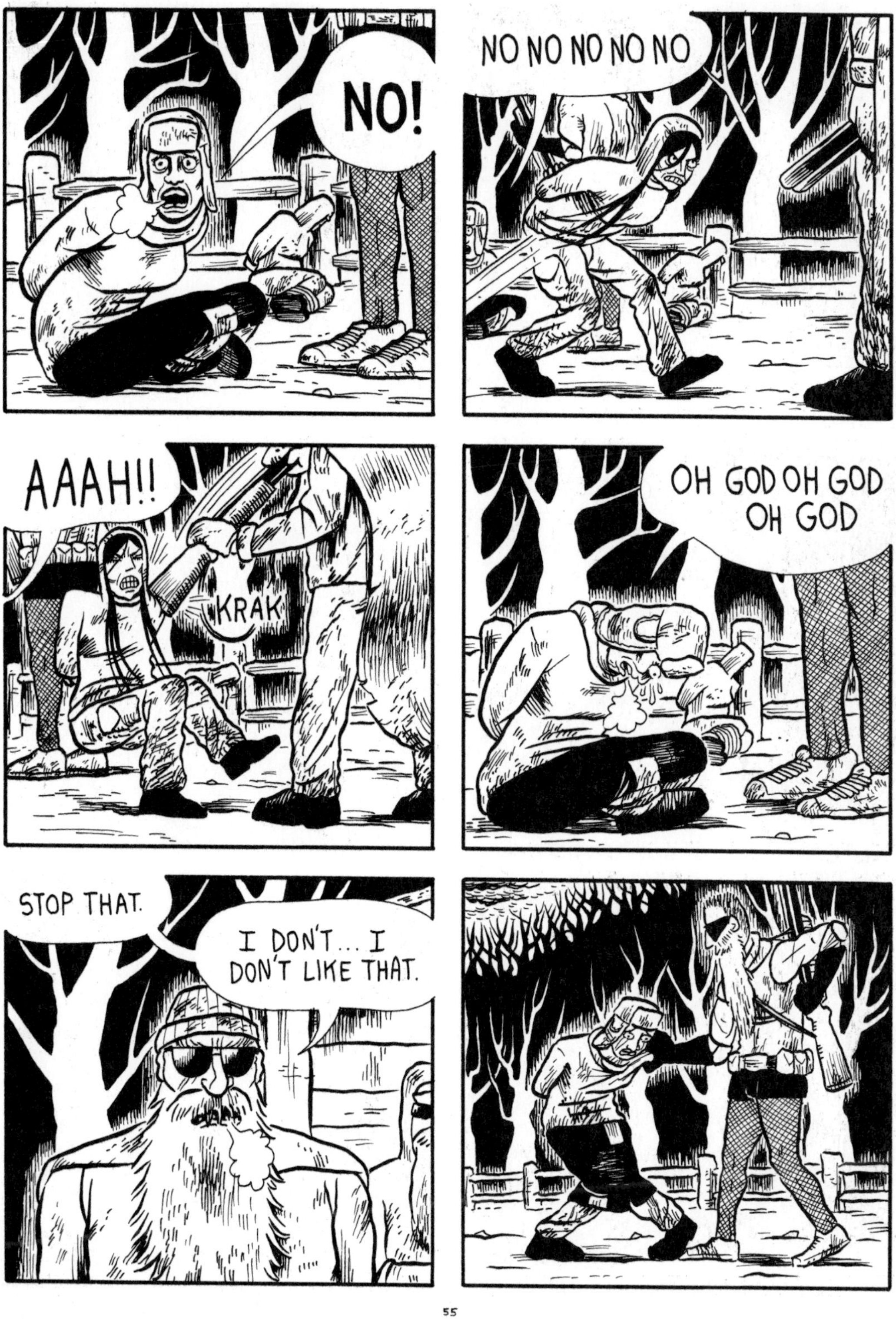
NO!
NO NO NO NO NO
AAAH!!
KRAK
OH GOD OH GOD OH GOD
STOP THAT.
I DON'T... I DON'T LIKE THAT.

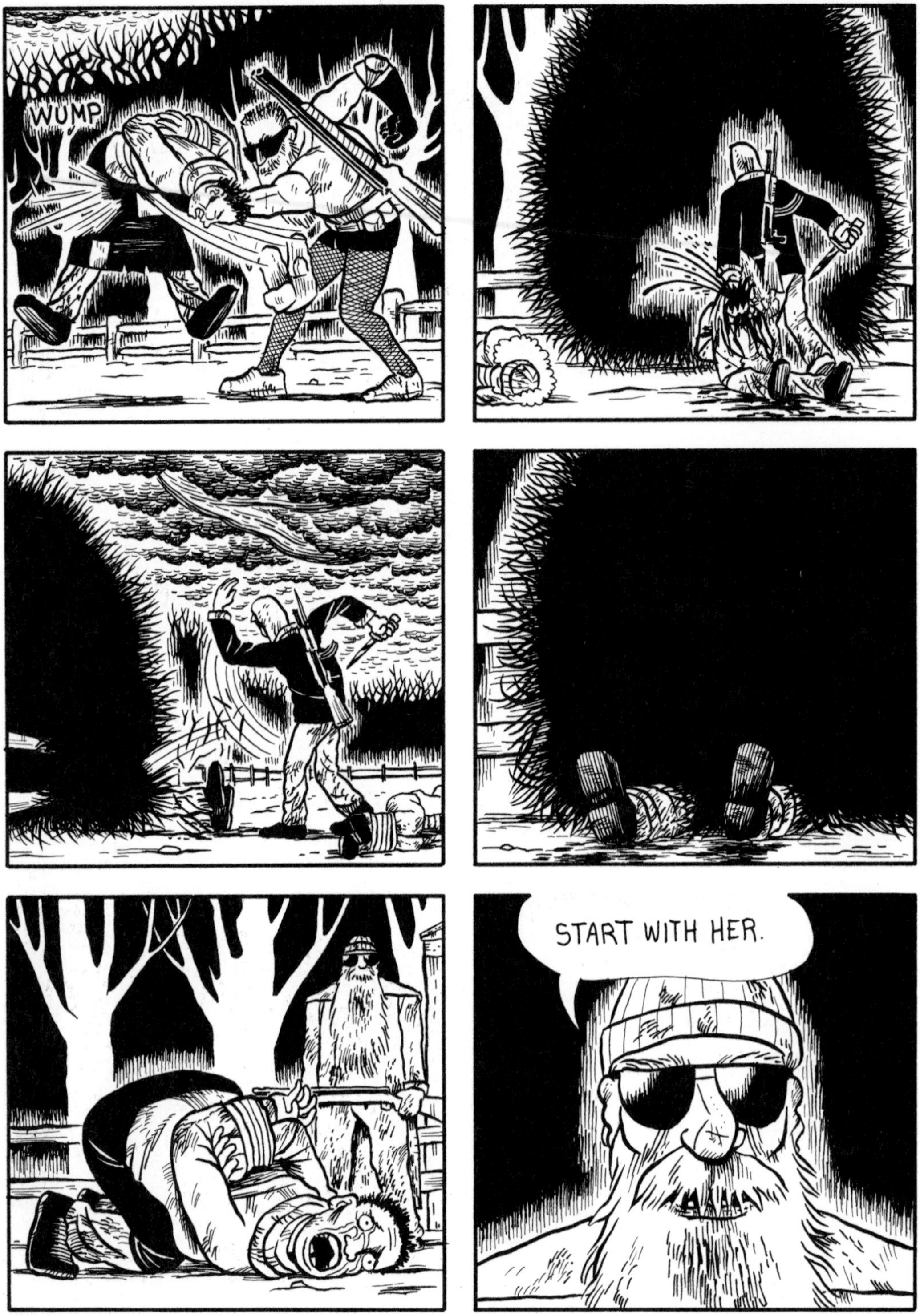
WUMP
START WITH HER.

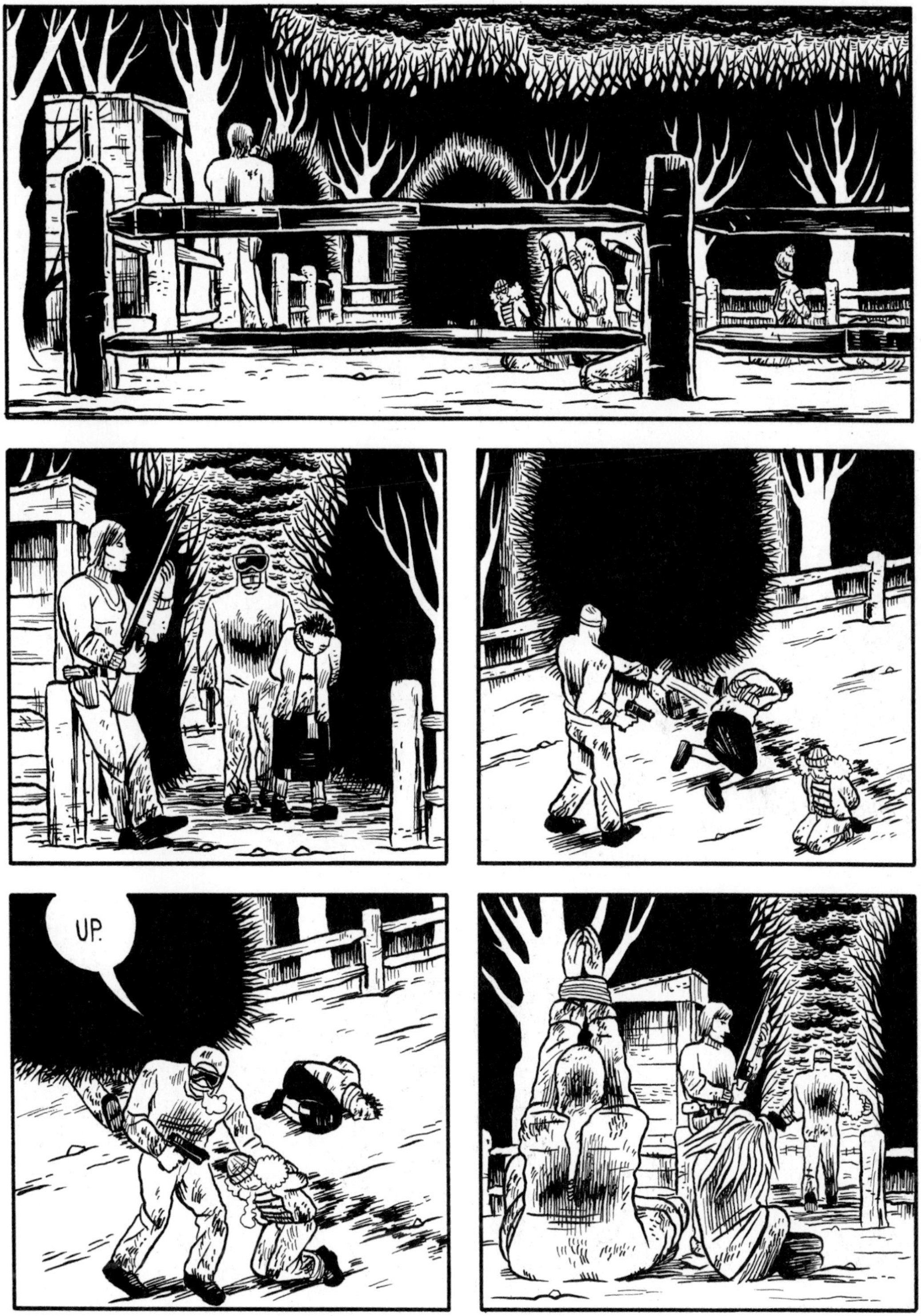
UP.

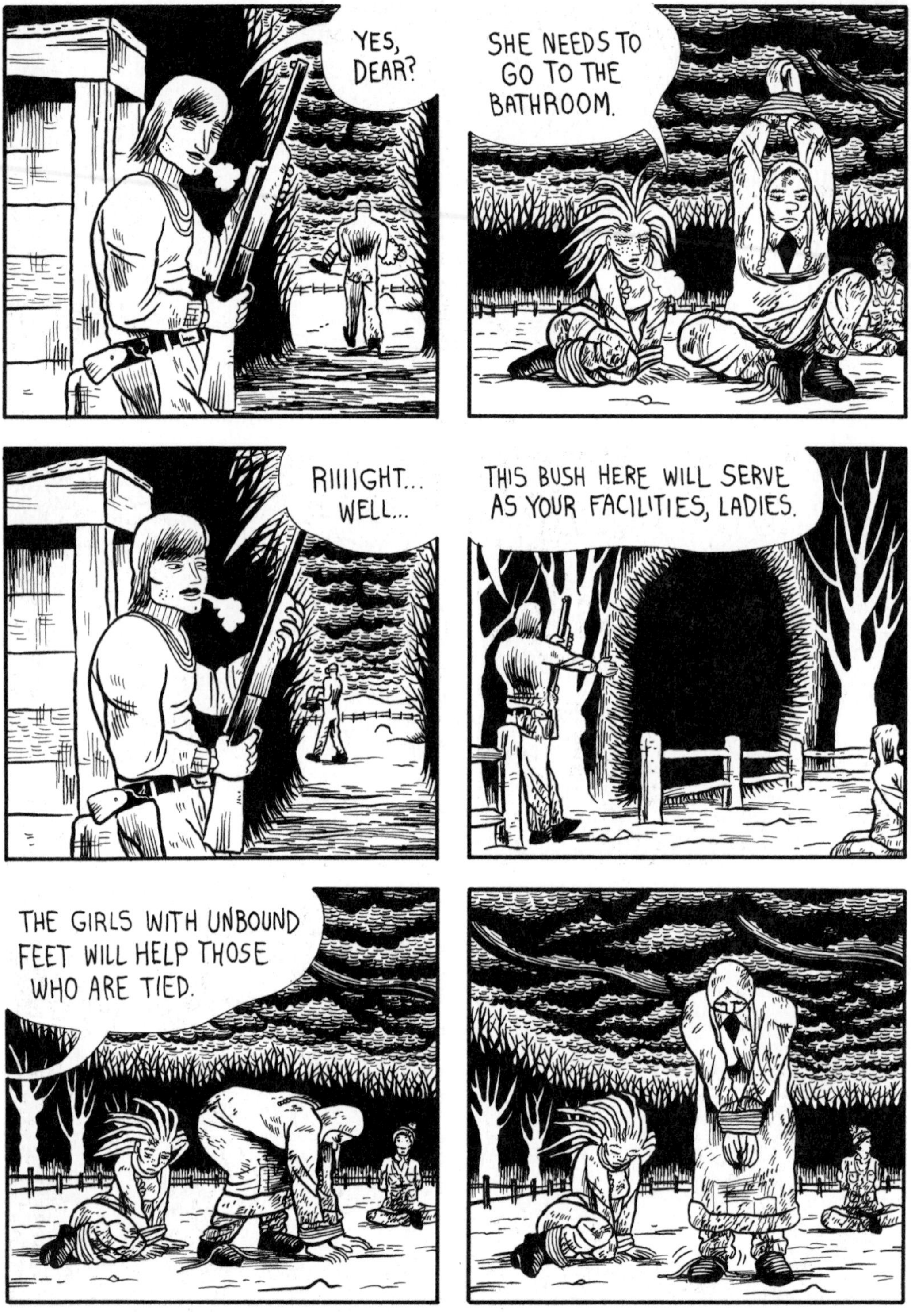
YES, DEAR?
SHE NEEDS TO GO TO THE BATHROOM.
RIIIIGHT... WELL...
THIS BUSH HERE WILL SERVE AS YOUR FACILITIES, LADIES.
THE GIRLS WITH UNBOUND FEET WILL HELP THOSE WHO ARE TIED.

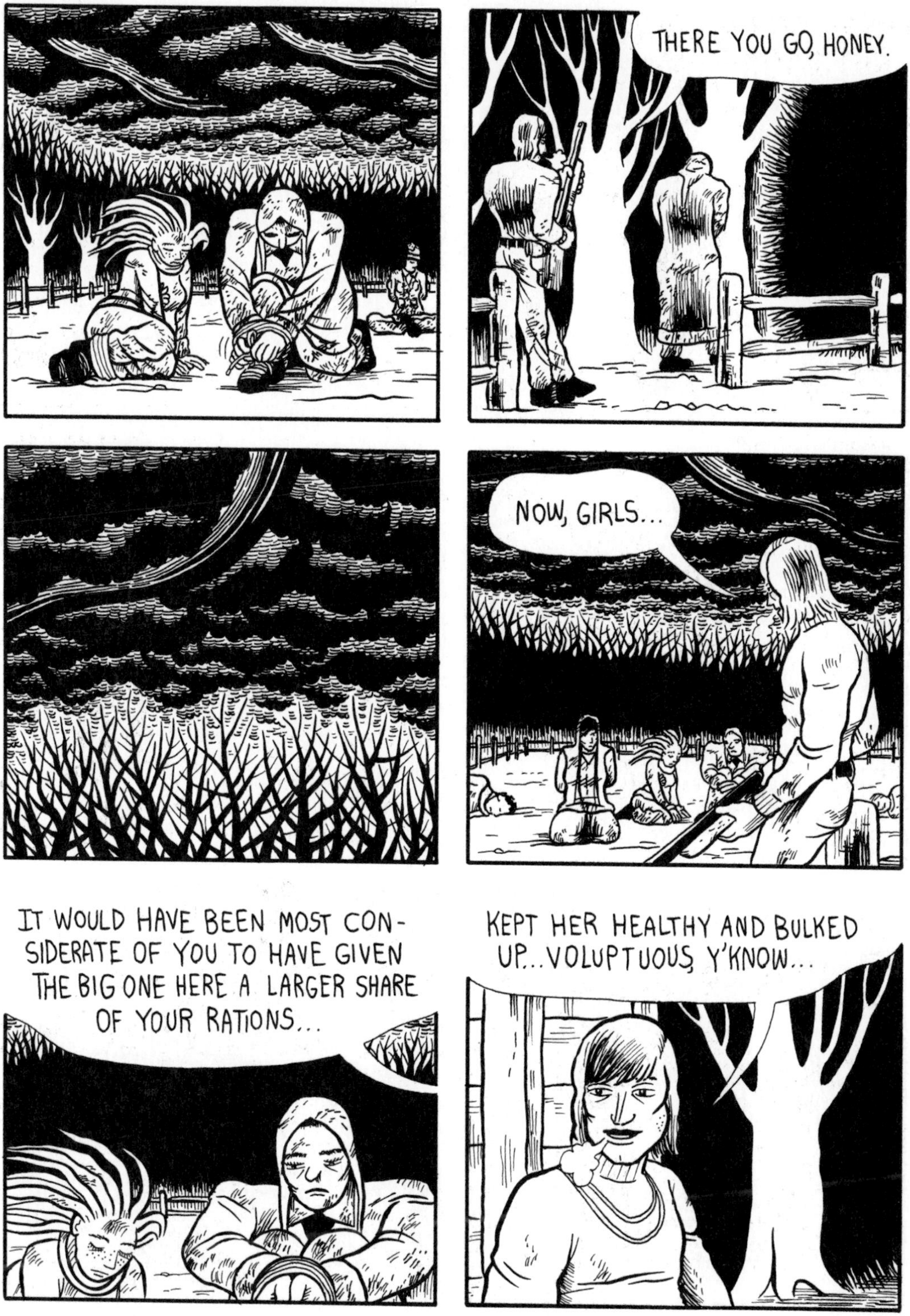
THERE YOU GO, HONEY.
NOW, GIRLS...
IT WOULD HAVE BEEN MOST CONSIDERATE OF YOU TO HAVE GIVEN THE BIG ONE HERE A LARGER SHARE OF YOUR RATIONS...
KEPT HER HEALTHY AND BULKED UP... VOLUPTUOUS, Y'KNOW...

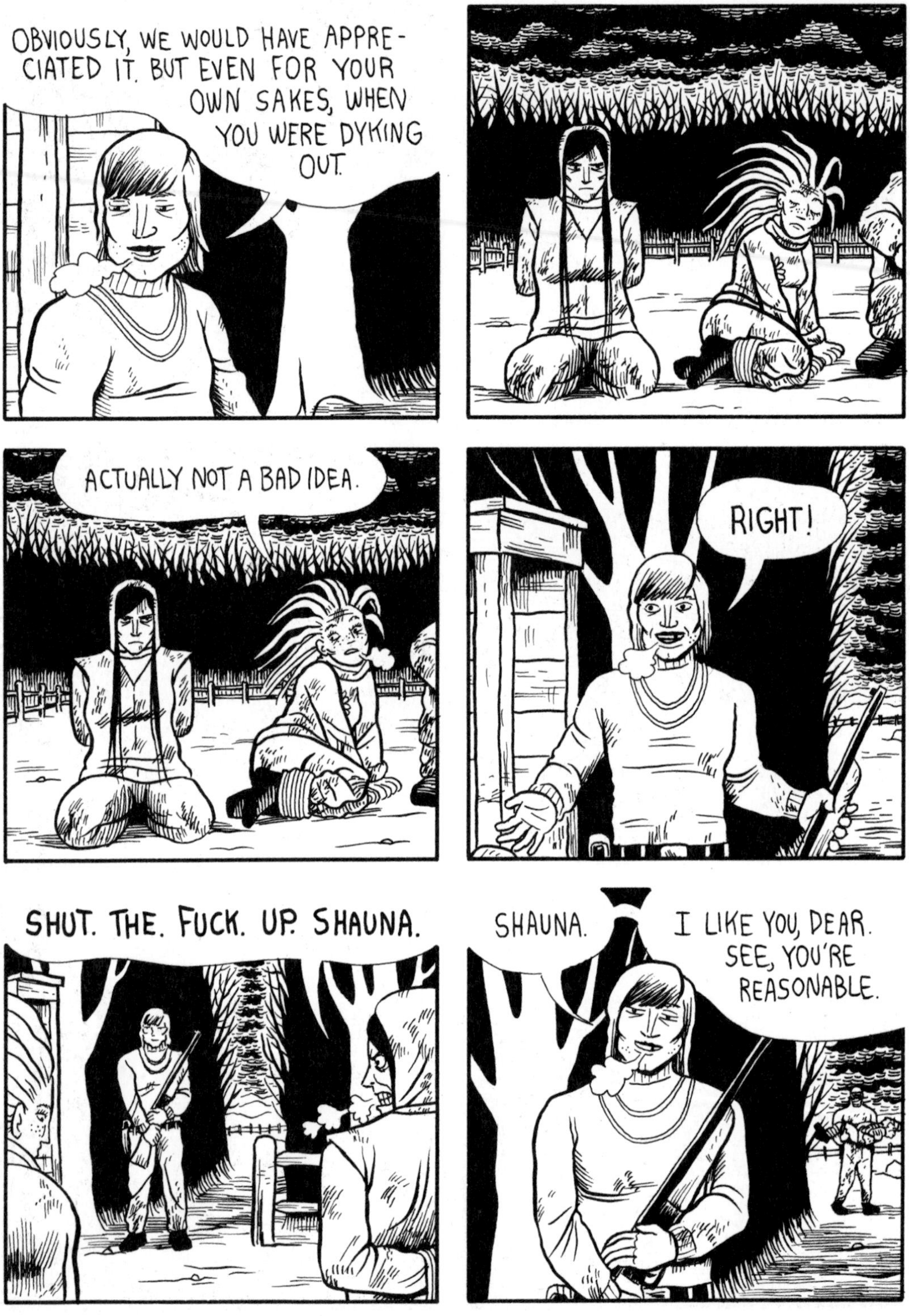
OBVIOUSLY, WE WOULD HAVE APPRECIATED IT. BUT EVEN FOR YOUR OWN SAKES, WHEN YOU WERE DYKING OUT.
ACTUALLY NOT A BAD IDEA.
RIGHT!
SHUT. THE. FUCK. UP. SHAUNA.
SHAUNA.
I LIKE YOU, DEAR. SEE, YOU'RE REASONABLE.

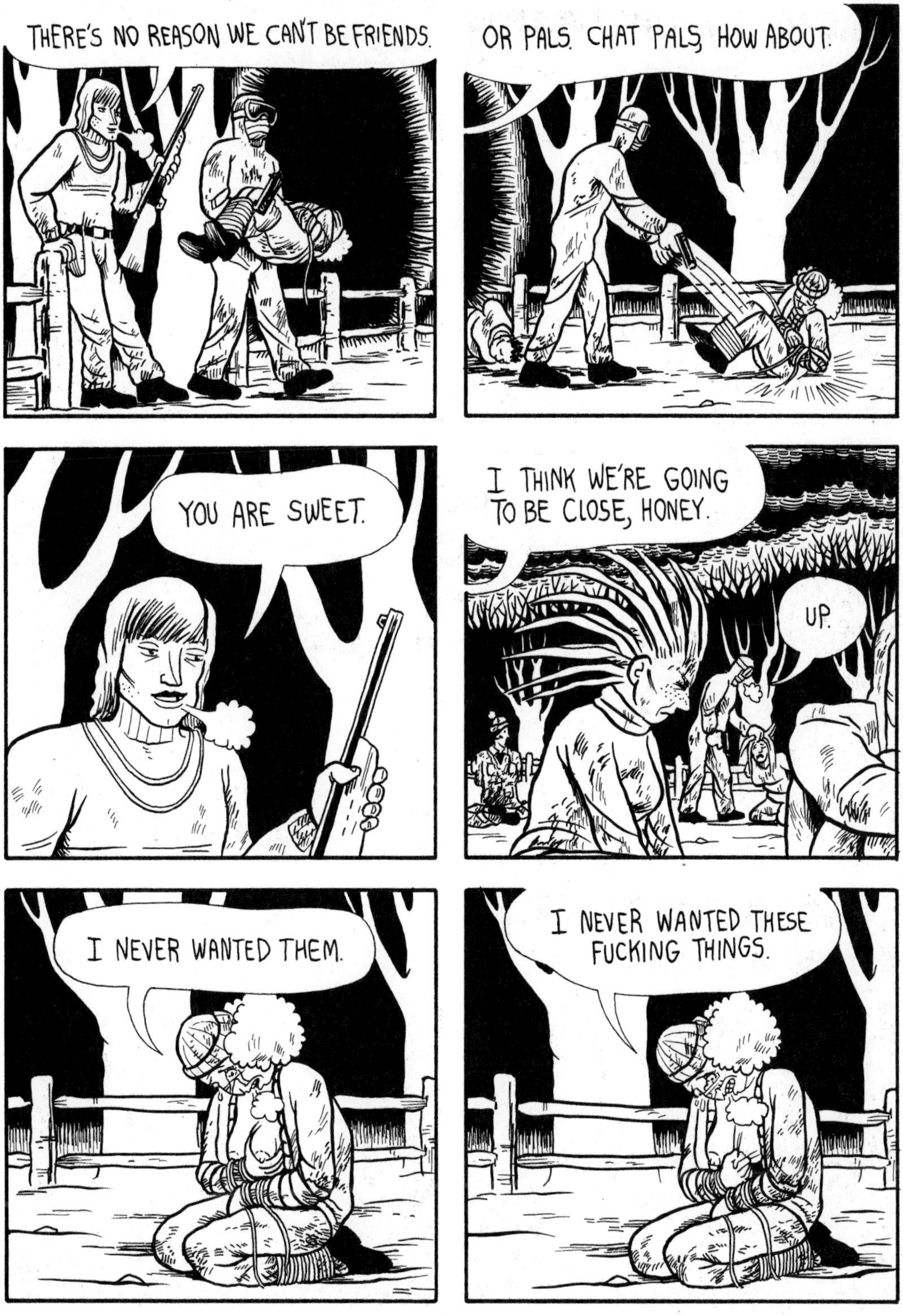
THERE'S NO REASON WE CAN'T BE FRIENDS.
OR PALS. CHAT PALS, HOW ABOUT.
YOU ARE SWEET.
I THINK WE'RE GOING TO BE CLOSE, HONEY.
UP.
I NEVER WANTED THEM.
I NEVER WANTED THESE FUCKING THINGS.

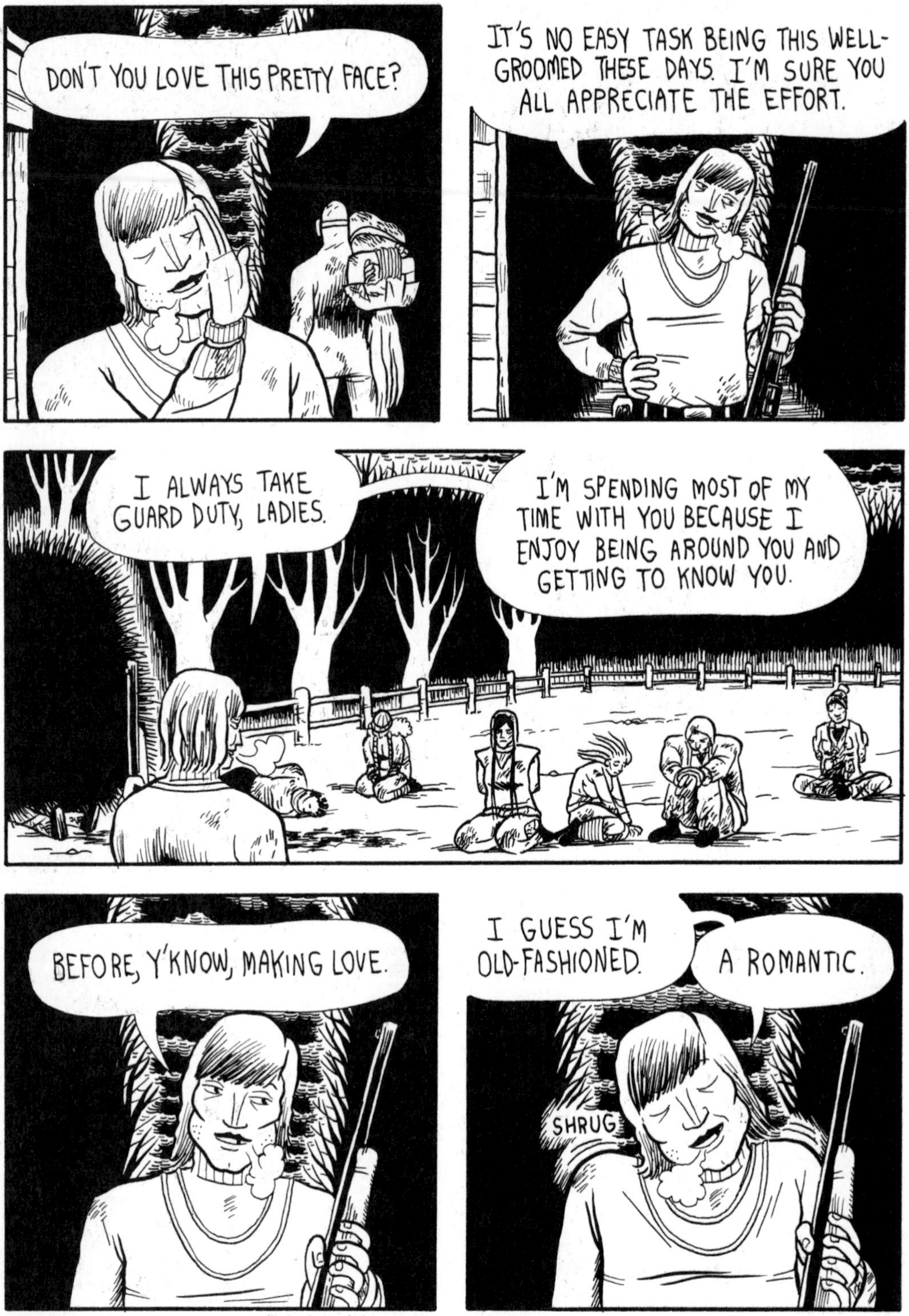
DON'T YOU LOVE THIS PRETTY FACE?
IT'S NO EASY TASK BEING THIS WELL-GROOMED THESE DAYS. I'M SURE YOU ALL APPRECIATE THE EFFORT.
I ALWAYS TAKE GUARD DUTY, LADIES.
I'M SPENDING MOST OF MY TIME WITH YOU BECAUSE I ENJOY BEING AROUND YOU AND GETTING TO KNOW YOU.
BEFORE, Y'KNOW, MAKING LOVE.
I GUESS I'M OLD-FASHIONED.
A ROMANTIC.
SHRUG

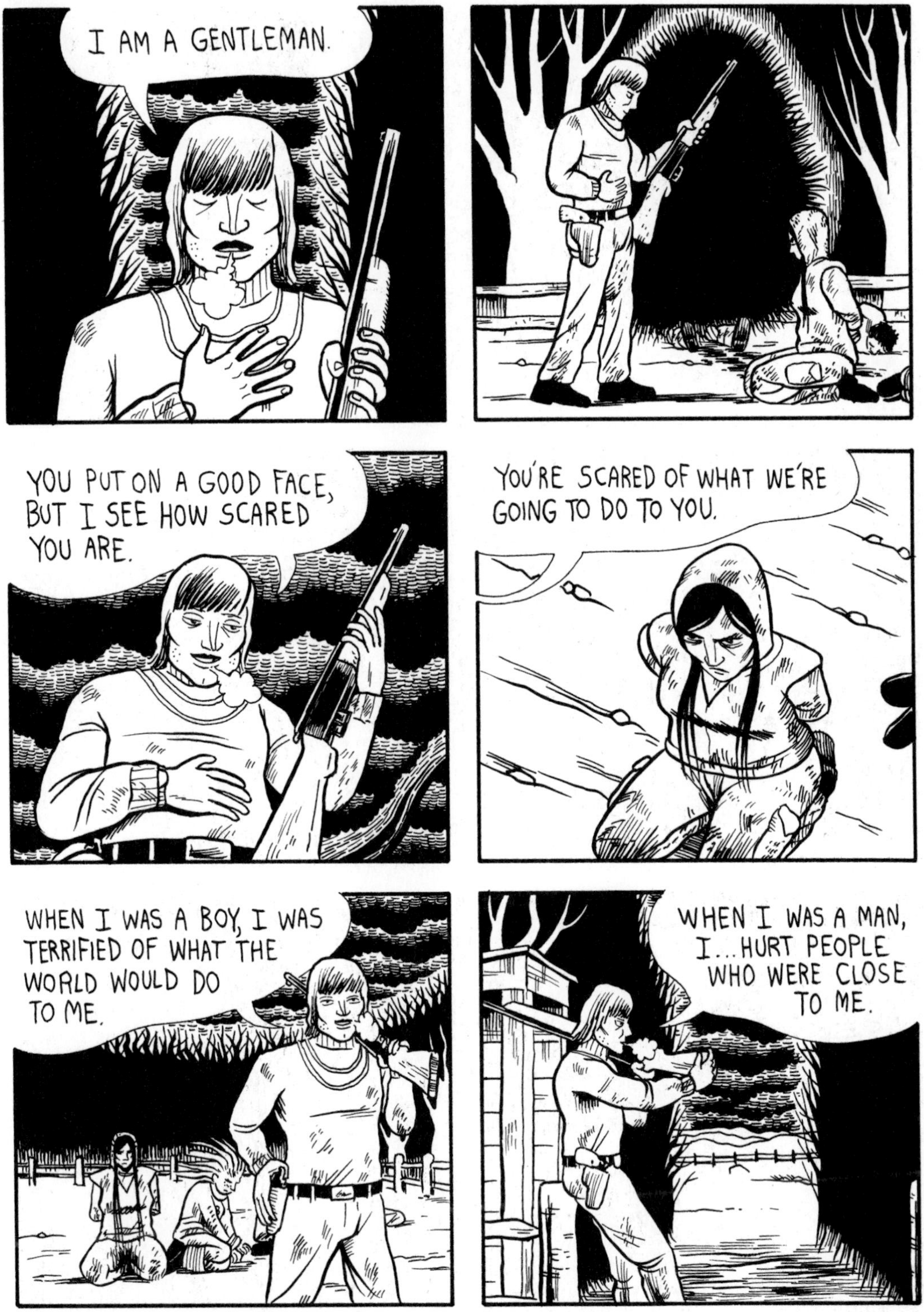
I AM A GENTLEMAN.
YOU PUT ON A GOOD FACE, BUT I SEE HOW SCARED YOU ARE.
YOU'RE SCARED OF WHAT WE'RE GOING TO DO TO YOU.
WHEN I WAS A BOY, I WAS TERRIFIED OF WHAT THE WORLD WOULD DO TO ME.
WHEN I WAS A MAN, I... HURT PEOPLE WHO WERE CLOSE TO ME.

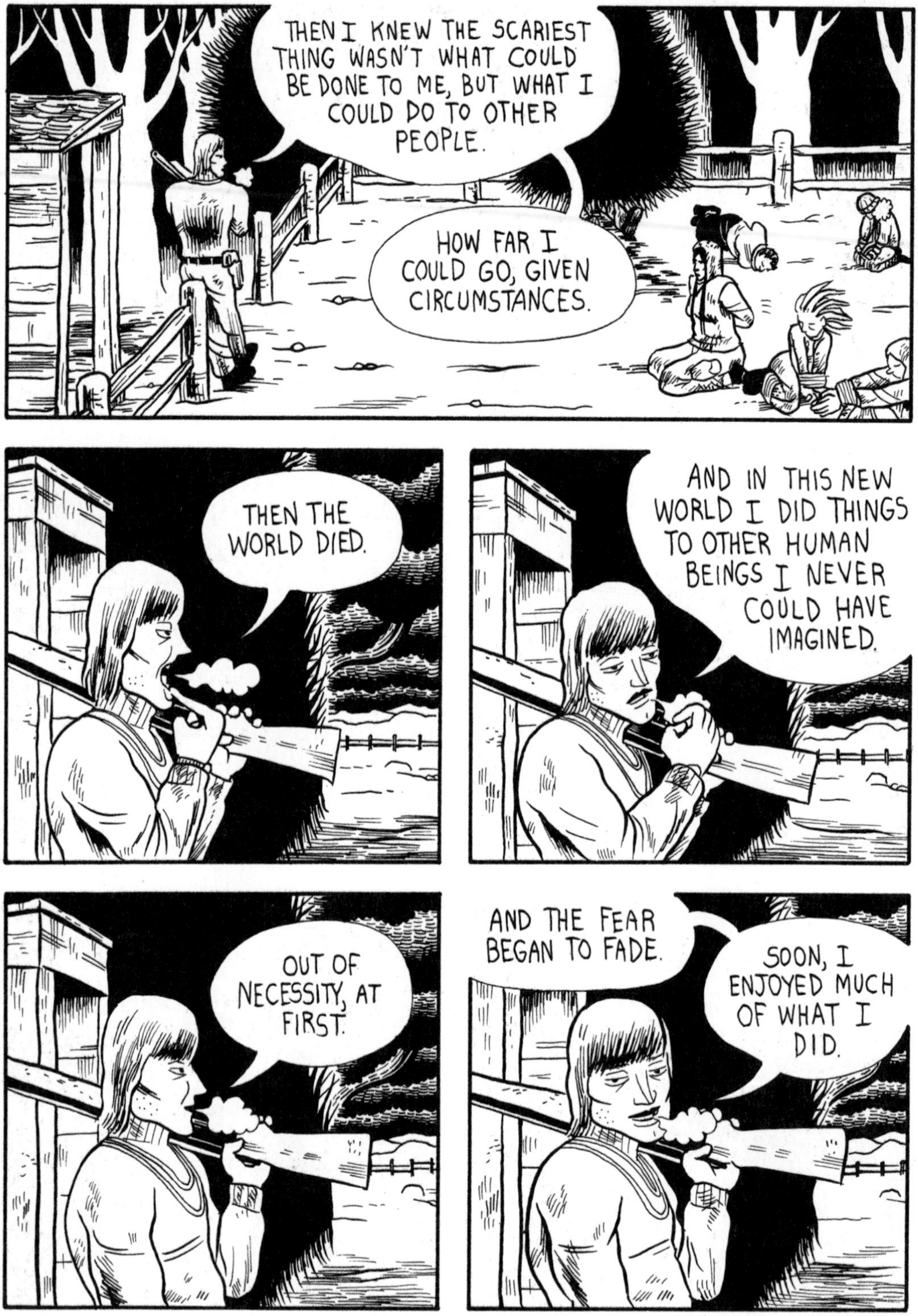
THEN I KNEW THE SCARIEST THING WASN'T WHAT COULD BE DONE TO ME, BUT WHAT I COULD DO TO OTHER PEOPLE.
HOW FAR I COULD GO, GIVEN CIRCUMSTANCES.
THEN THE WORLD DIED.
AND IN THIS NEW WORLD I DID THINGS TO OTHER HUMAN BEINGS I NEVER COULD HAVE IMAGINED.
OUT OF NECESSITY, AT FIRST.
AND THE FEAR BEGAN TO FADE.
SOON, I ENJOYED MUCH OF WHAT I DID.

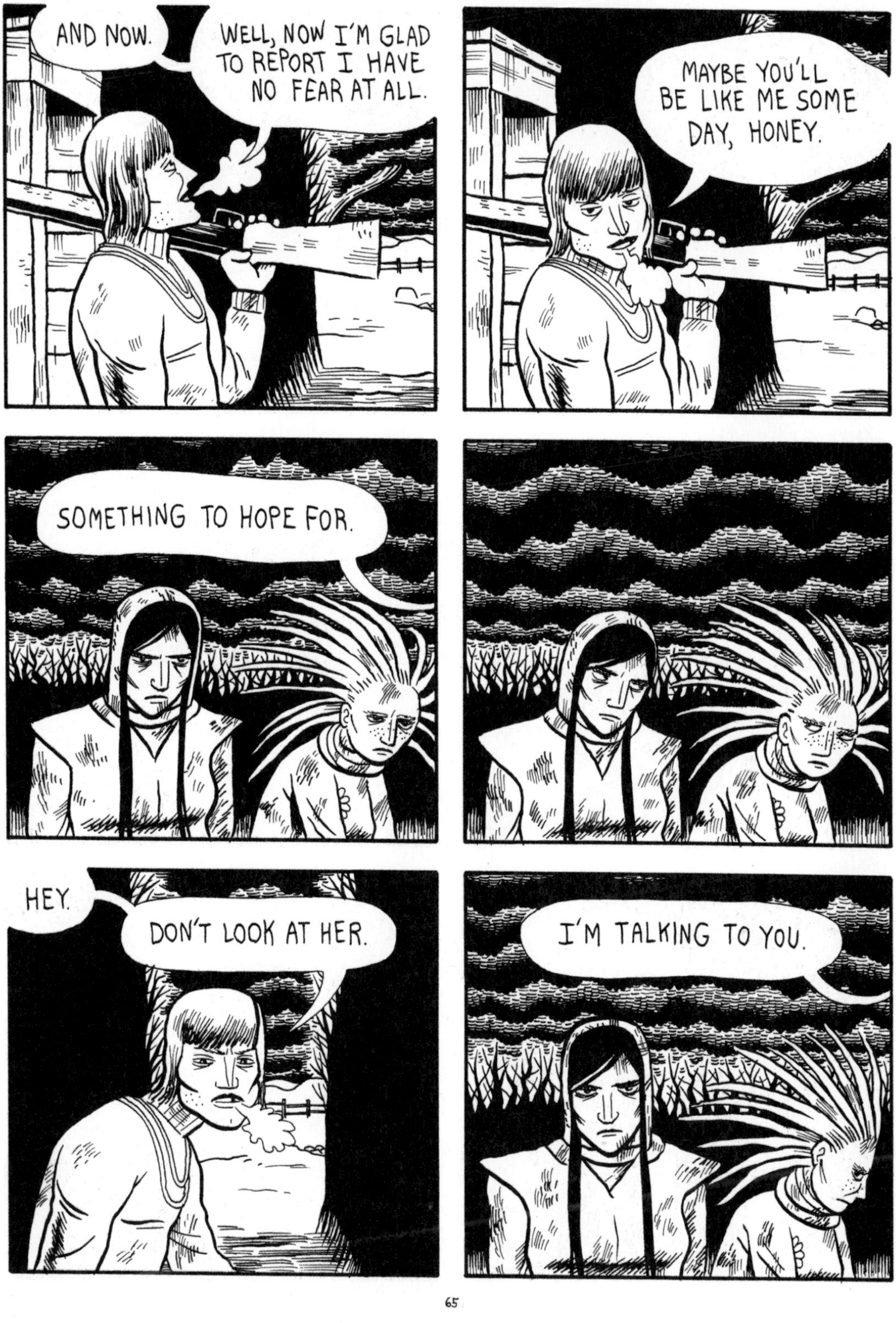
AND NOW.
WELL, NOW I'M GLAD TO REPORT I HAVE NO FEAR AT ALL.
MAYBE YOU'LL BE LIKE ME SOME DAY, HONEY.
SOMETHING TO HOPE FOR.
HEY.
DON'T LOOK AT HER.
I'M TALKING TO YOU.

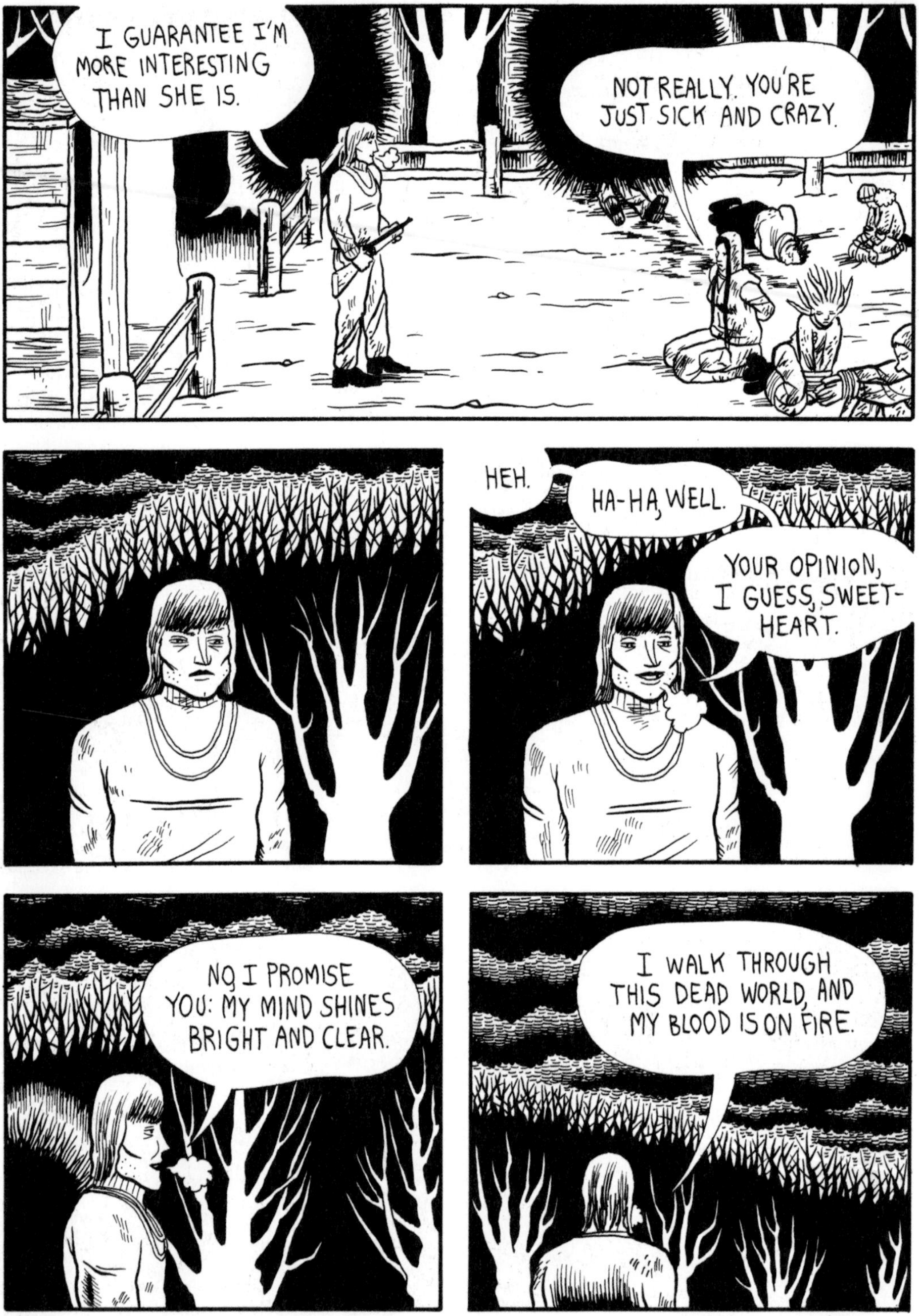
I GUARANTEE I'M MORE INTERESTING THAN SHE IS.
NOT REALLY. YOU'RE JUST SICK AND CRAZY.
HEH.
HA-HA, WELL.
YOUR OPINION, I GUESS, SWEETHEART.
NO, I PROMISE YOU: MY MIND SHINES BRIGHT AND CLEAR.
I WALK THROUGH THIS DEAD WORLD, AND MY BLOOD IS ON FIRE.

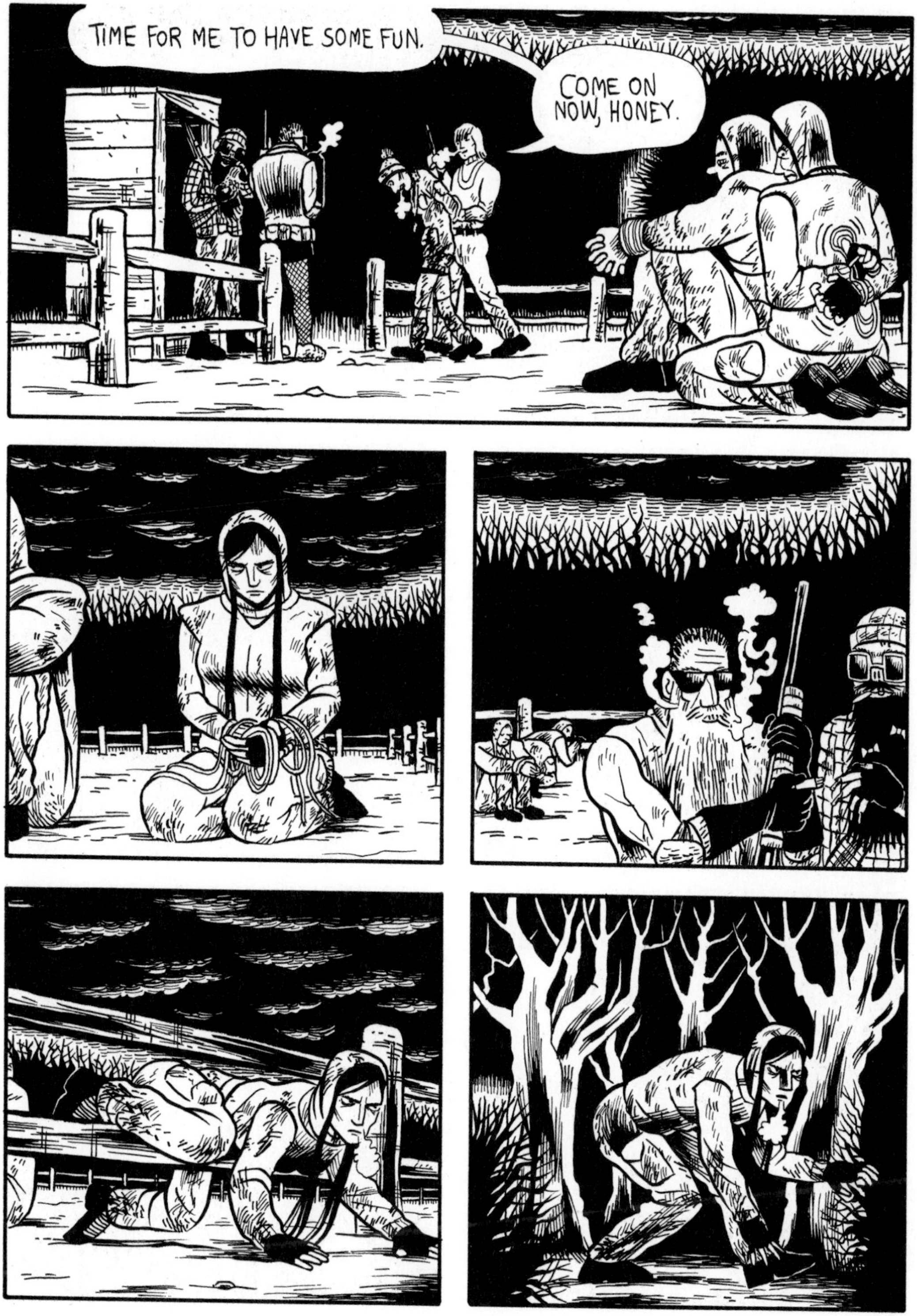
TIME FOR ME TO HAVE SOME FUN.
COME ON NOW, HONEY.

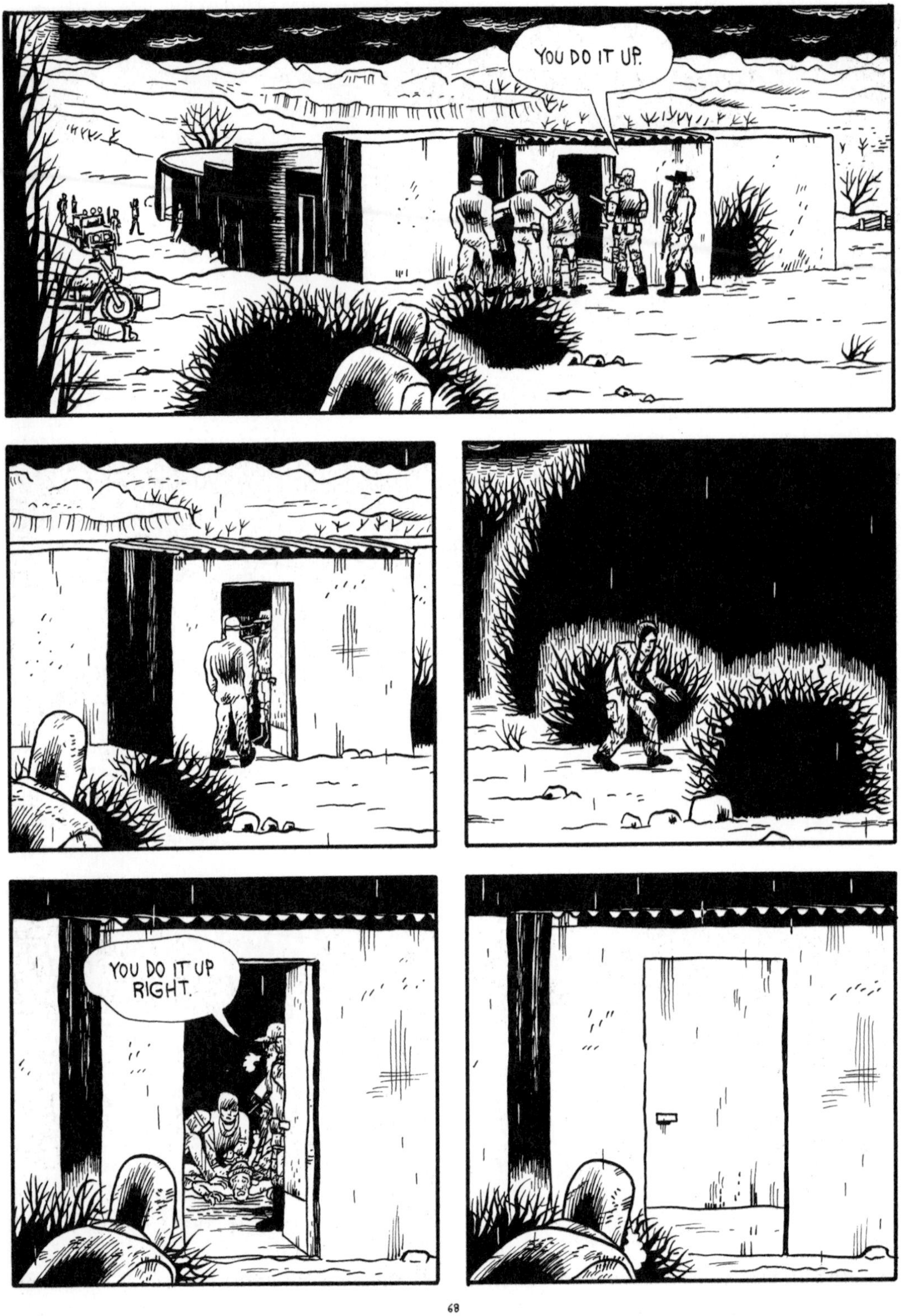
YOU DO IT UP.
YOU DO IT UP RIGHT.

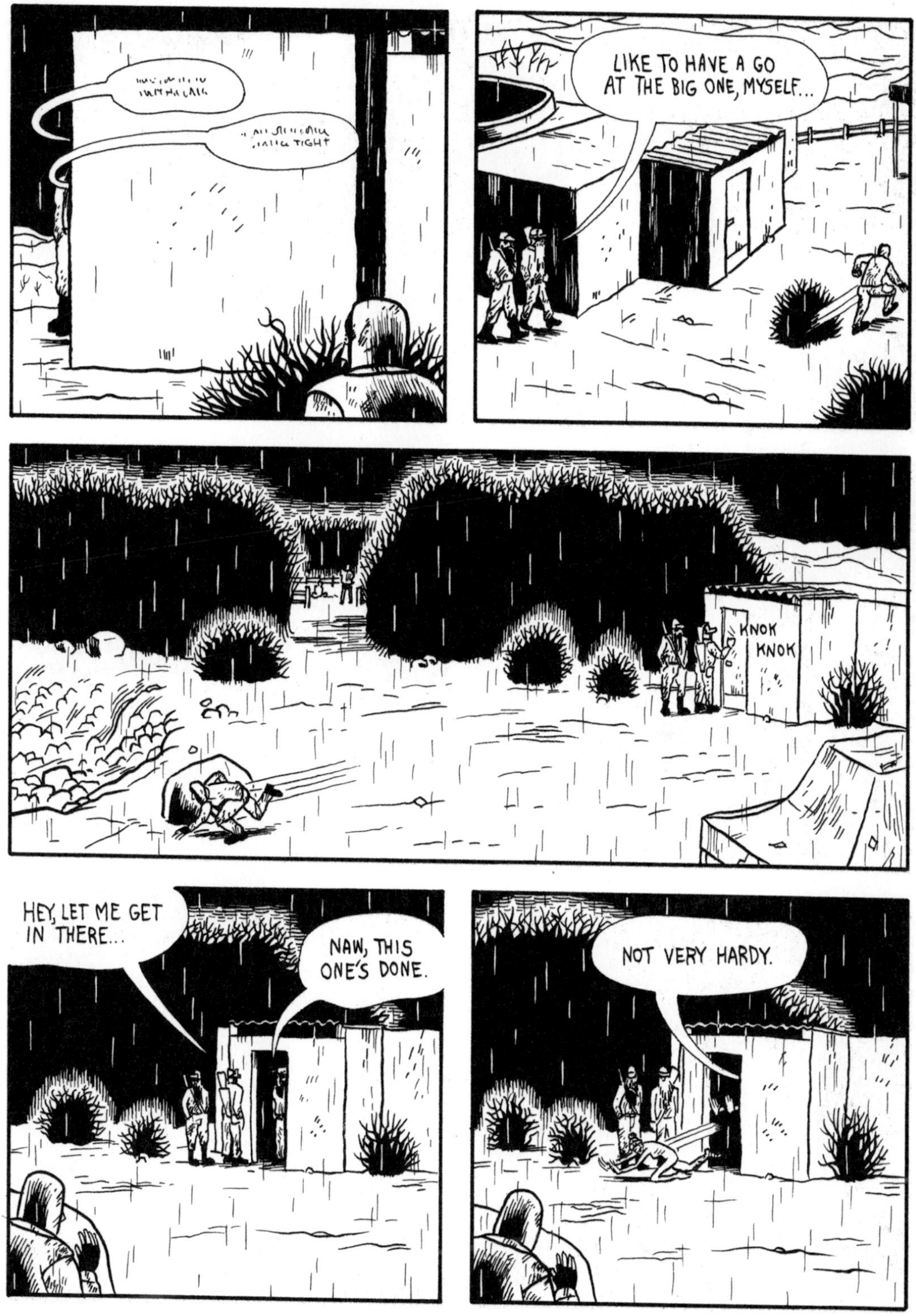
LIKE TO HAVE A GO AT THE BIG ONE, MYSELF...
KNOK KNOK
HEY, LET ME GET IN THERE...
NAW, THIS ONE'S DONE.
NOT VERY HARDY.

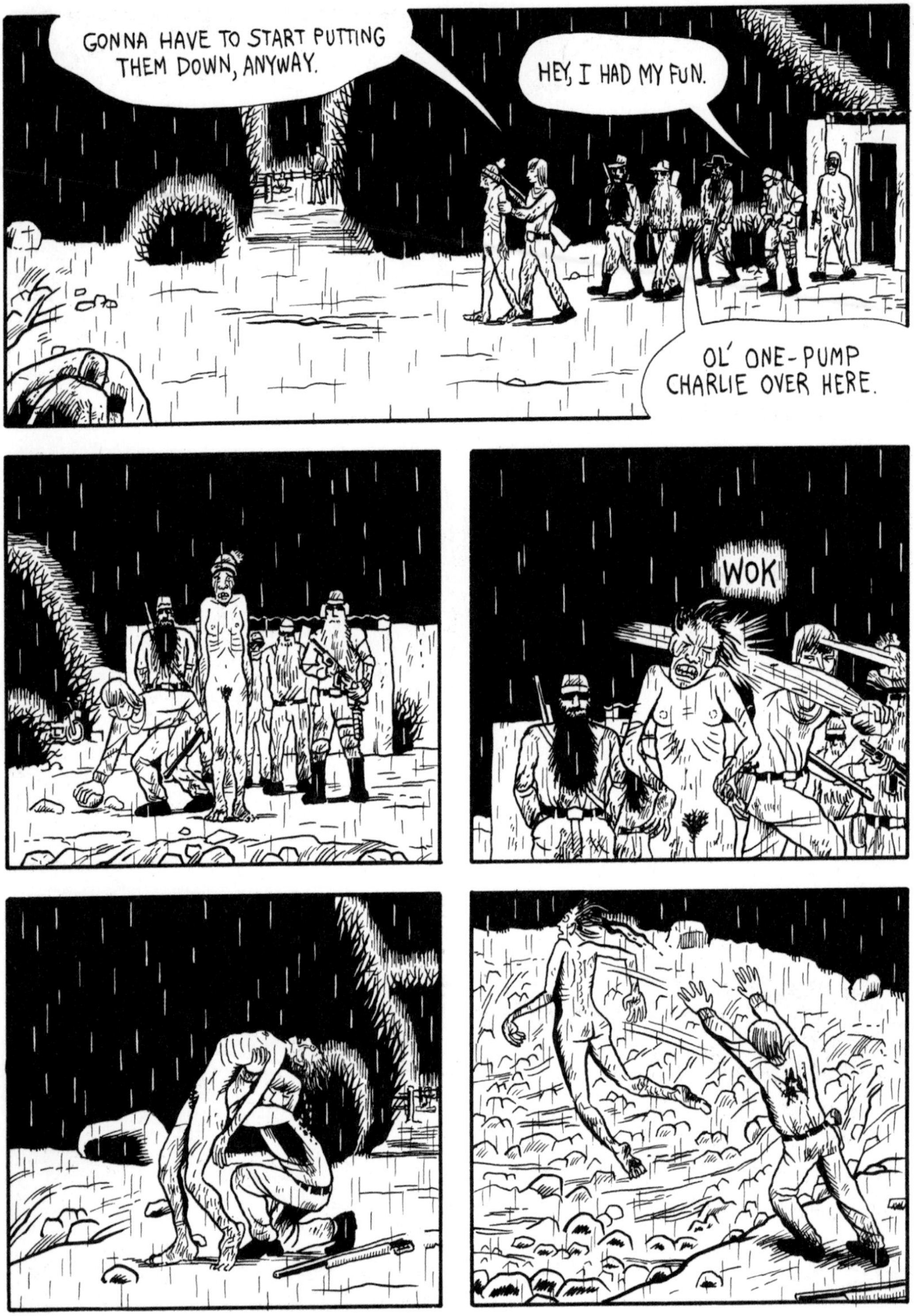
GONNA HAVE TO START PUTTING THEM DOWN, ANYWAY.
HEY, I HAD MY FUN.
OL' ONE-PUMP CHARLIE OVER HERE.
WOK

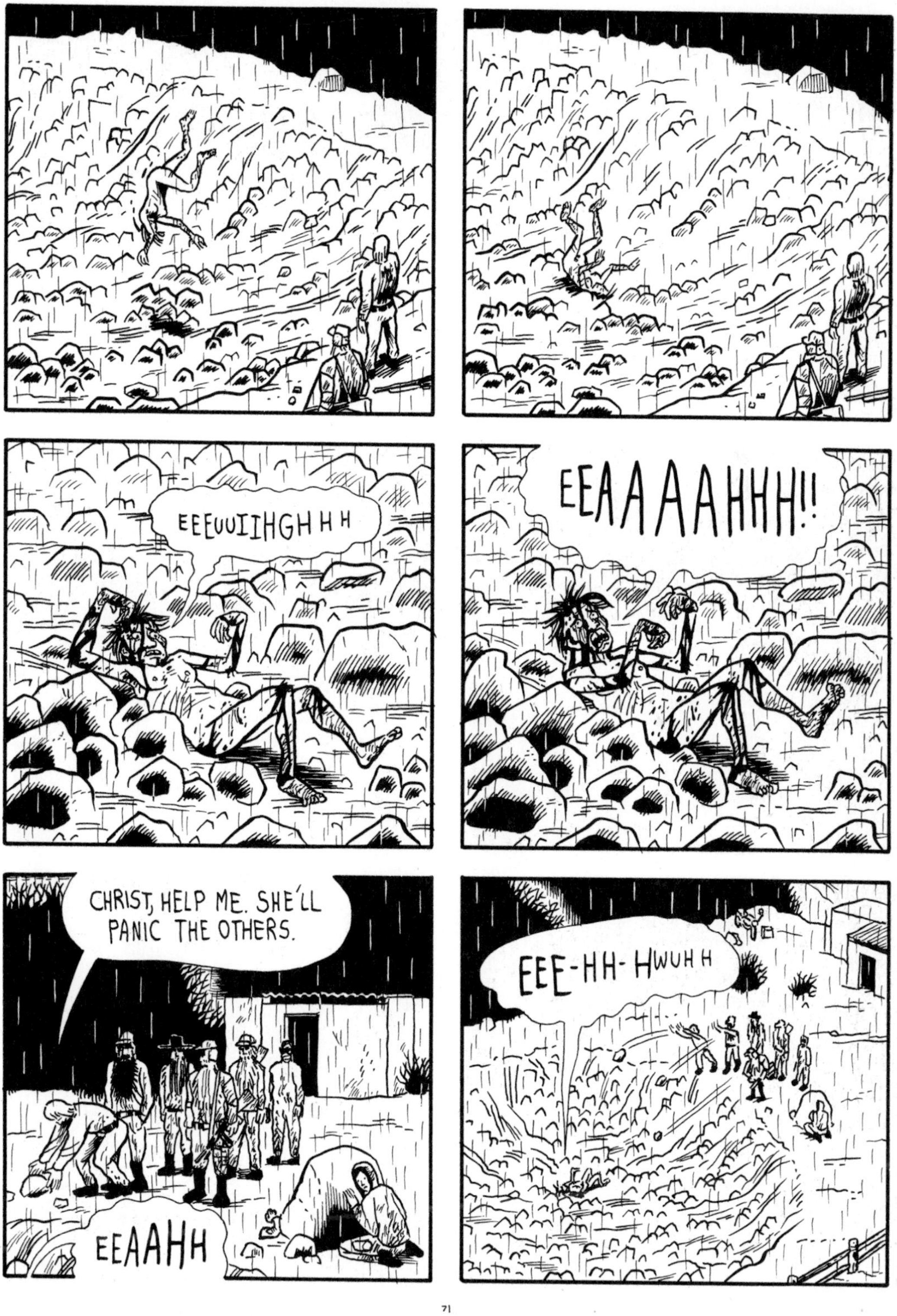
EEEUUIIHGH H H
EEAAAAHHH!!
CHRIST, HELP ME. SHE'LL PANIC THE OTHERS.
EEAAHH
EEE-HH-HWUH H

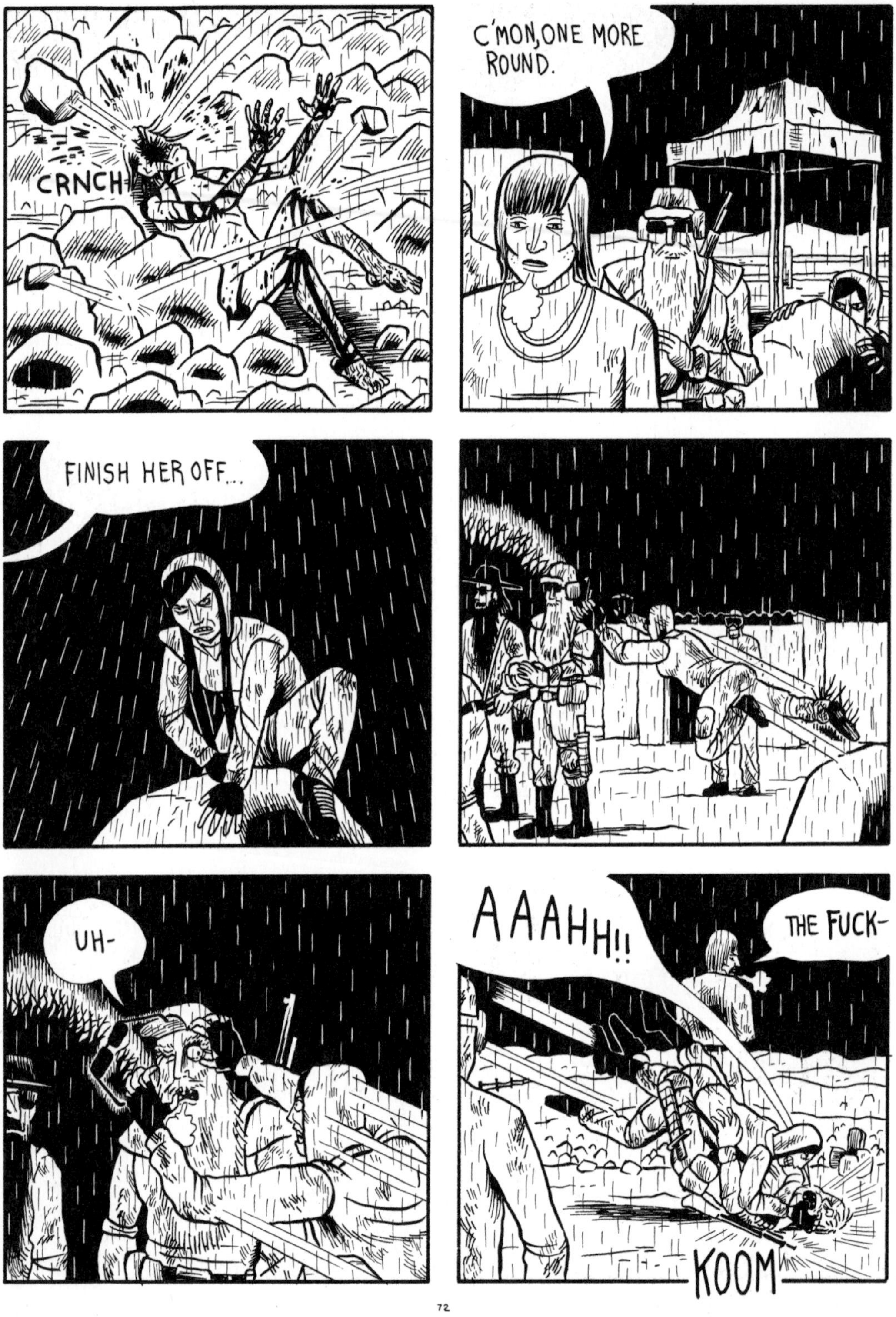
CRNCH
C'MON, ONE MORE ROUND.
FINISH HER OFF...
UH-
AAAHH!!
THE FUCK-
KOOM

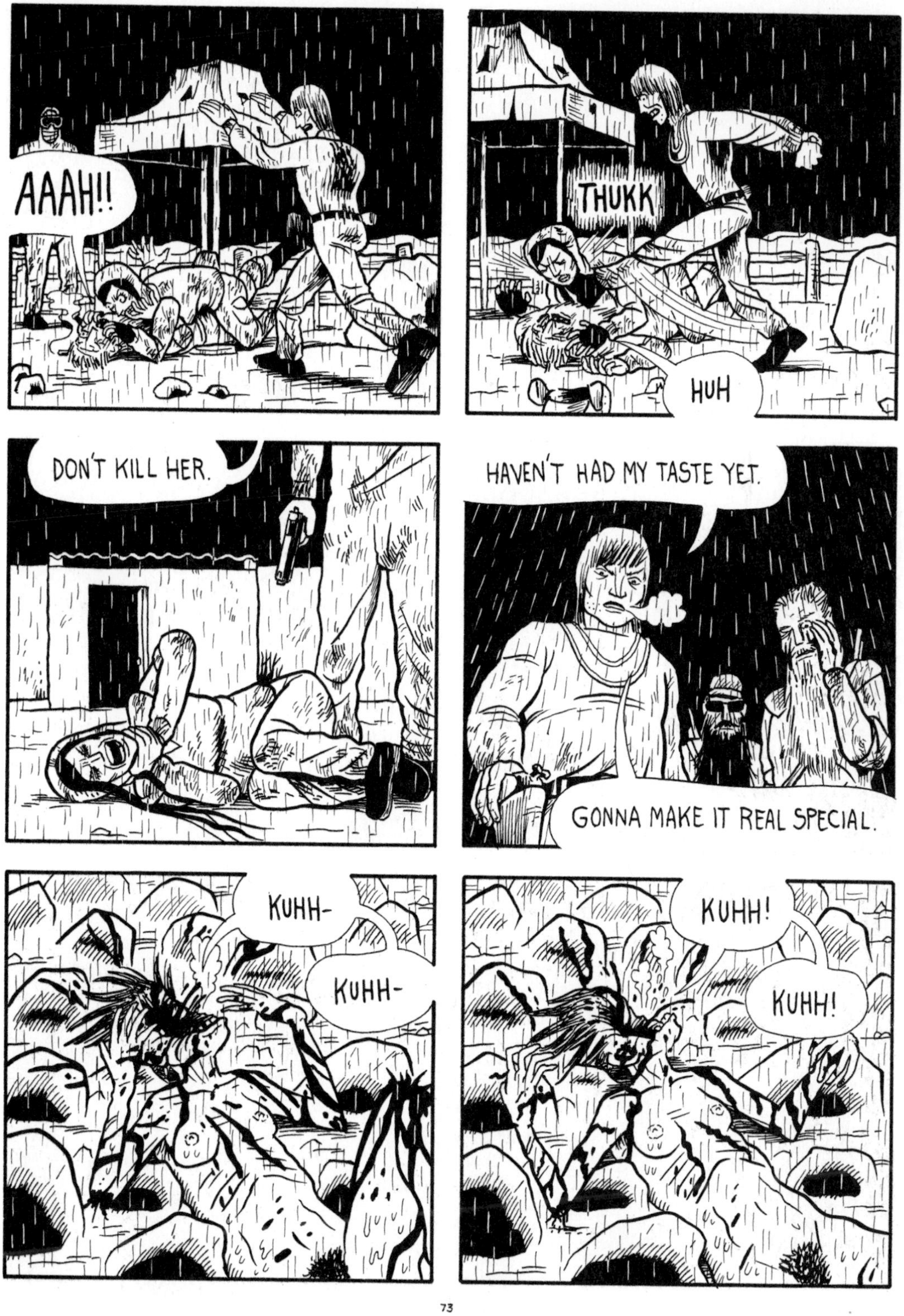
AAAH!!
THUKK
HUH
DON'T KILL HER.
HAVEN'T HAD MY TASTE YET.
GONNA MAKE IT REAL SPECIAL.
KUHH-
KUHH-
KUHH!
KUHH!

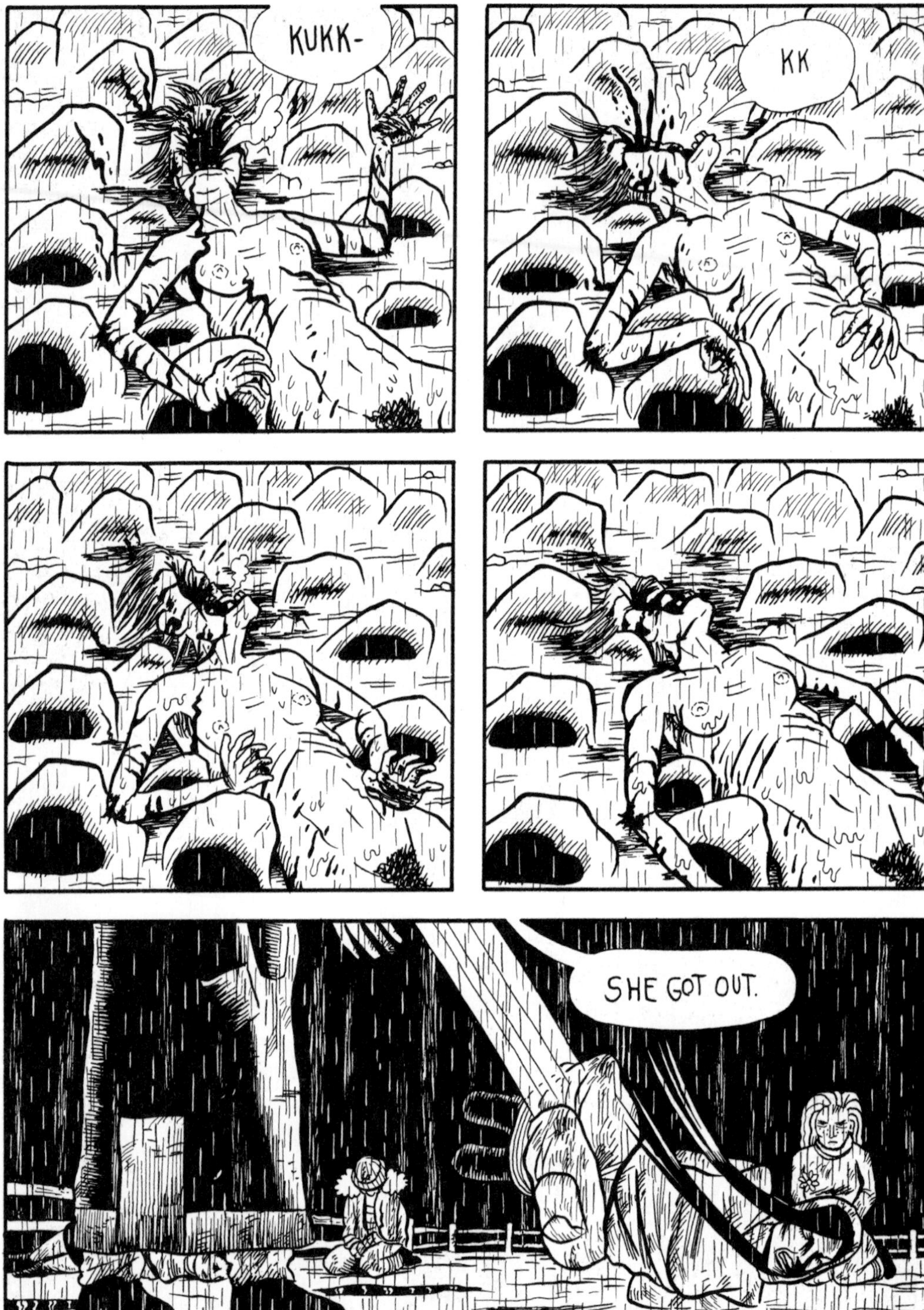
KUKK-
KK
SHE GOT OUT.

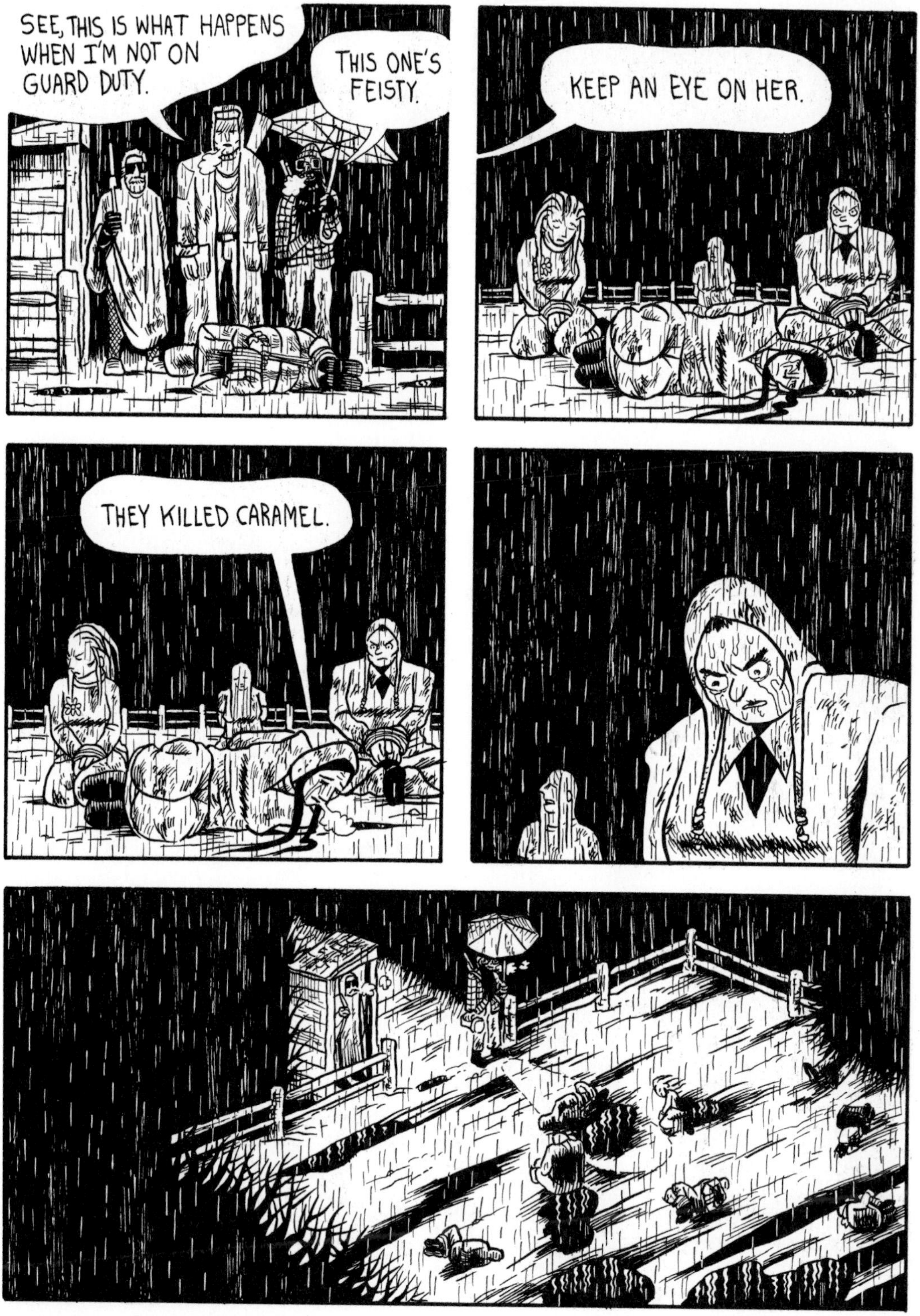
SEE, THIS IS WHAT HAPPENS WHEN I'M NOT ON GUARD DUTY.
THIS ONE'S FEISTY.
KEEP AN EYE ON HER.
THEY KILLED CARAMEL.

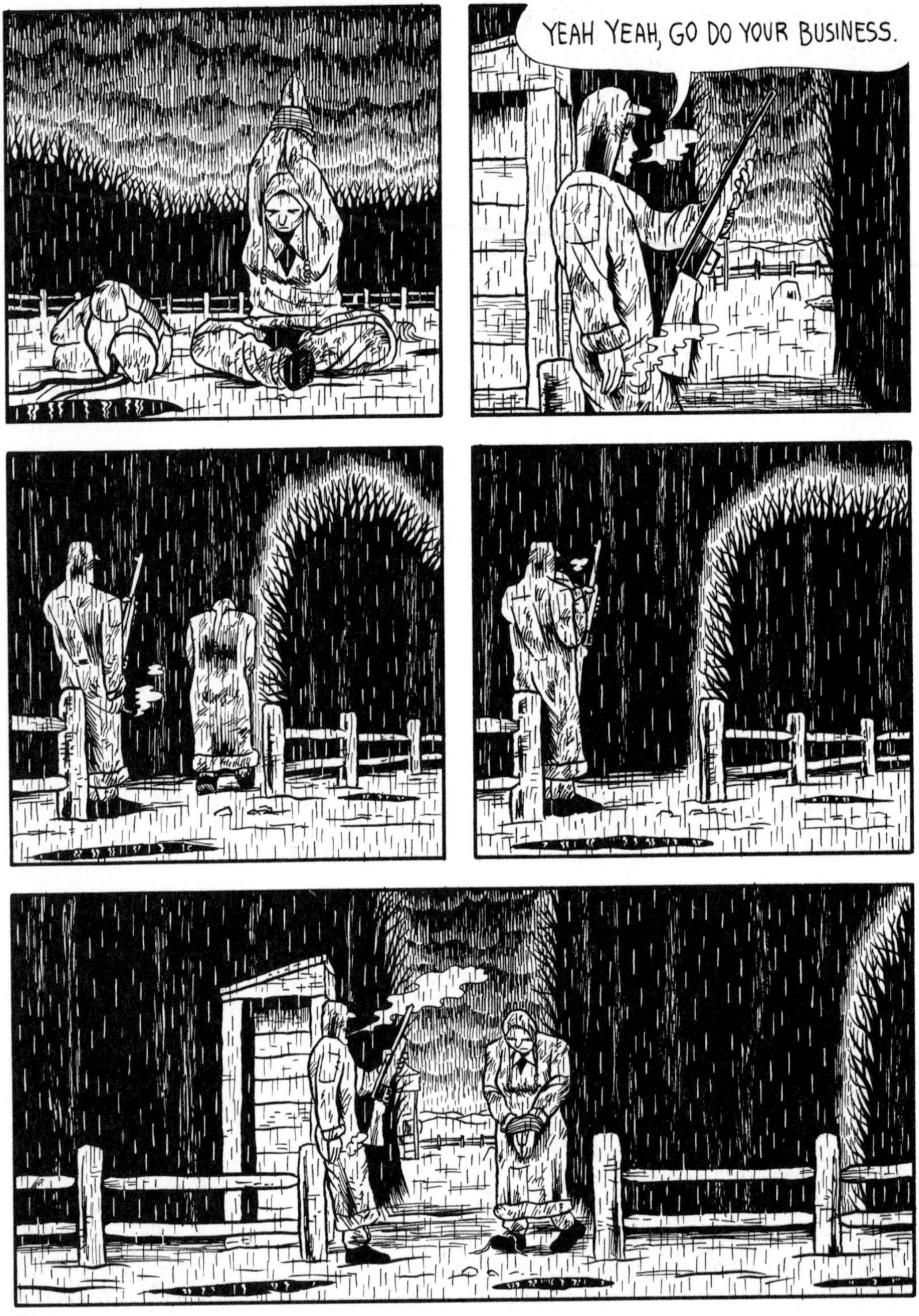
YEAH YEAH, GO DO YOUR BUSINESS.

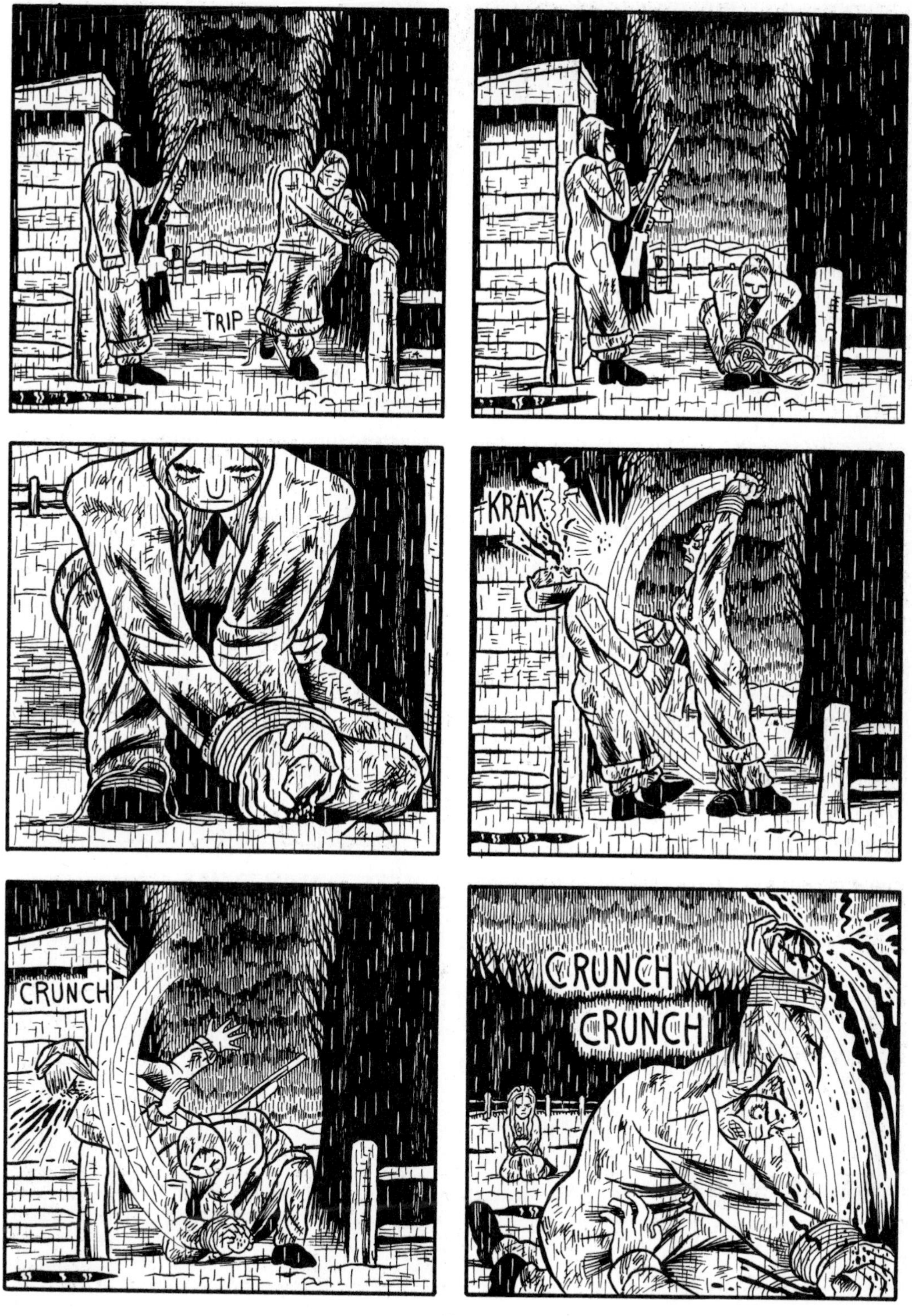
TRIP
KRAK
CRUNCH
CRUNCH
CRUNCH

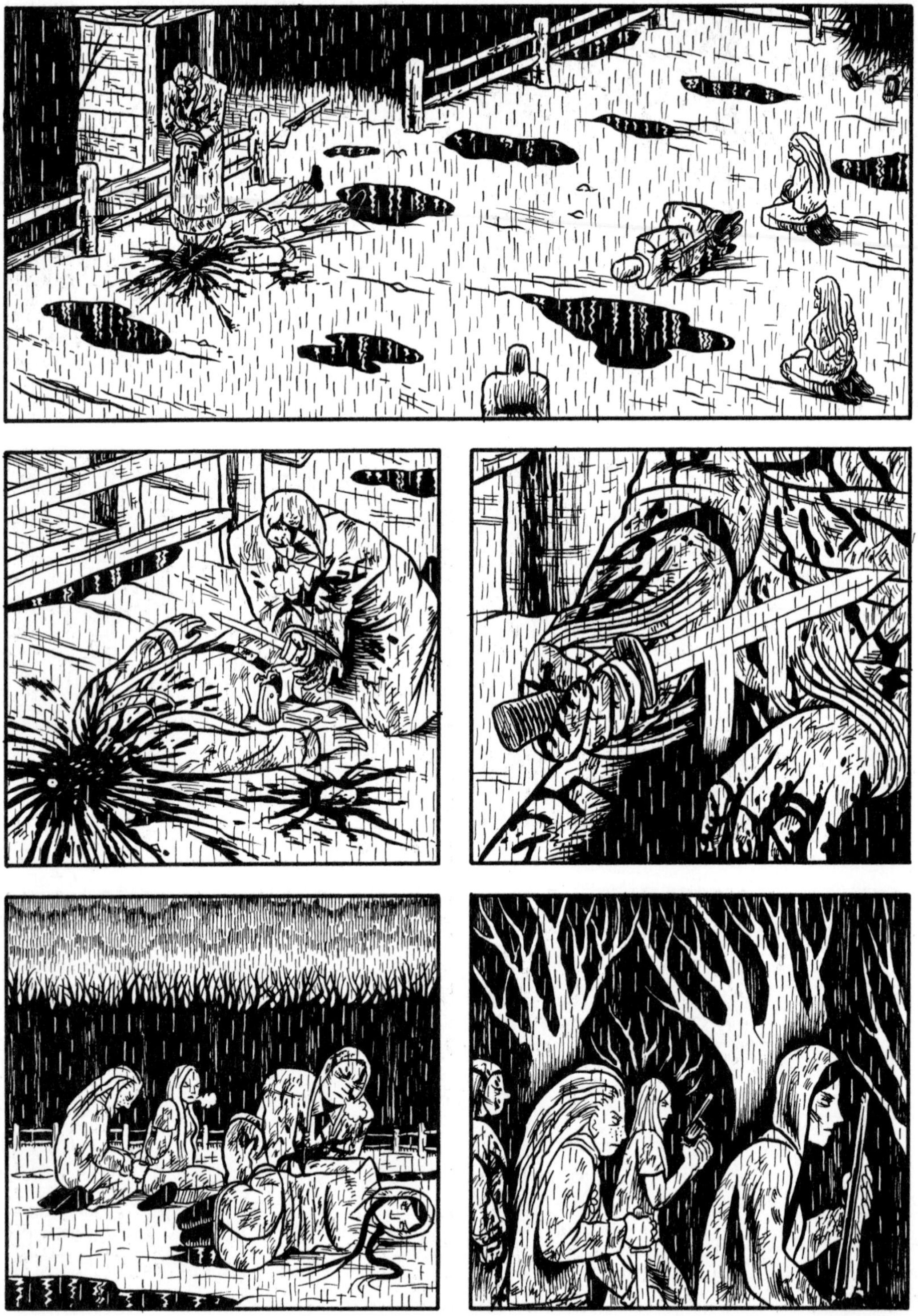

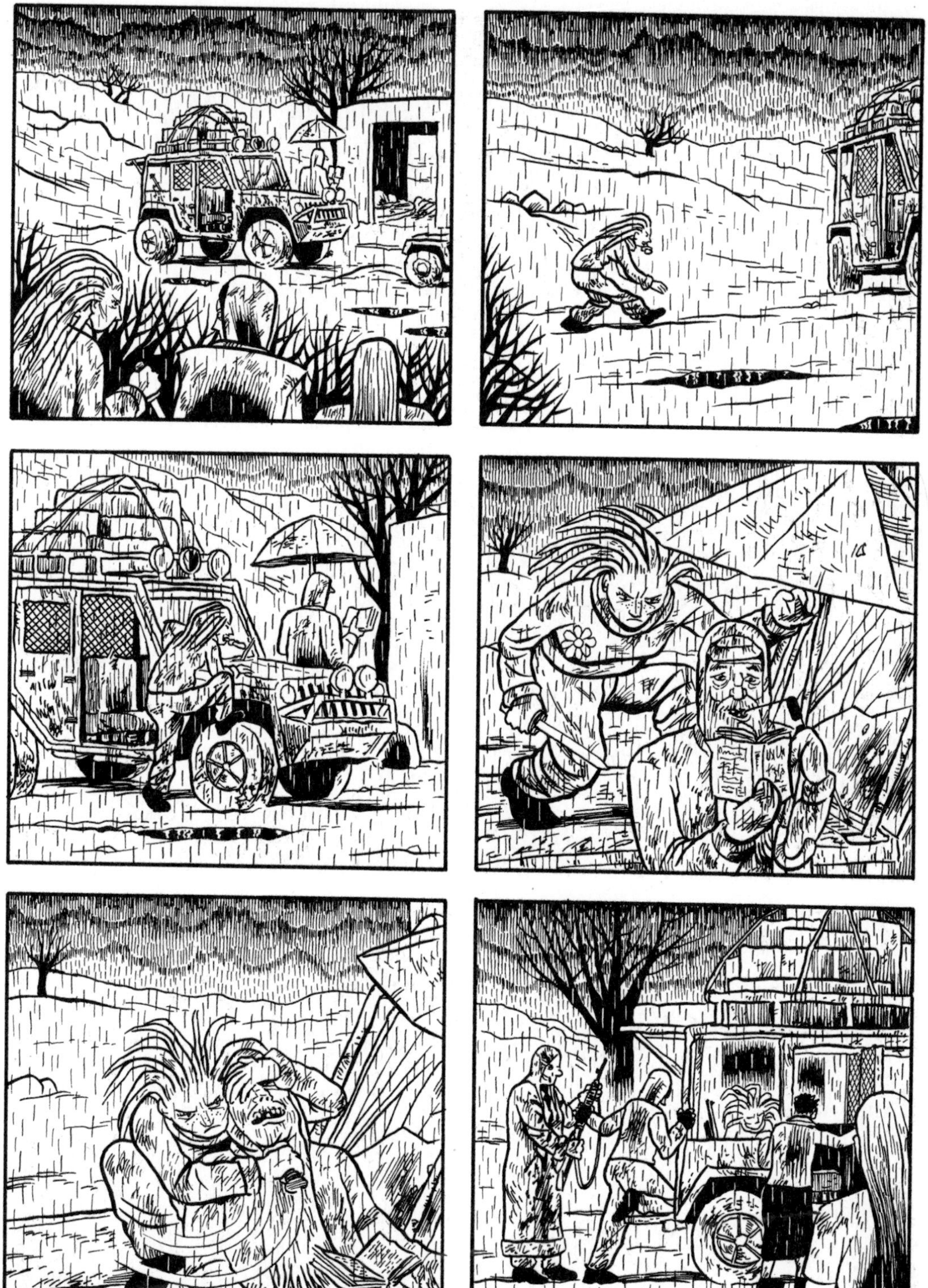

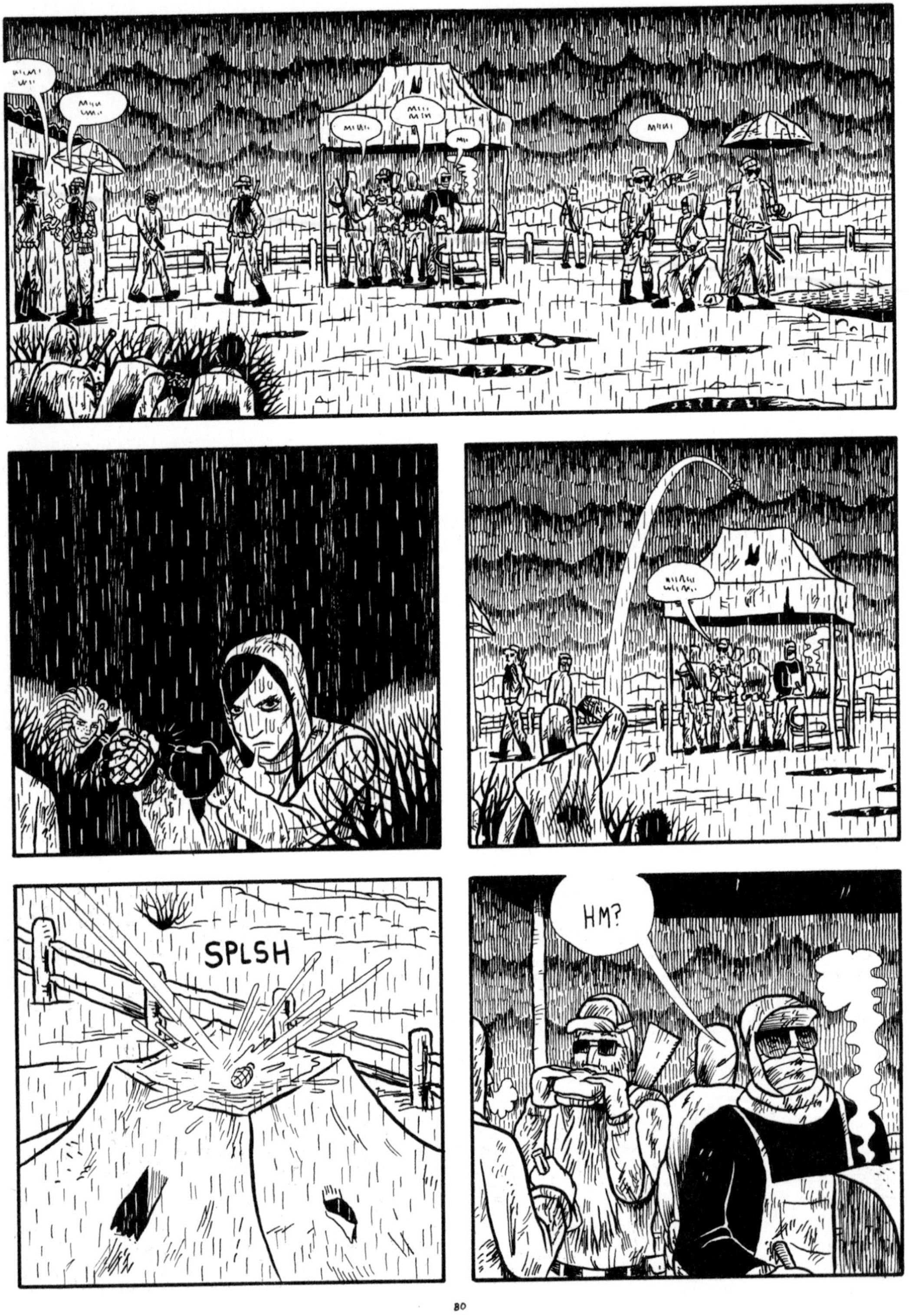
SPLSH
HM?

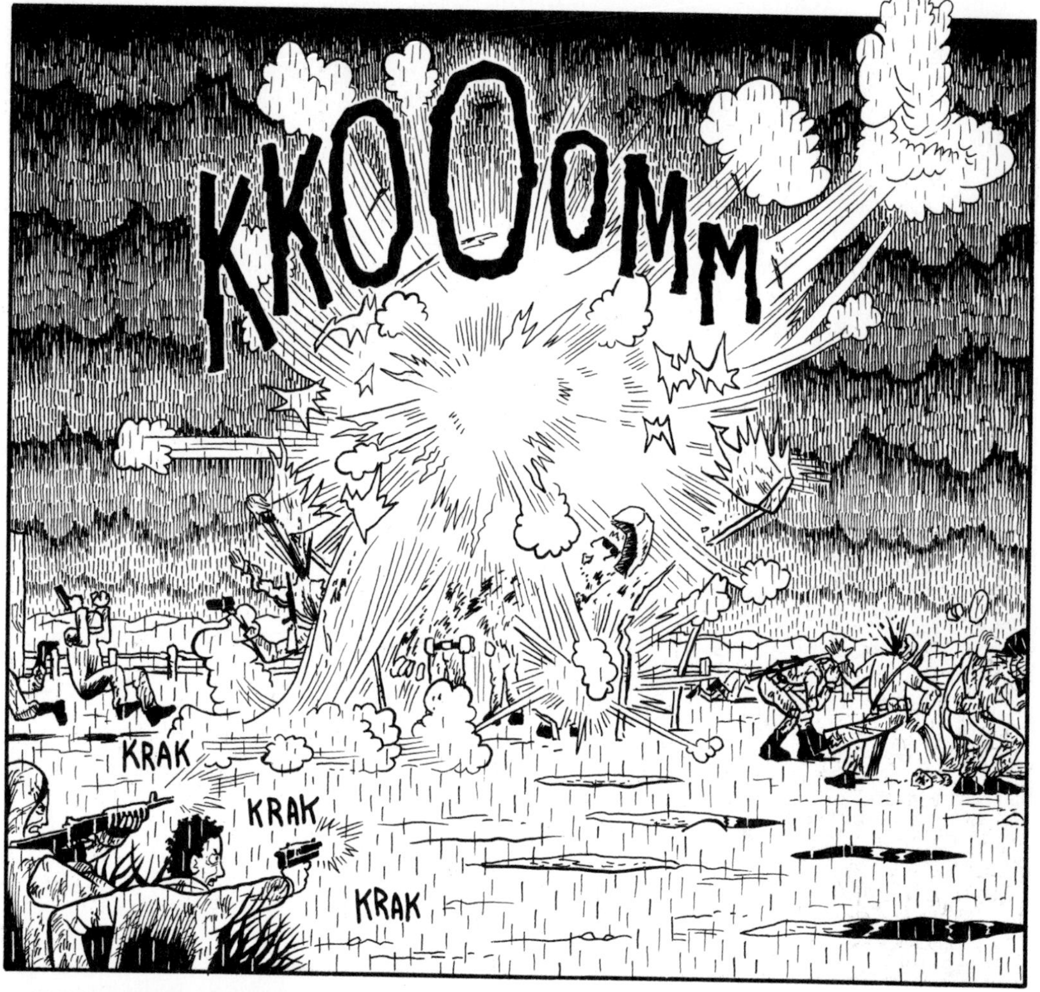
KKOOOMM
KRAK
KRAK
KRAK

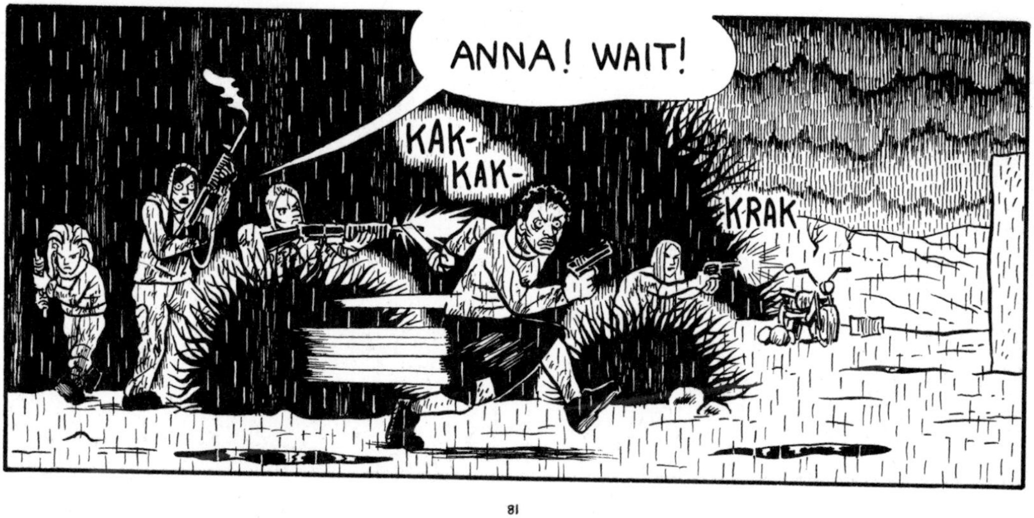
ANNA! WAIT!
KAK-
KAK-
KRAK

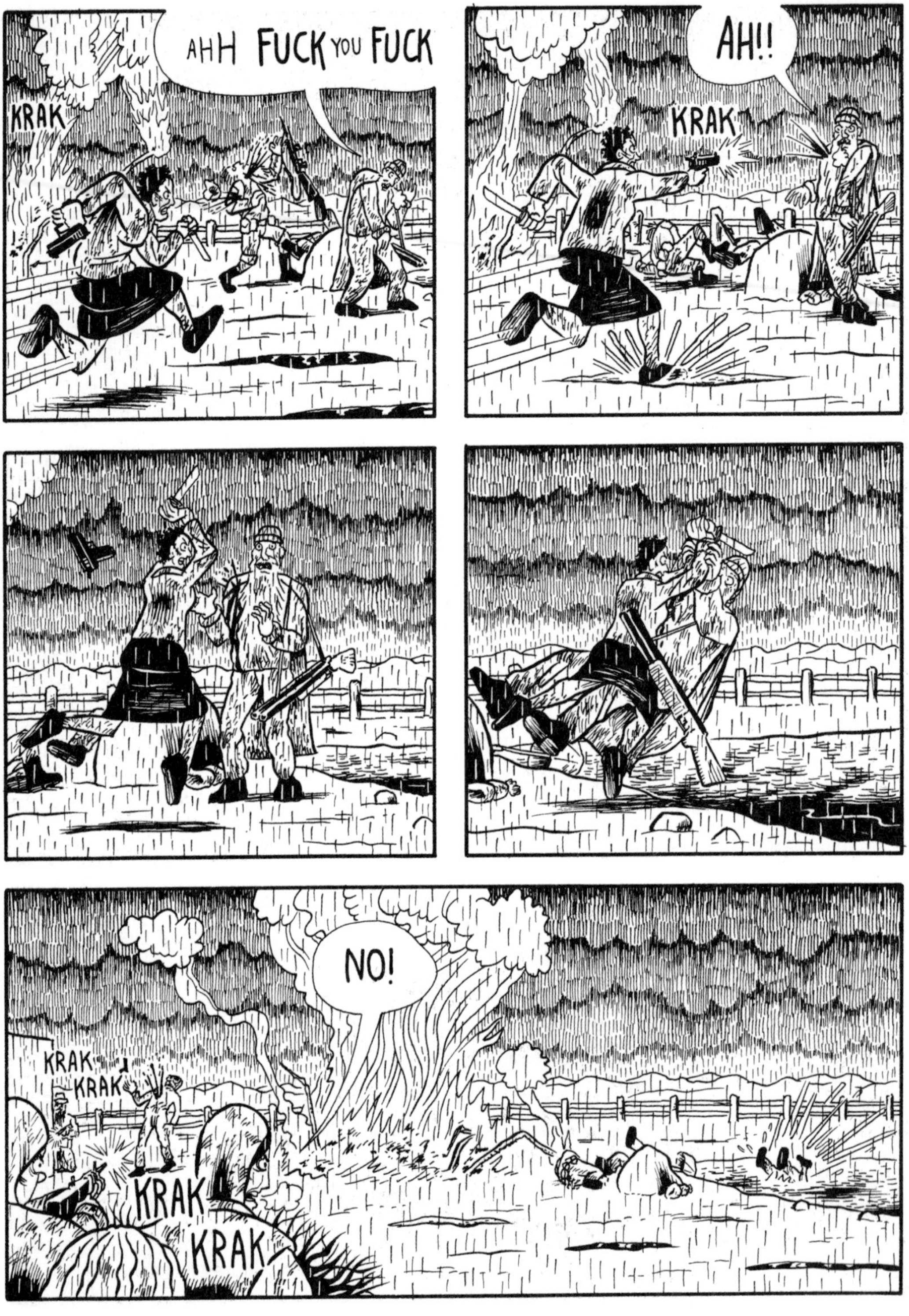
KRAK
AHH FUCK YOU FUCK
KRAK
AH!!
NO!
KRAK
KRAK
KRAK
KRAK

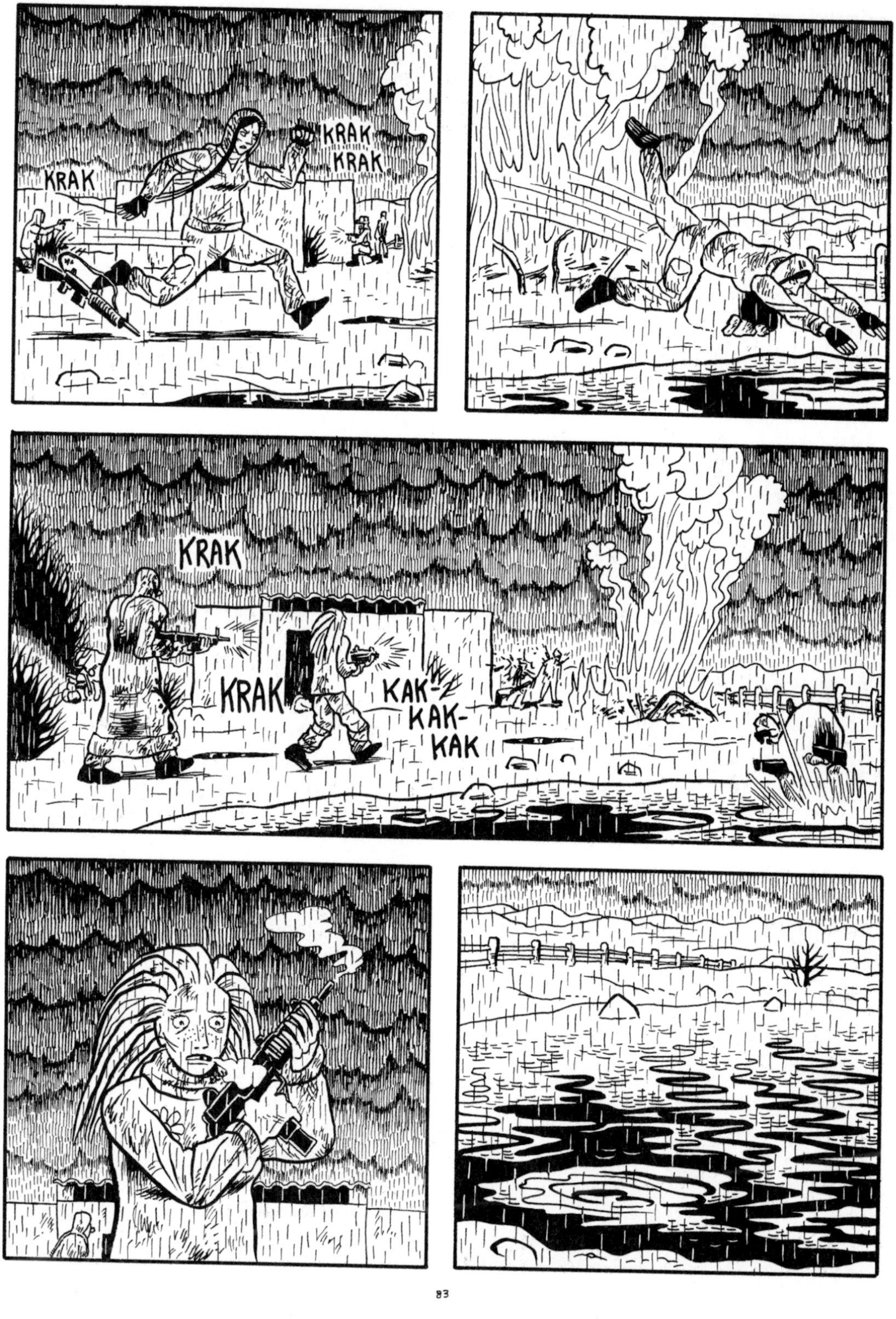
KRAK
KRAK
KRAK
KRAK
KRAK
KAK-
KAK-
KAK

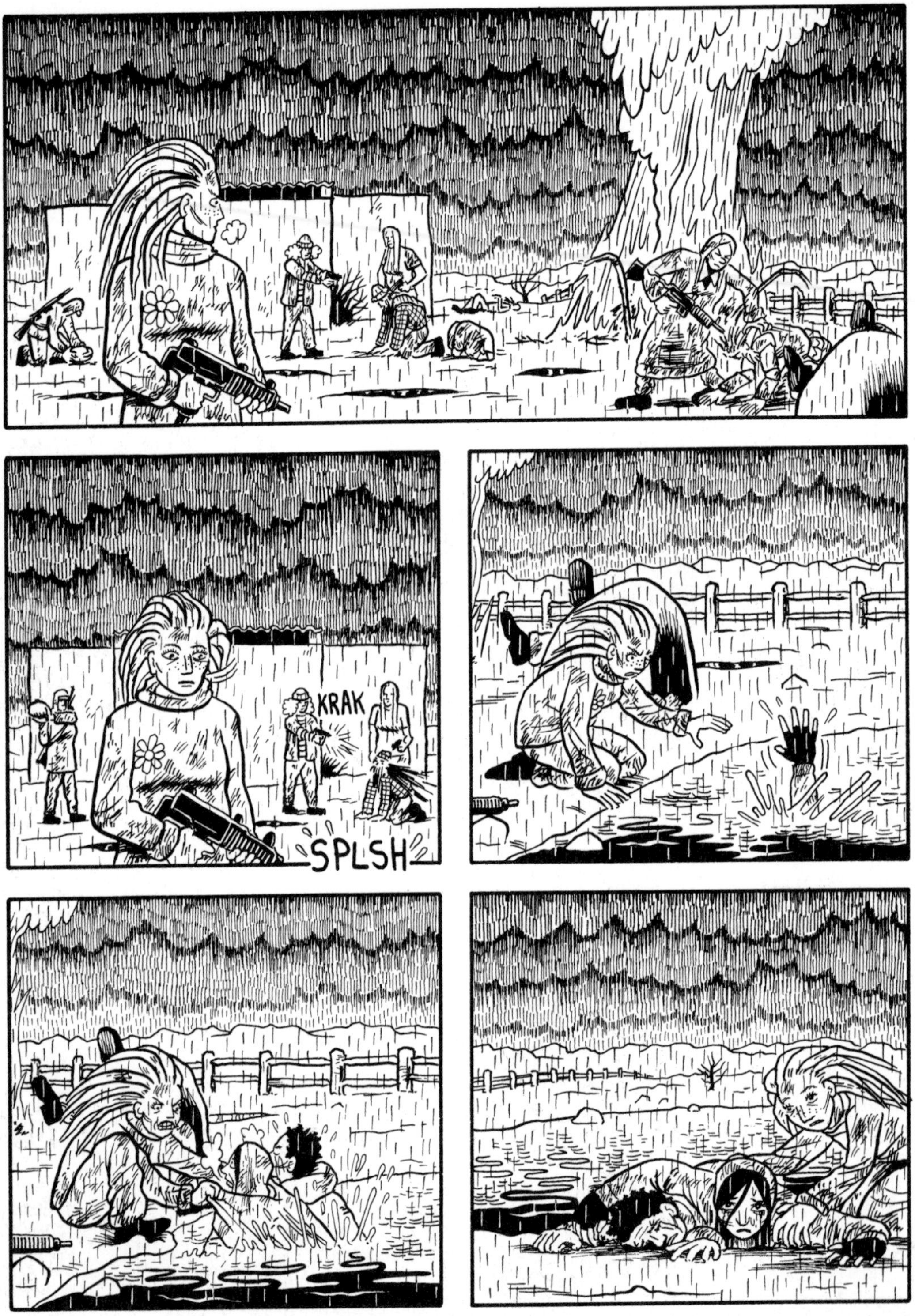
KRAK
SPLSH

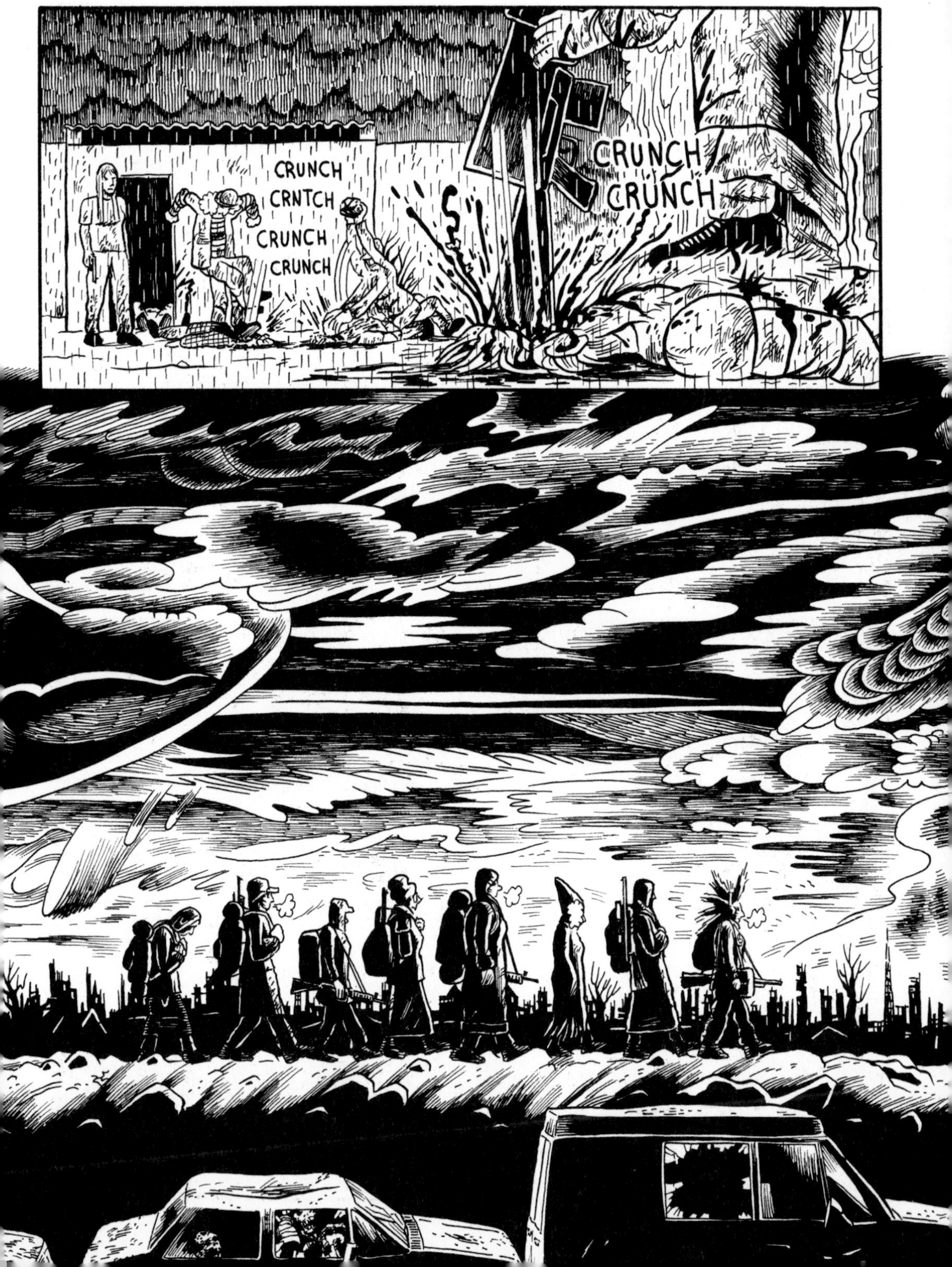
CRUNCH
CRNTCH
CRUNCH
CRUNCH
CRUNCH
CRUNCH

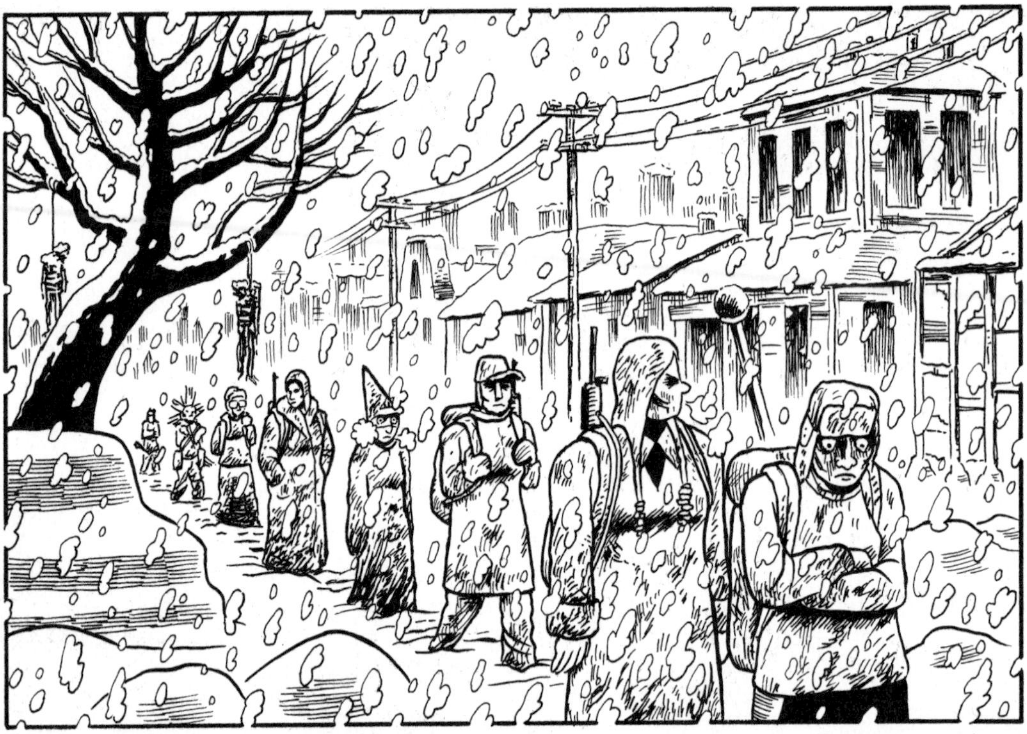

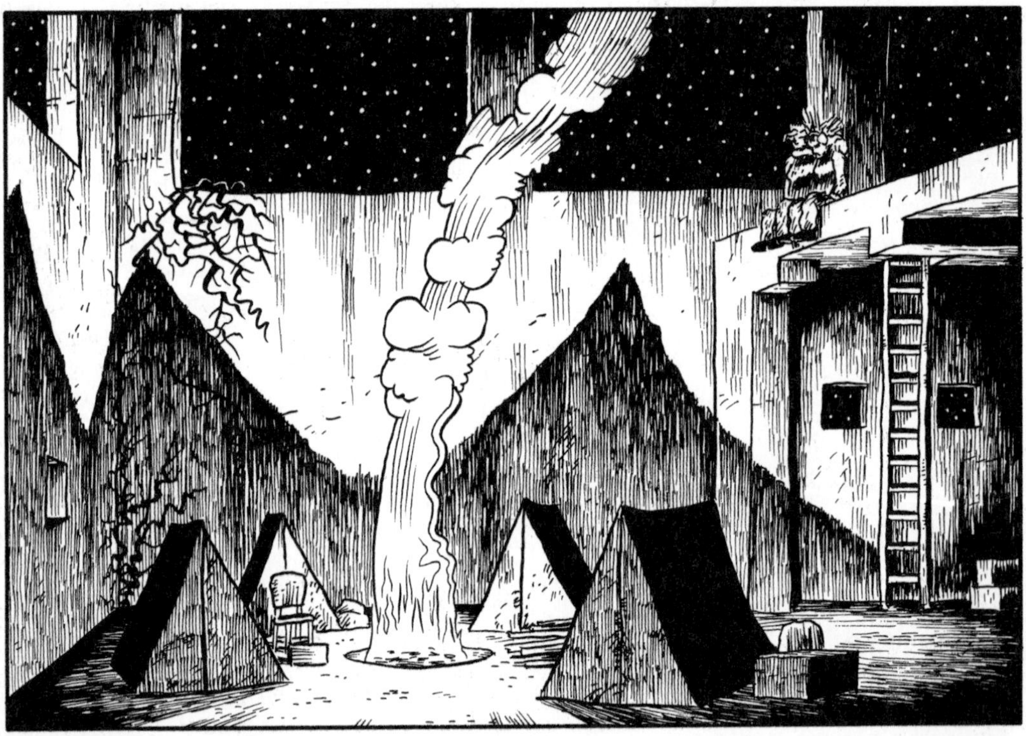

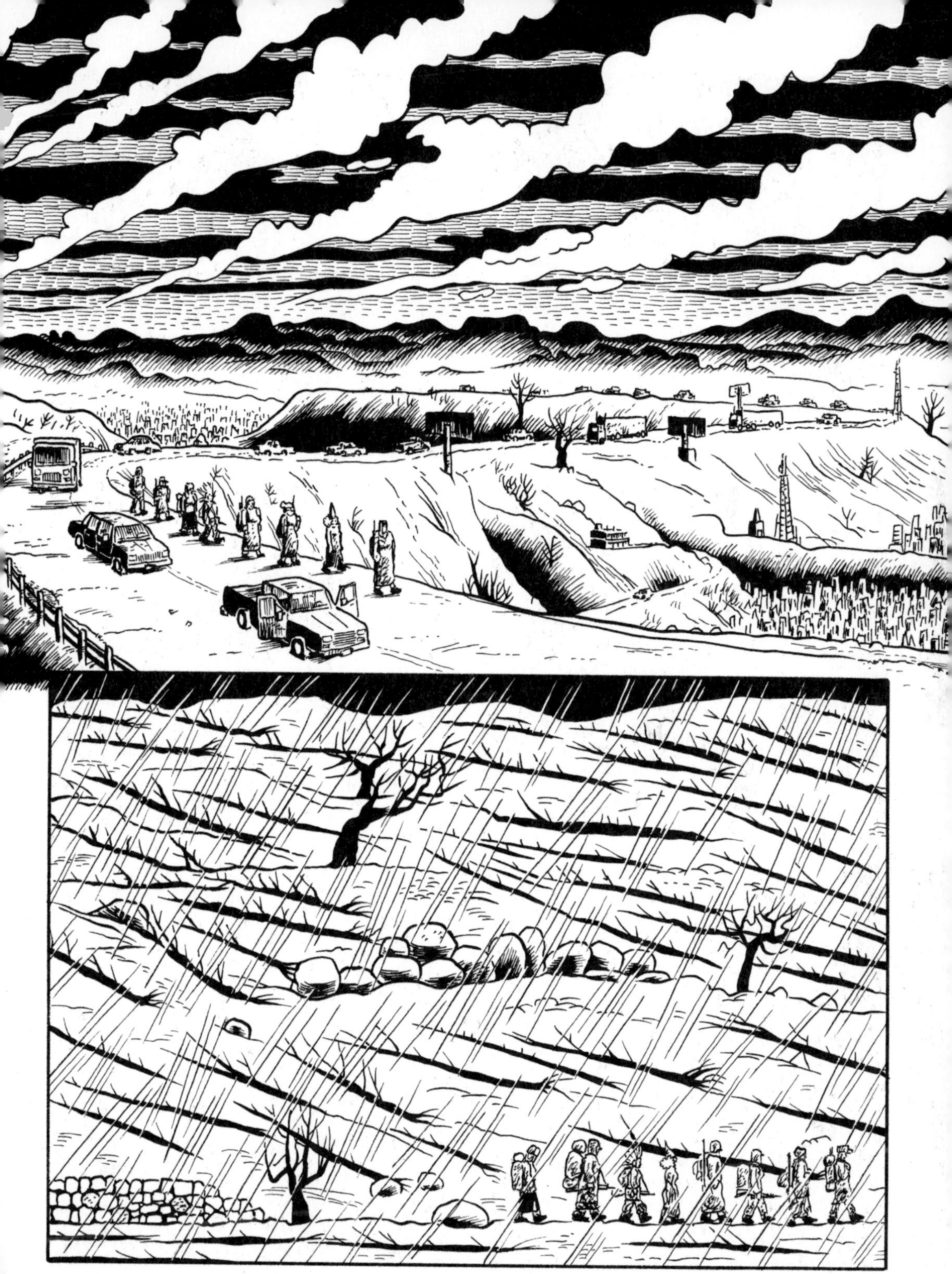

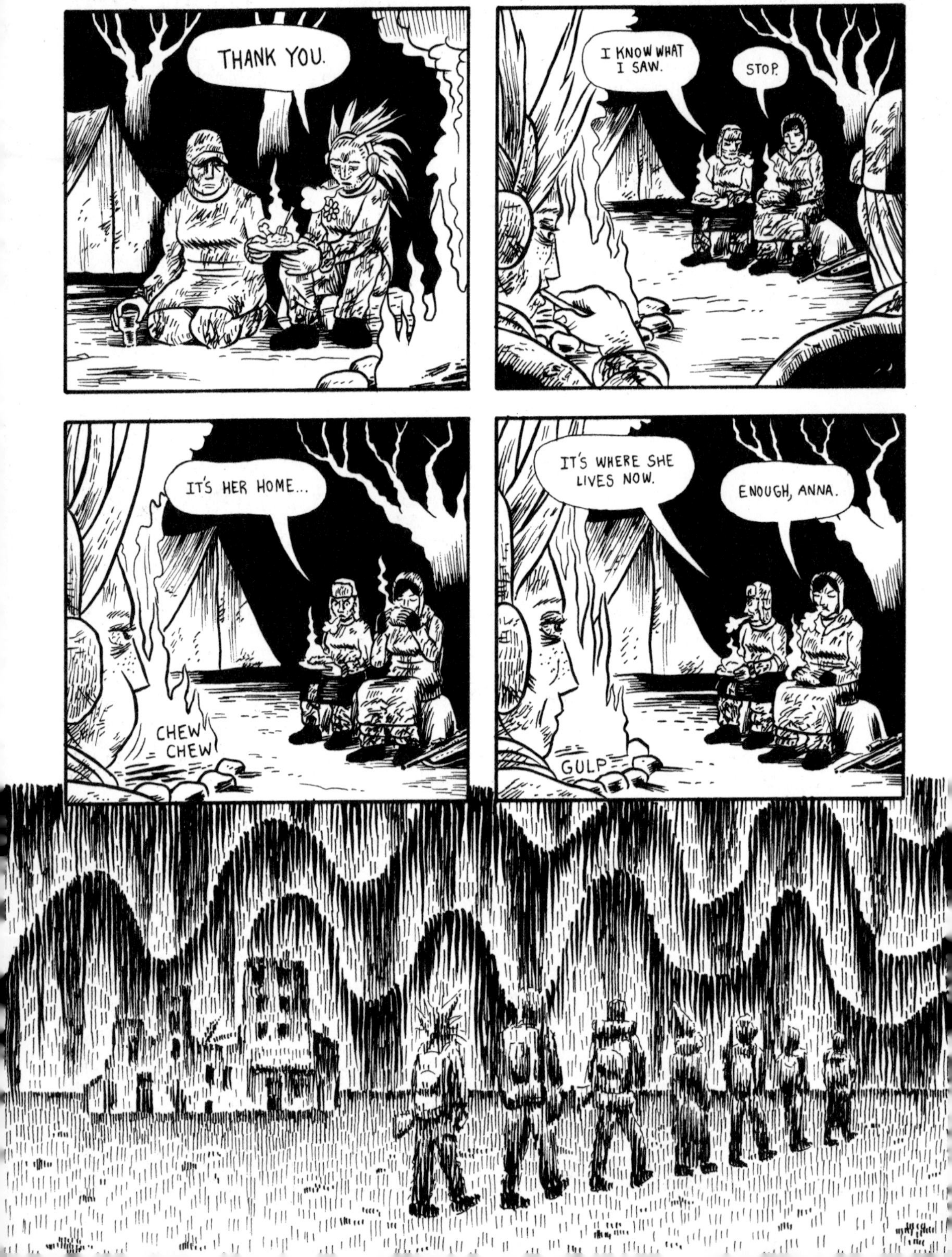
THANK YOU.
I KNOW WHAT I SAW.
STOP.
IT'S HER HOME...
CHEW CHEW
IT'S WHERE SHE LIVES NOW.
ENOUGH, ANNA.
GULP

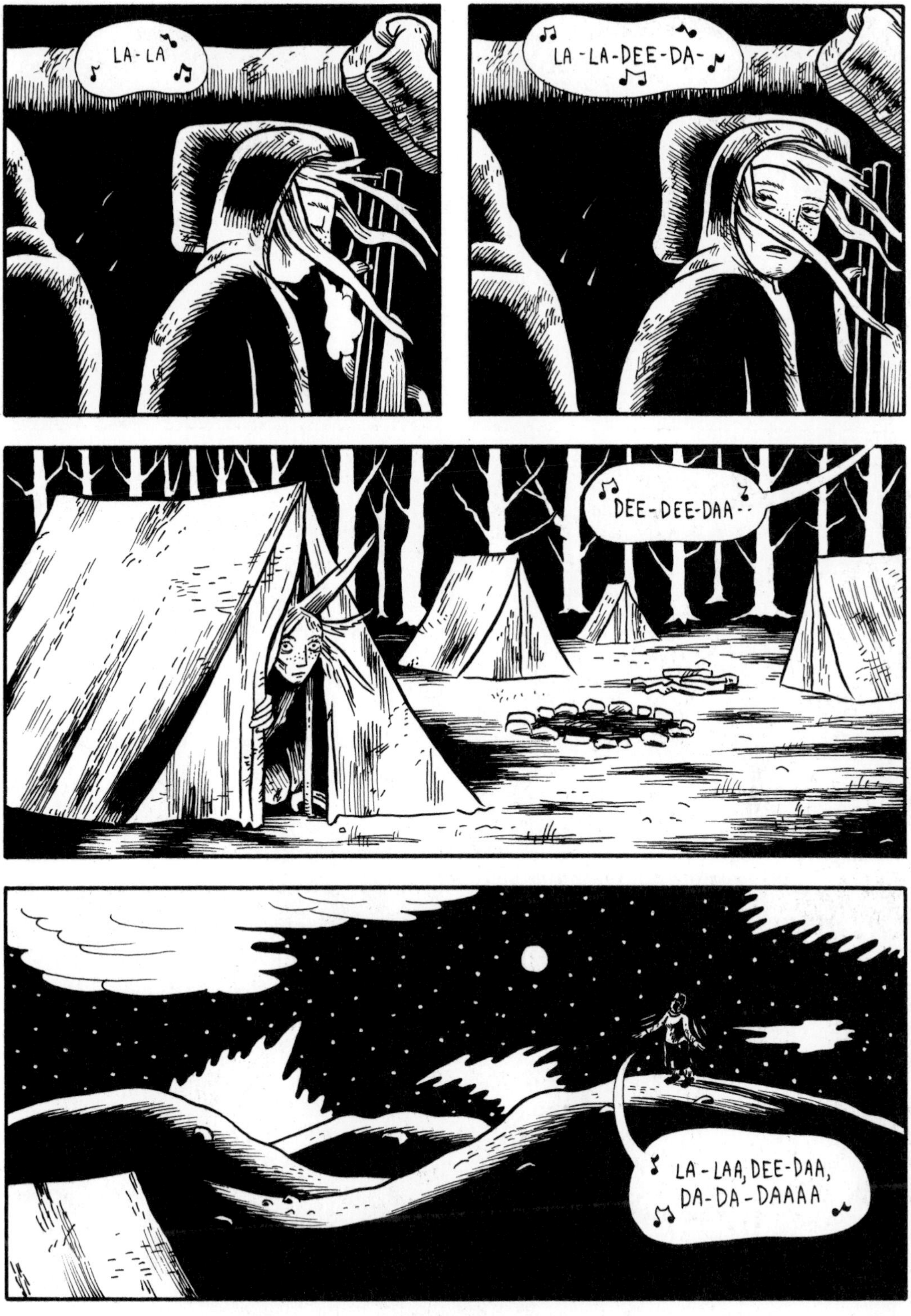
LA-LA
LA-LA-DEE-DA-
DEE-DEE-DAA...
LA-LAA, DEE-DAA, DA-DA-DAAAA

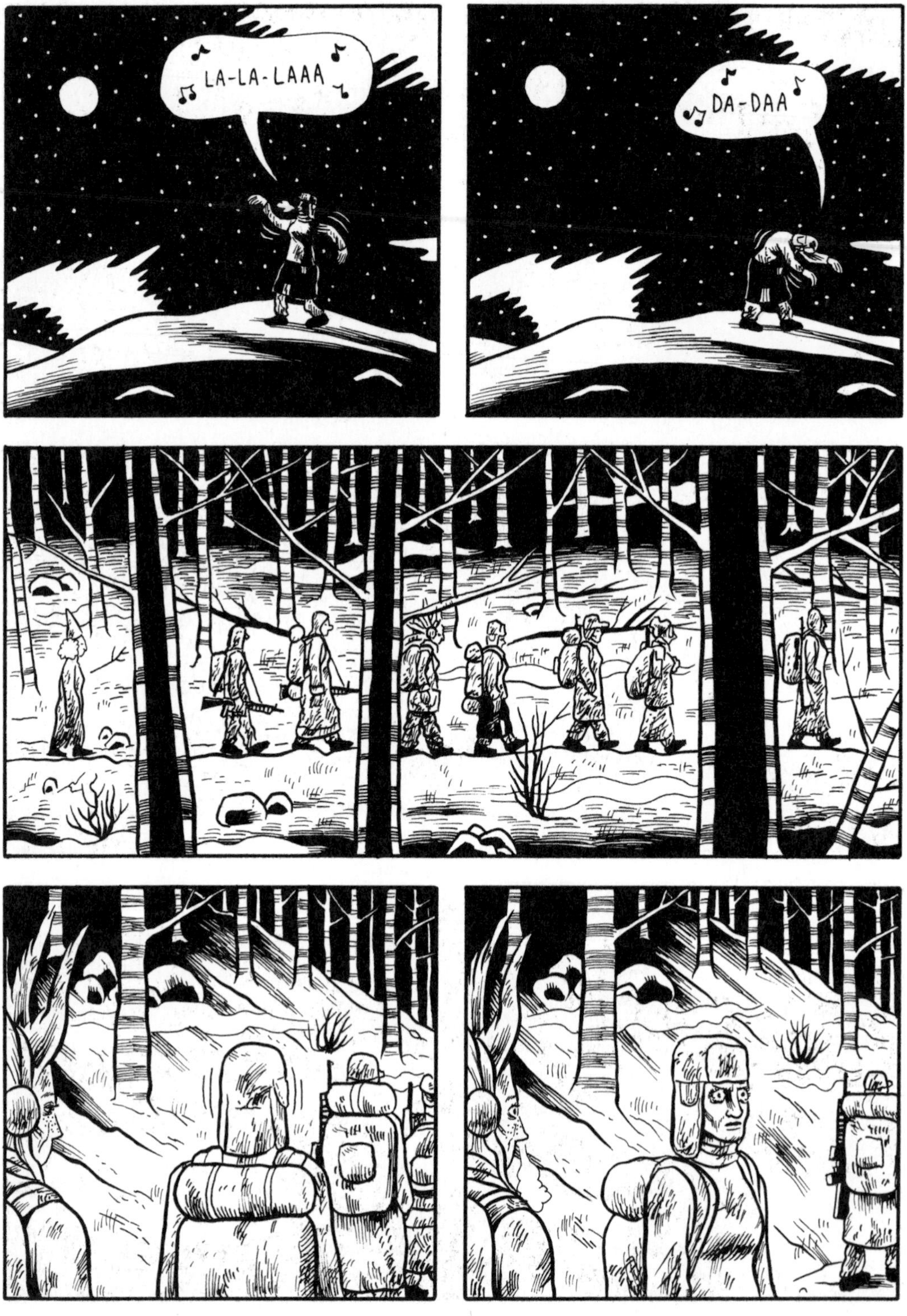
LA-LA-LAAA
DA-DAA

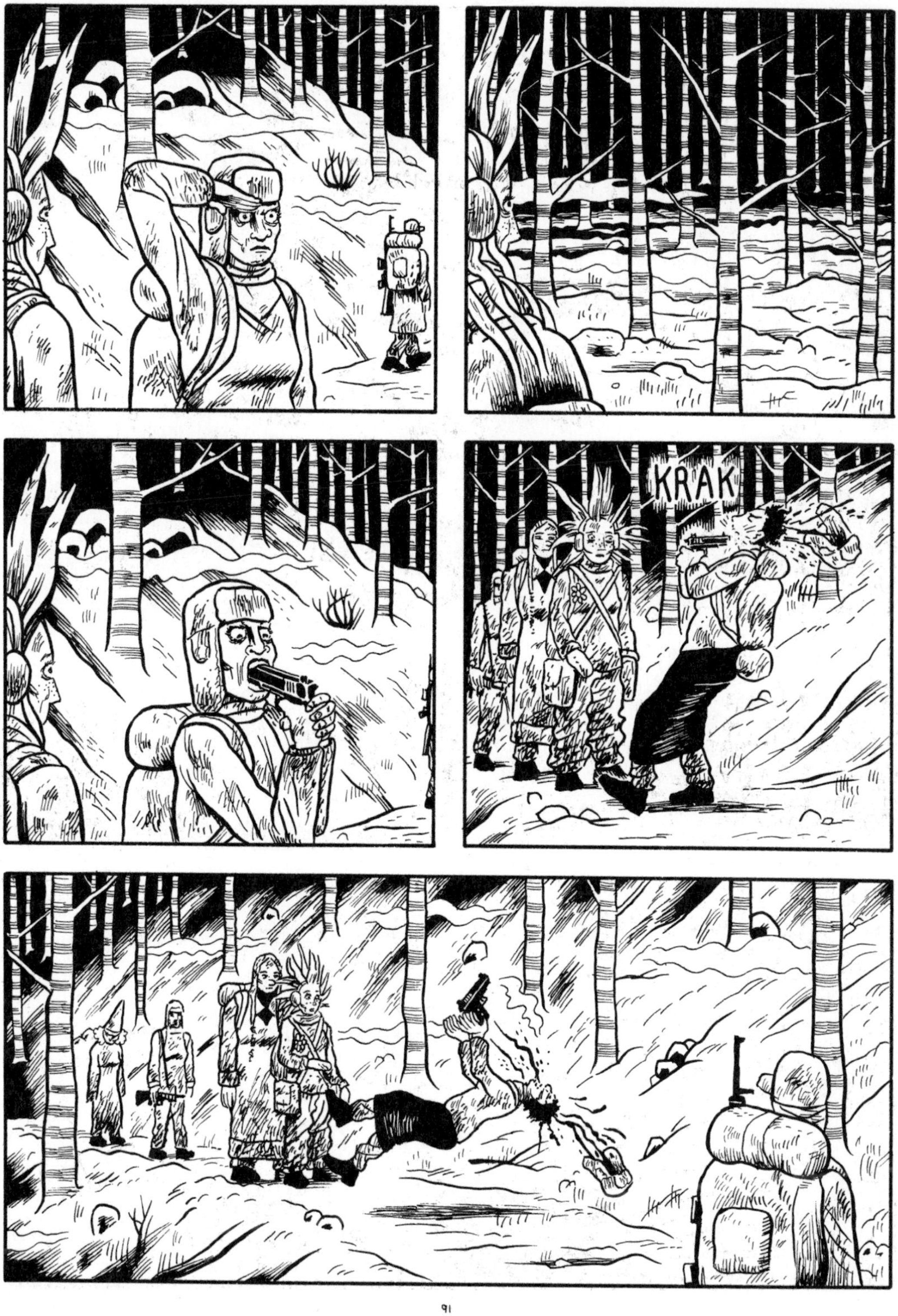
KRAK

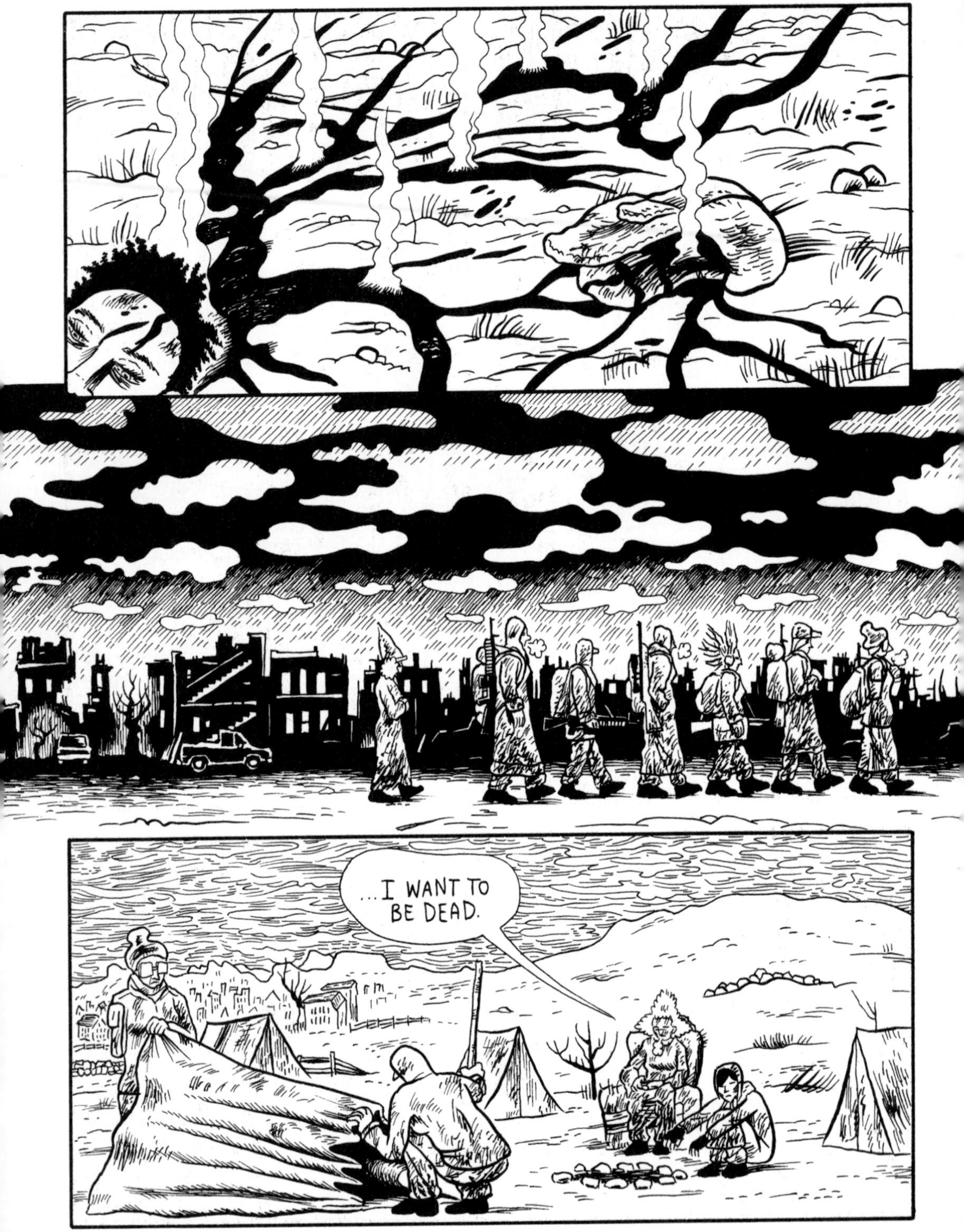
...I WANT TO BE DEAD.

I WANT TO DISAPPEAR. I WANT EVERY-ONE TO FORGET ME.

I DON'T WANT TO LEAVE A TRACE THAT I EVER EXISTED IN THIS WORLD.

I'M SO RIDICULOUS...

WE HUMOR EACH OTHER.

SNNNNIP

WE'RE ALL JUST WEIRD AND STUPID.

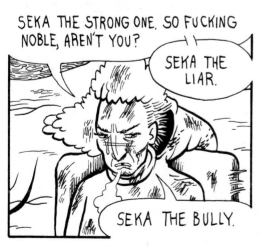

SEKA THE STRONG ONE. SO FUCKING NOBLE, AREN'T YOU?

SEKA THE LIAR.

SEKA THE BULLY.

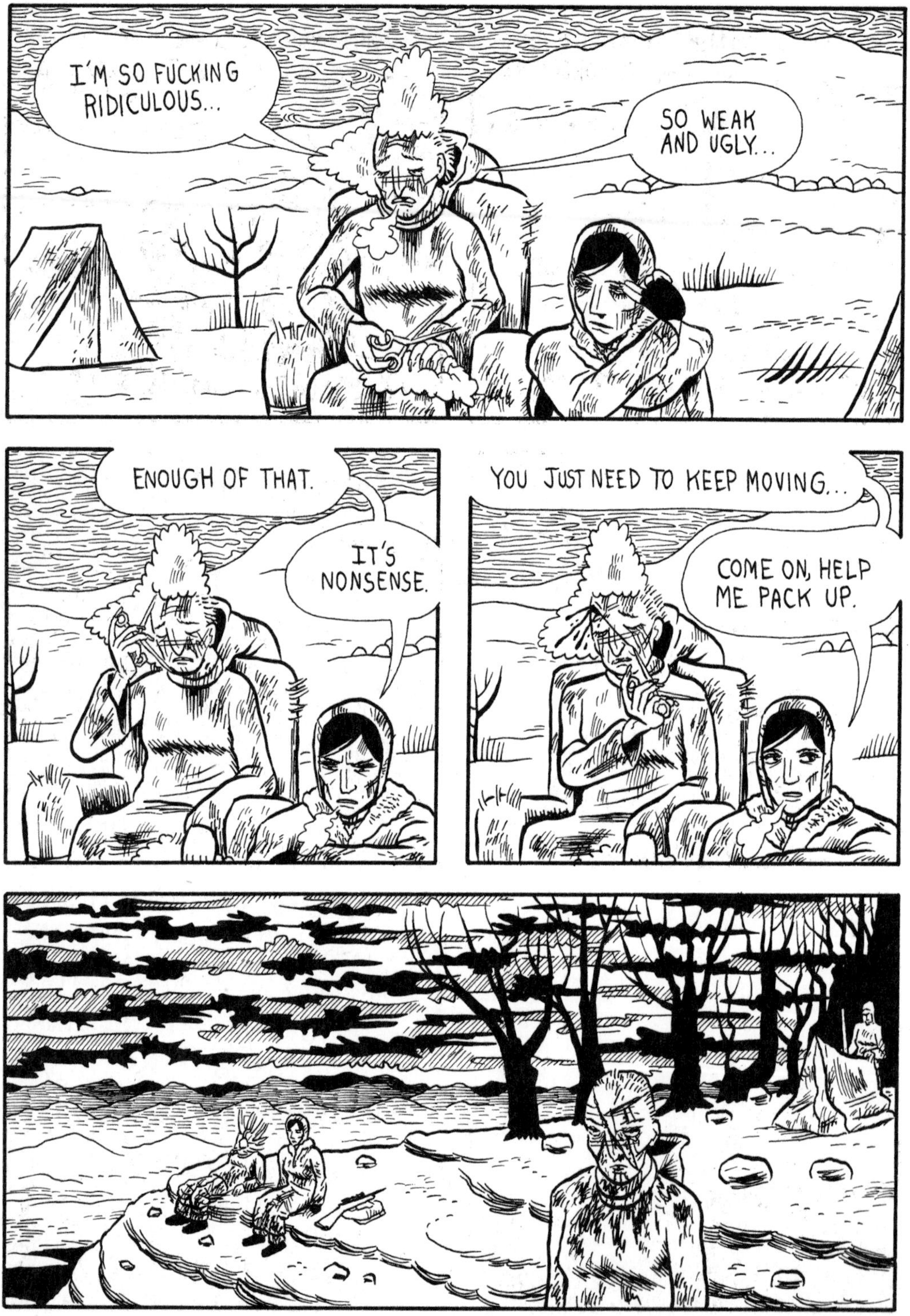
I'M SO FUCKING RIDICULOUS...
SO WEAK AND UGLY...
ENOUGH OF THAT.
IT'S NONSENSE.
YOU JUST NEED TO KEEP MOVING...
COME ON, HELP ME PACK UP.

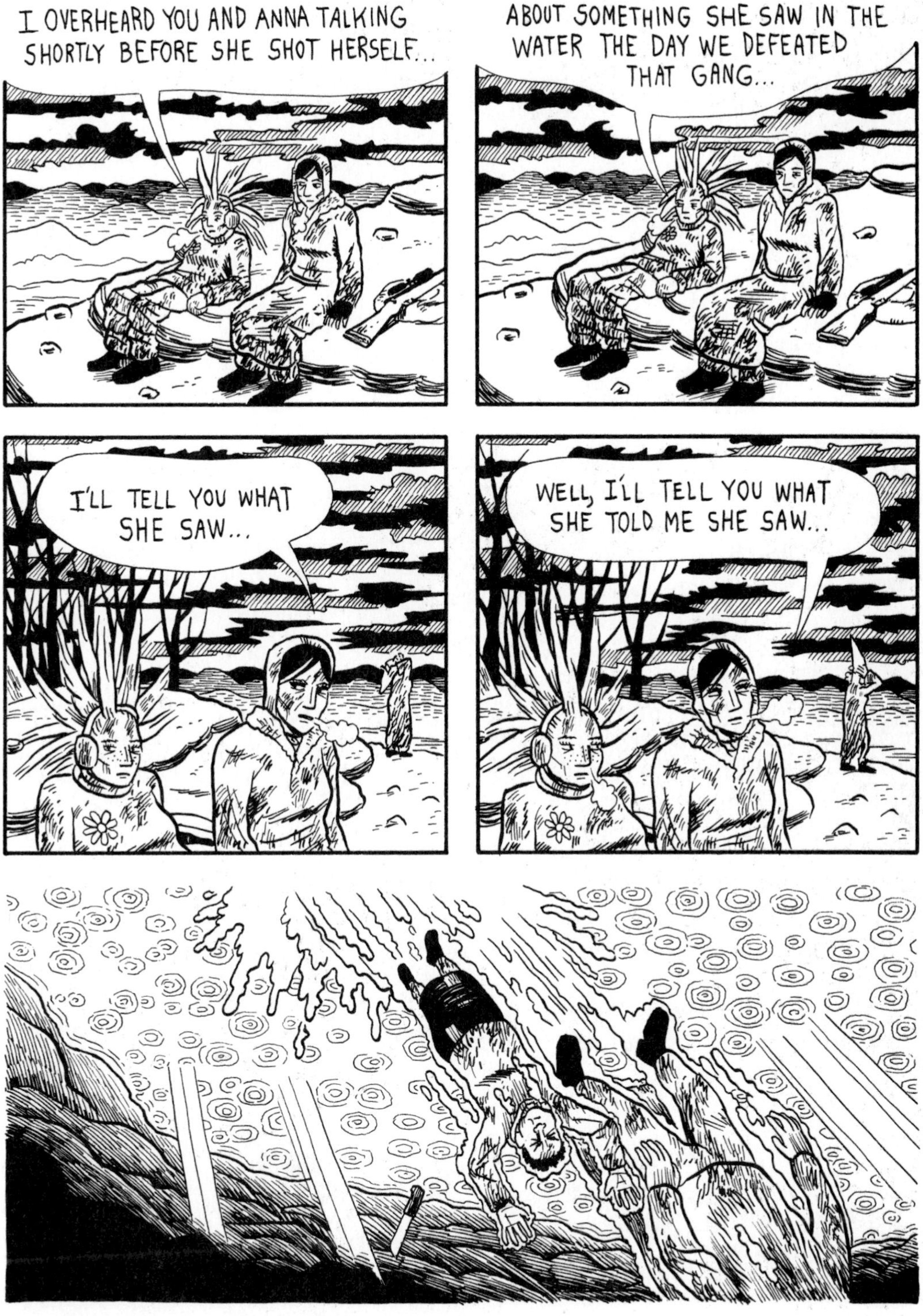

I OVERHEARD YOU AND ANNA TALKING SHORTLY BEFORE SHE SHOT HERSELF...
ABOUT SOMETHING SHE SAW IN THE WATER THE DAY WE DEFEATED THAT GANG...
I'LL TELL YOU WHAT SHE SAW...
WELL, I'LL TELL YOU WHAT SHE TOLD ME SHE SAW...

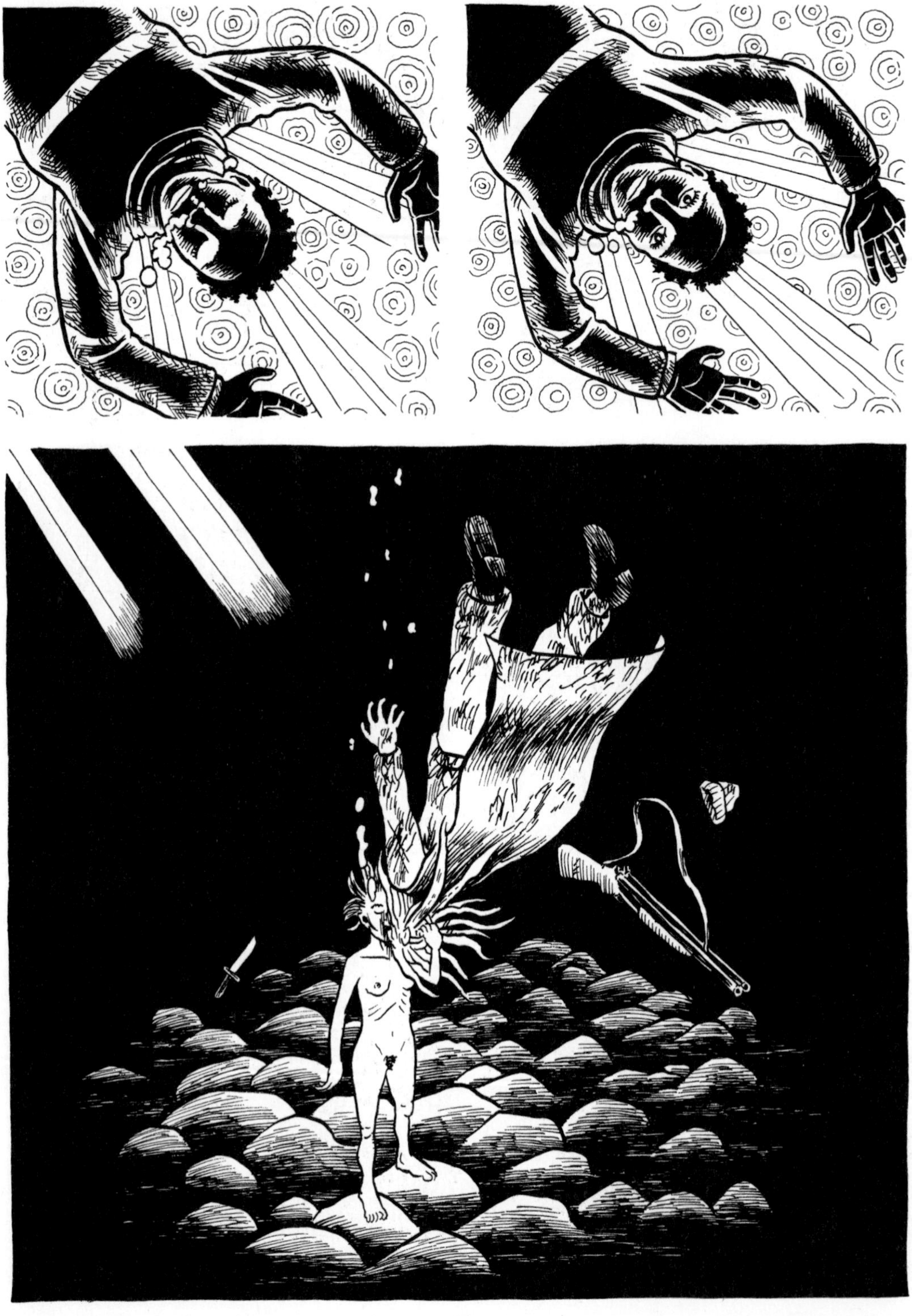

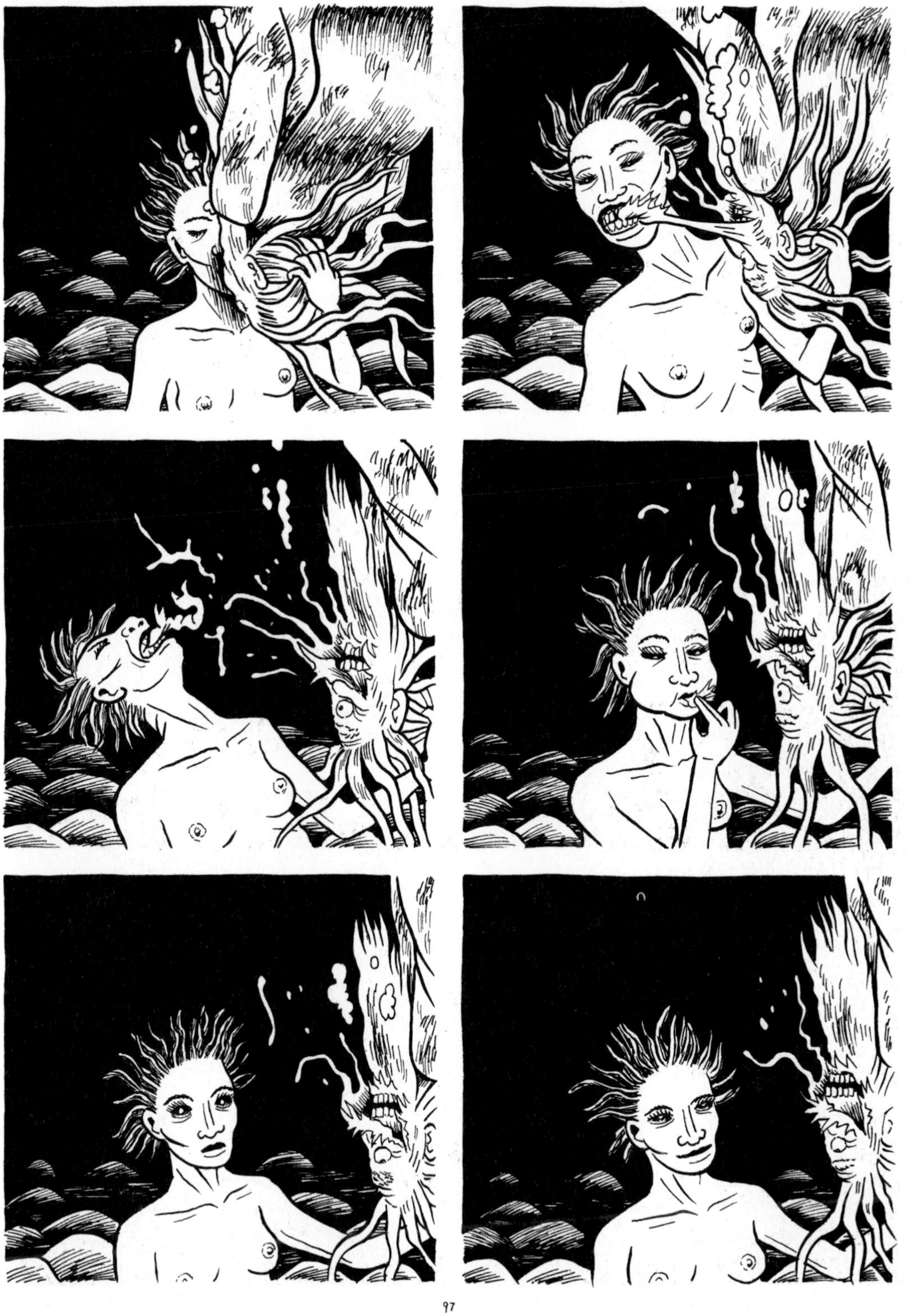

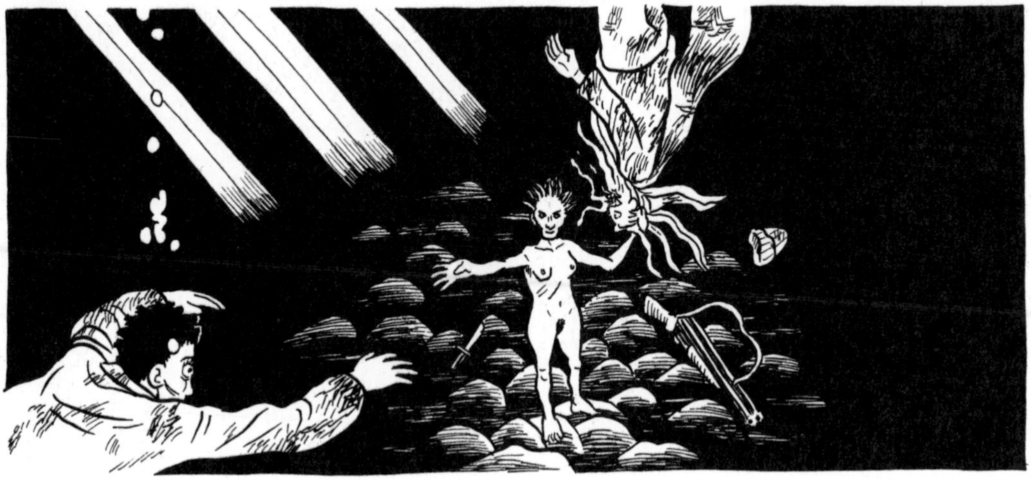
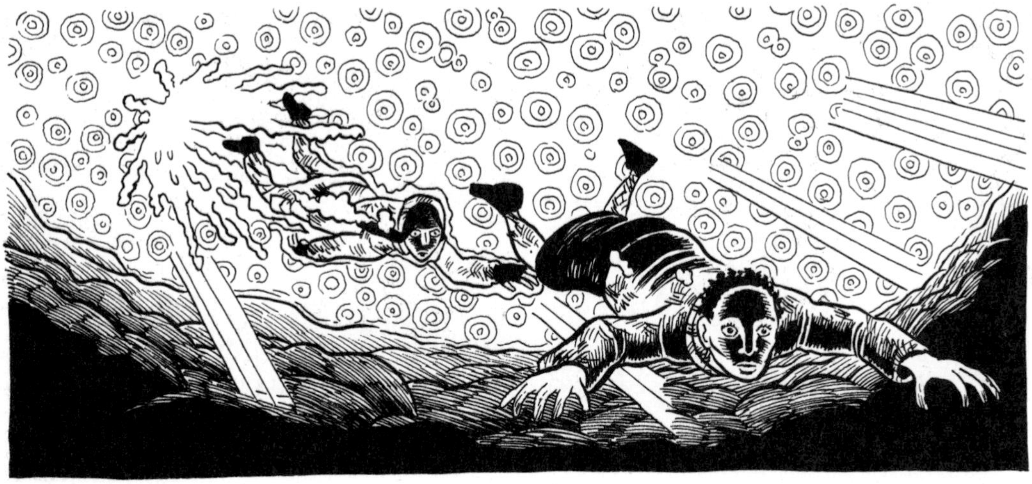
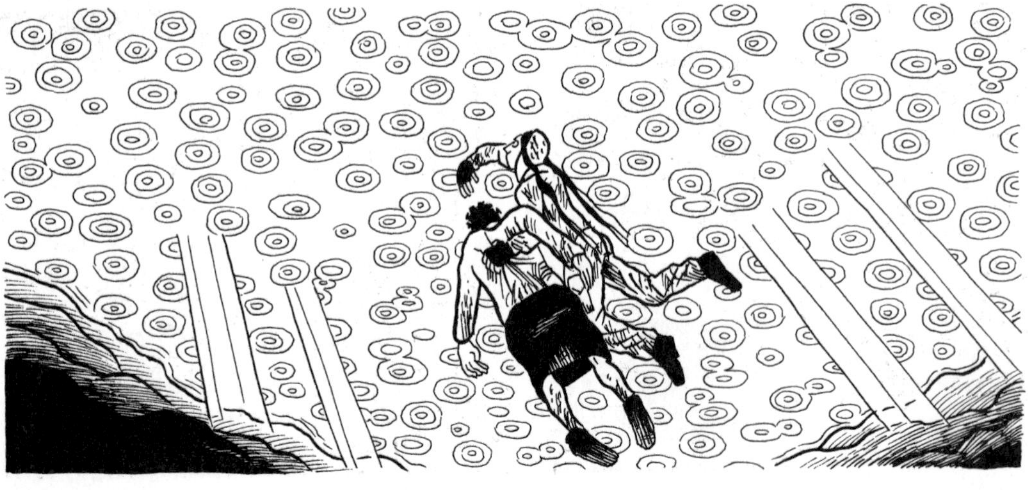

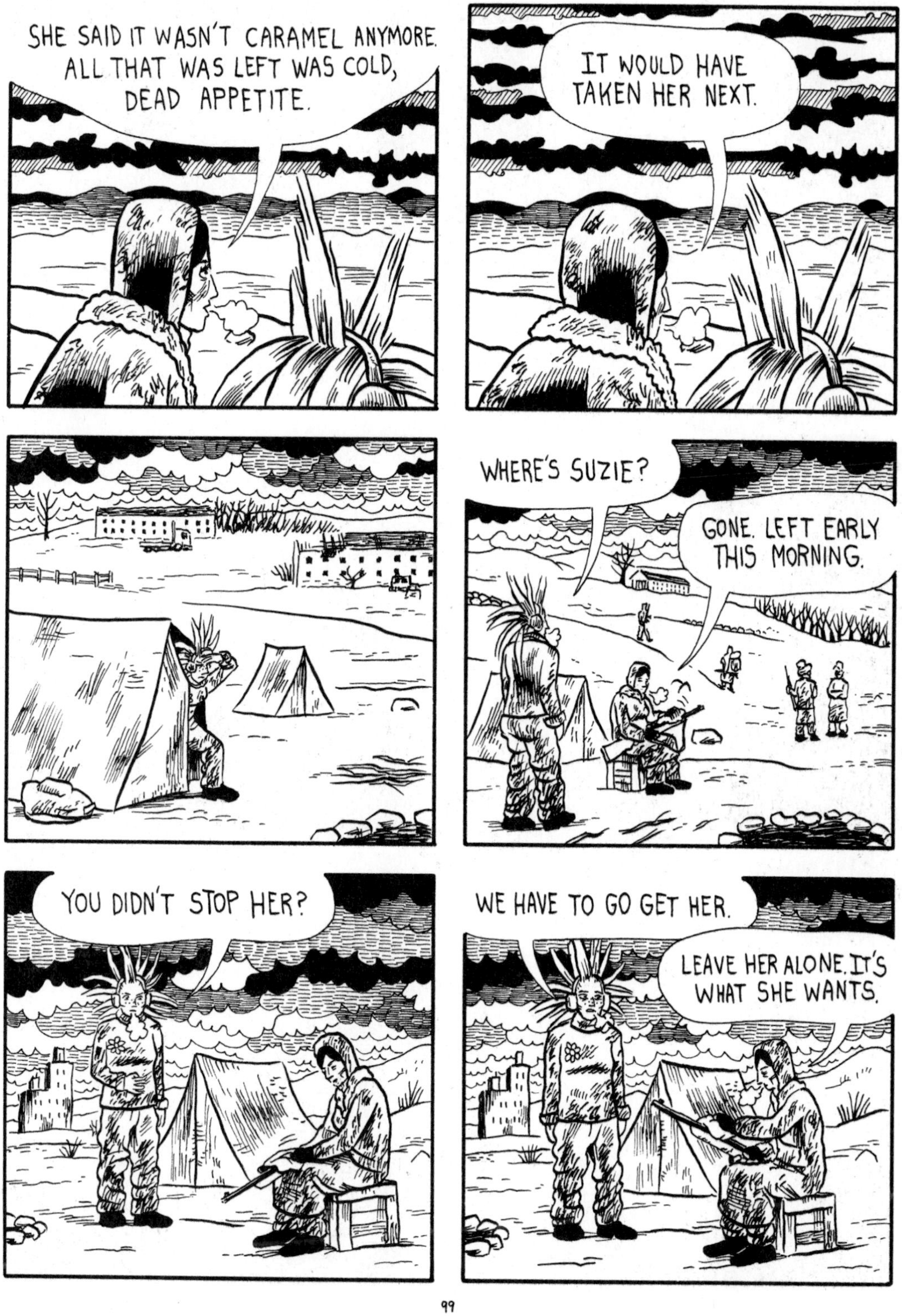
SHE SAID IT WASN'T CARAMEL ANYMORE. ALL THAT WAS LEFT WAS COLD, DEAD APPETITE.
IT WOULD HAVE TAKEN HER NEXT.
WHERE'S SUZIE?
GONE. LEFT EARLY THIS MORNING.
YOU DIDN'T STOP HER?
WE HAVE TO GO GET HER.
LEAVE HER ALONE. IT'S WHAT SHE WANTS.

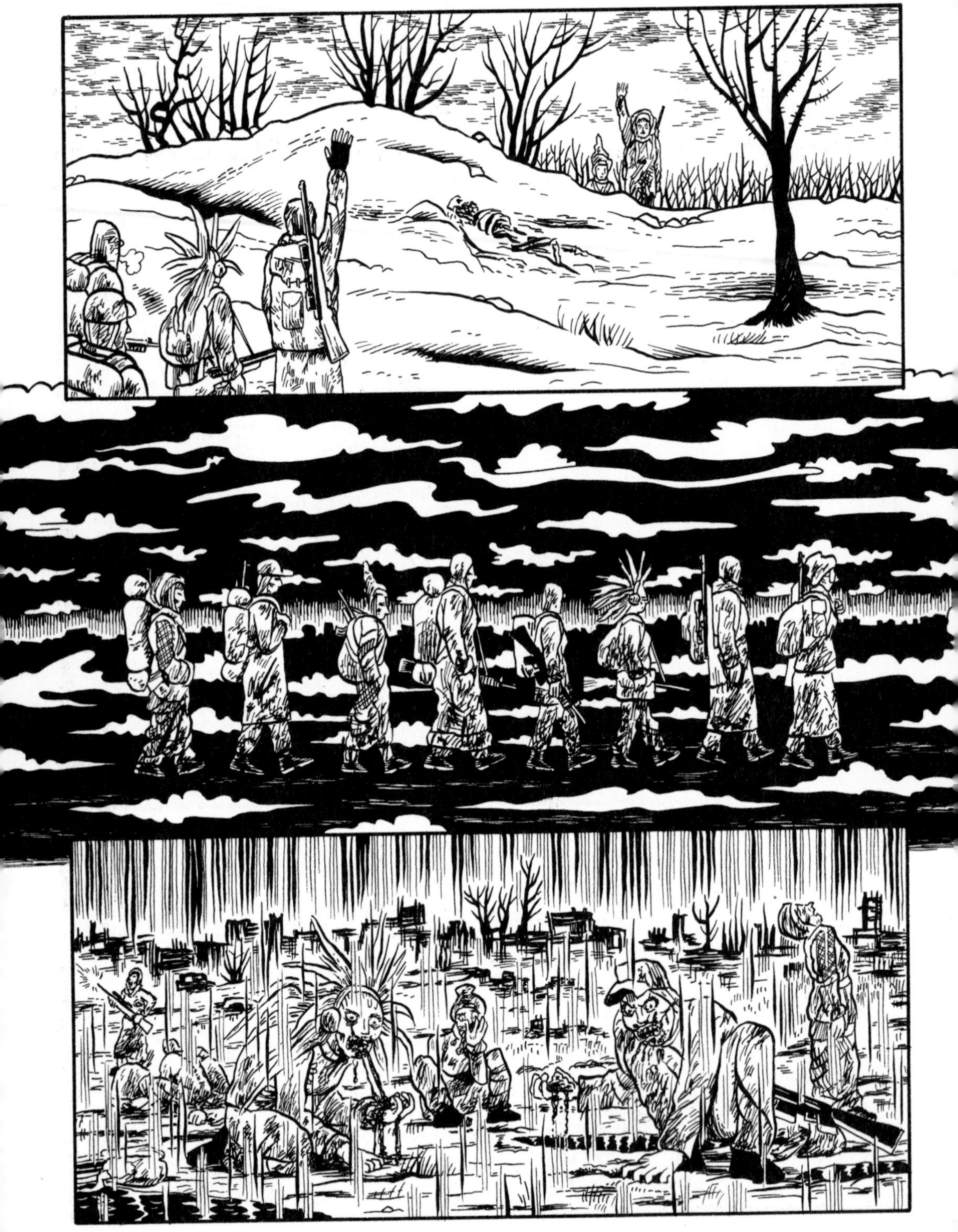

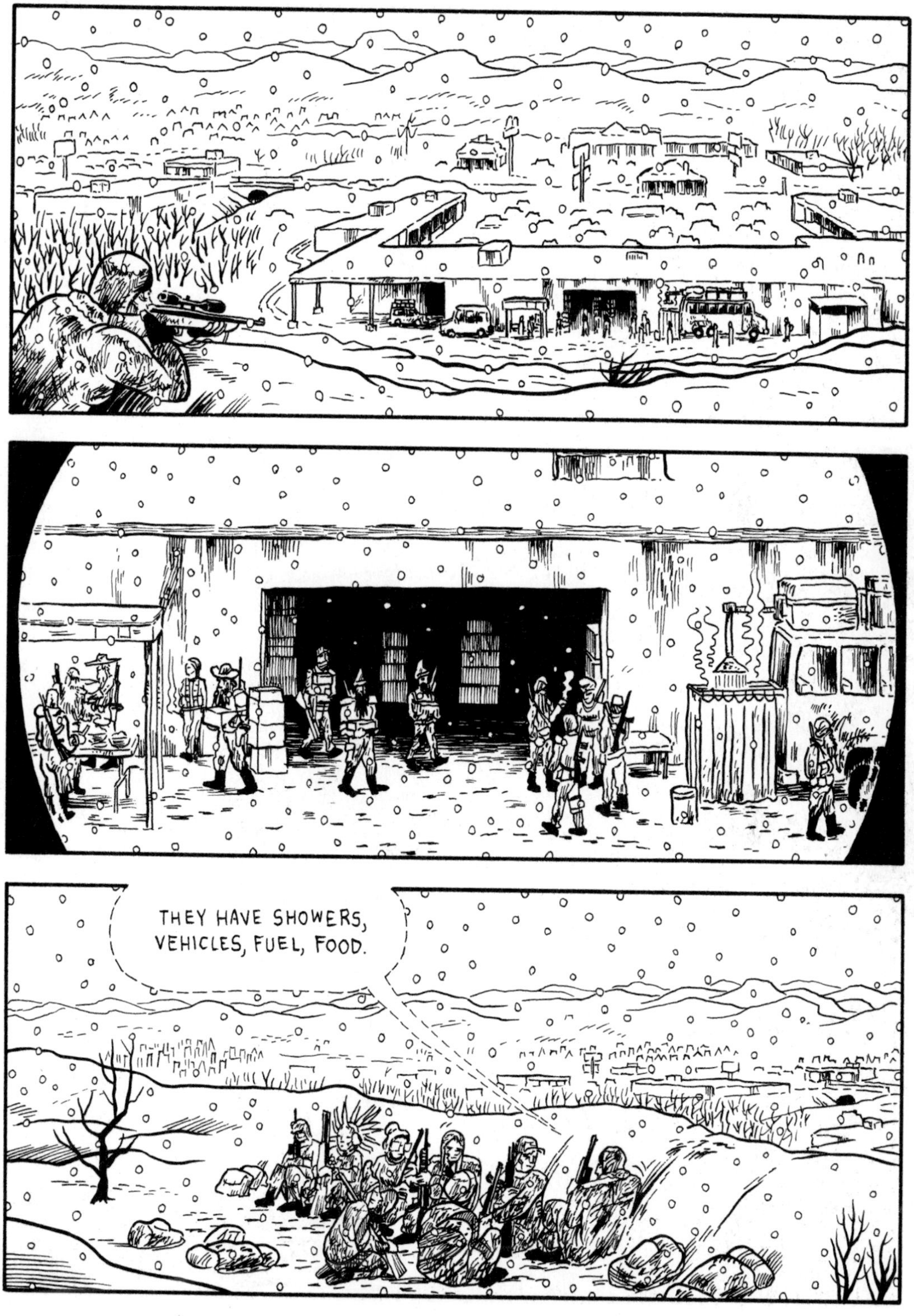
THEY HAVE SHOWERS, VEHICLES, FUEL, FOOD.

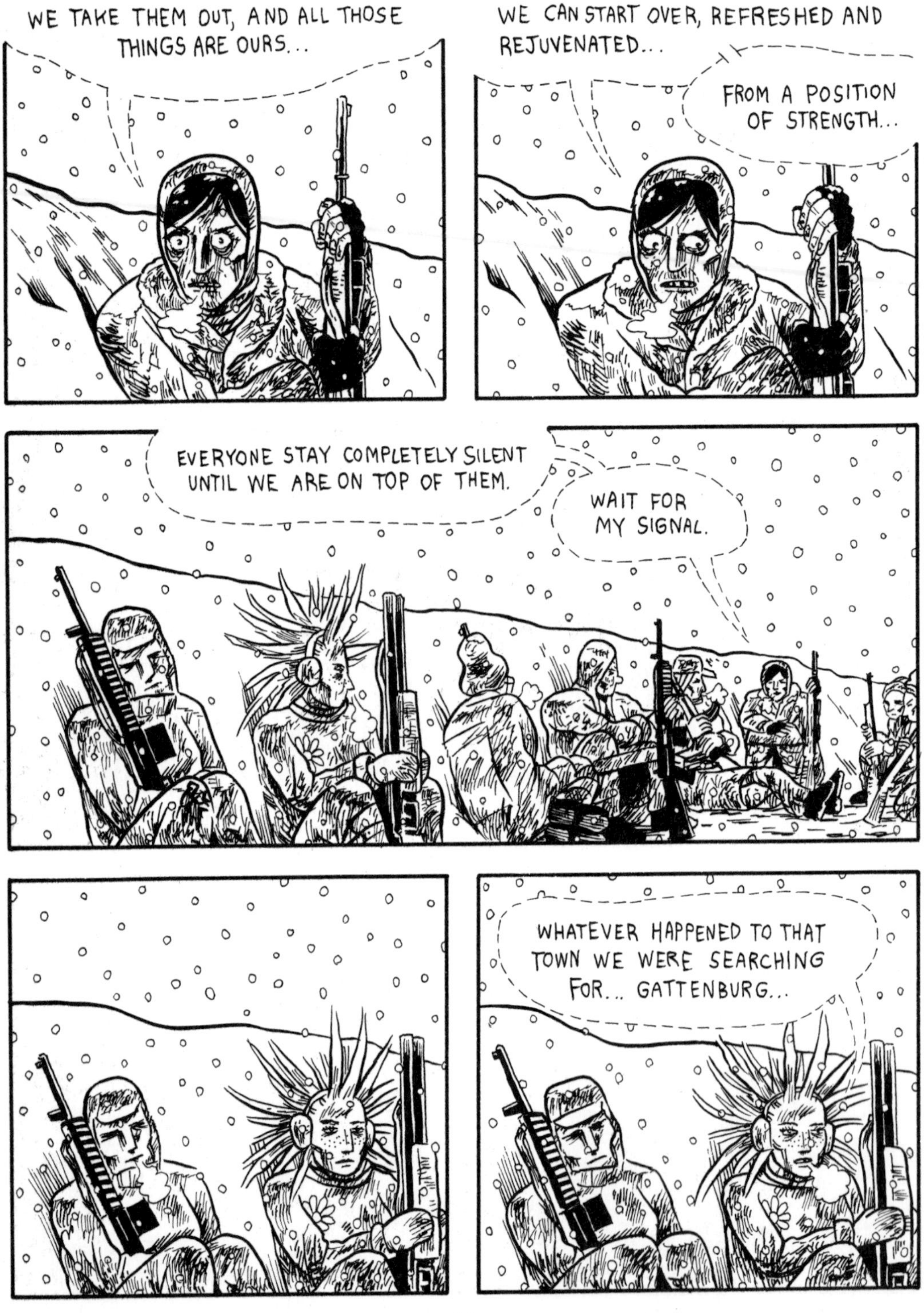
WE TAKE THEM OUT, AND ALL THOSE THINGS ARE OURS...
WE CAN START OVER, REFRESHED AND REJUVENATED...
FROM A POSITION OF STRENGTH...
EVERYONE STAY COMPLETELY SILENT UNTIL WE ARE ON TOP OF THEM.
WAIT FOR MY SIGNAL.
WHATEVER HAPPENED TO THAT TOWN WE WERE SEARCHING FOR... GATTENBURG...

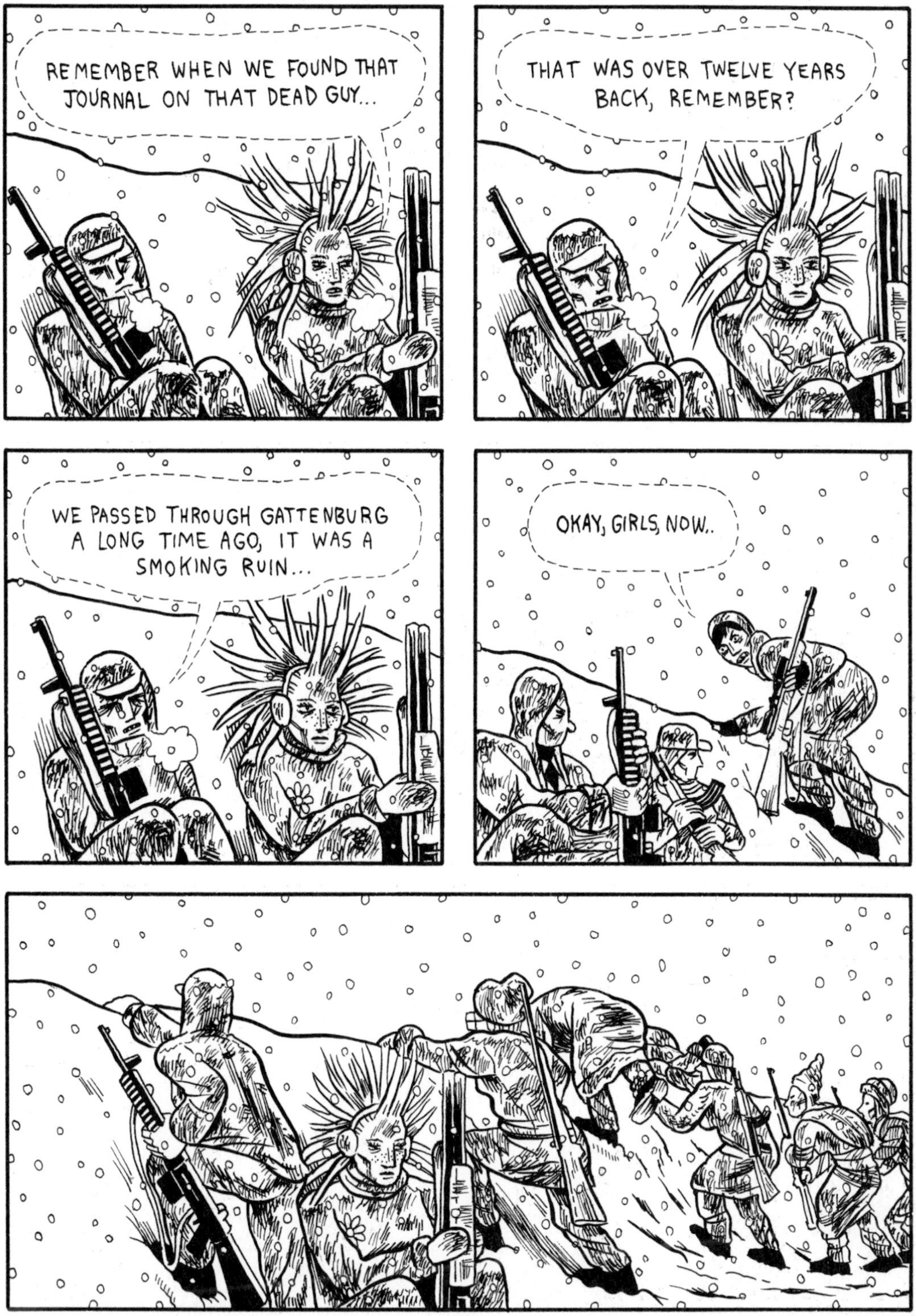
REMEMBER WHEN WE FOUND THAT JOURNAL ON THAT DEAD GUY...
THAT WAS OVER TWELVE YEARS BACK, REMEMBER?
WE PASSED THROUGH GATTENBURG A LONG TIME AGO, IT WAS A SMOKING RUIN...
OKAY, GIRLS, NOW..

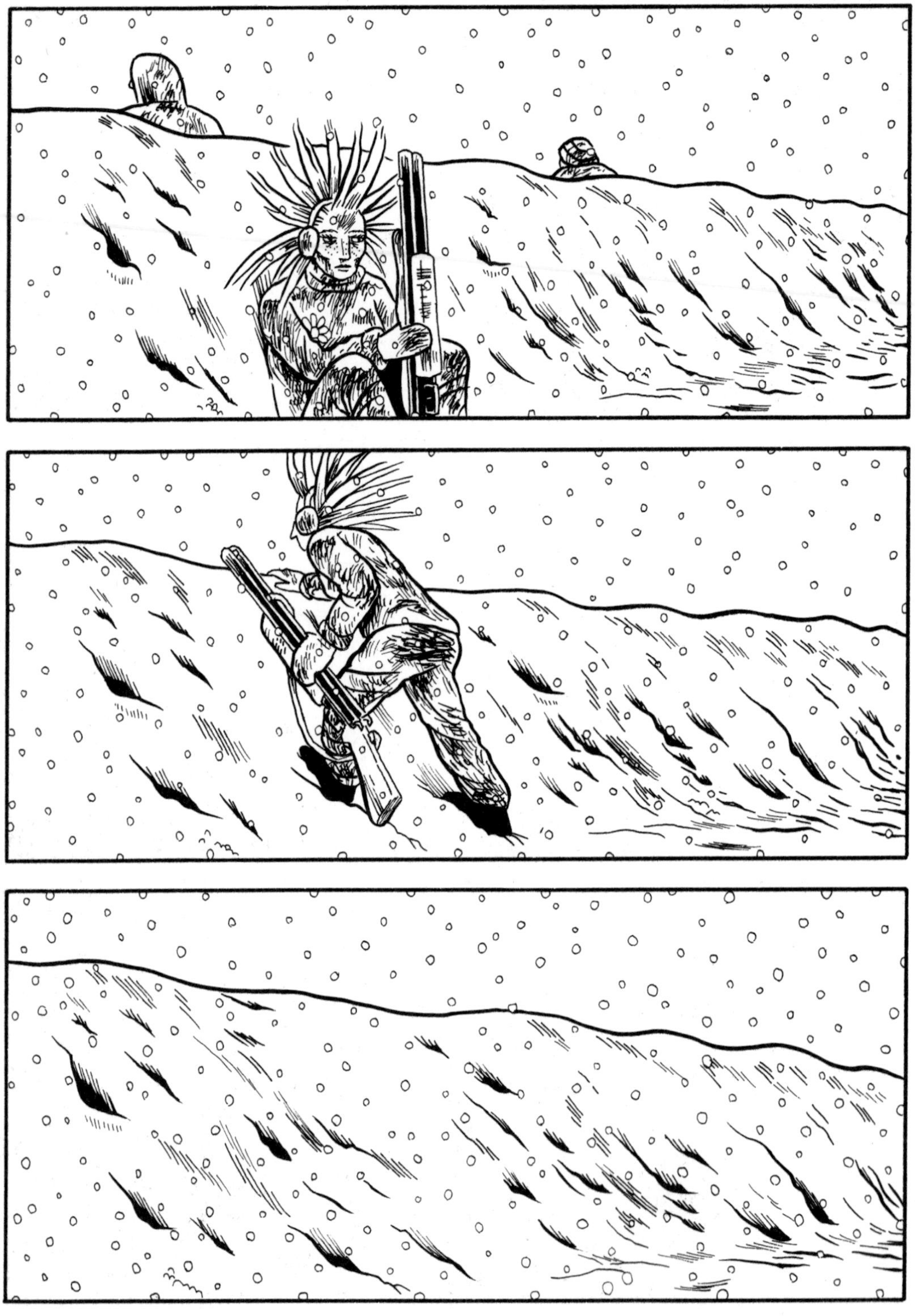

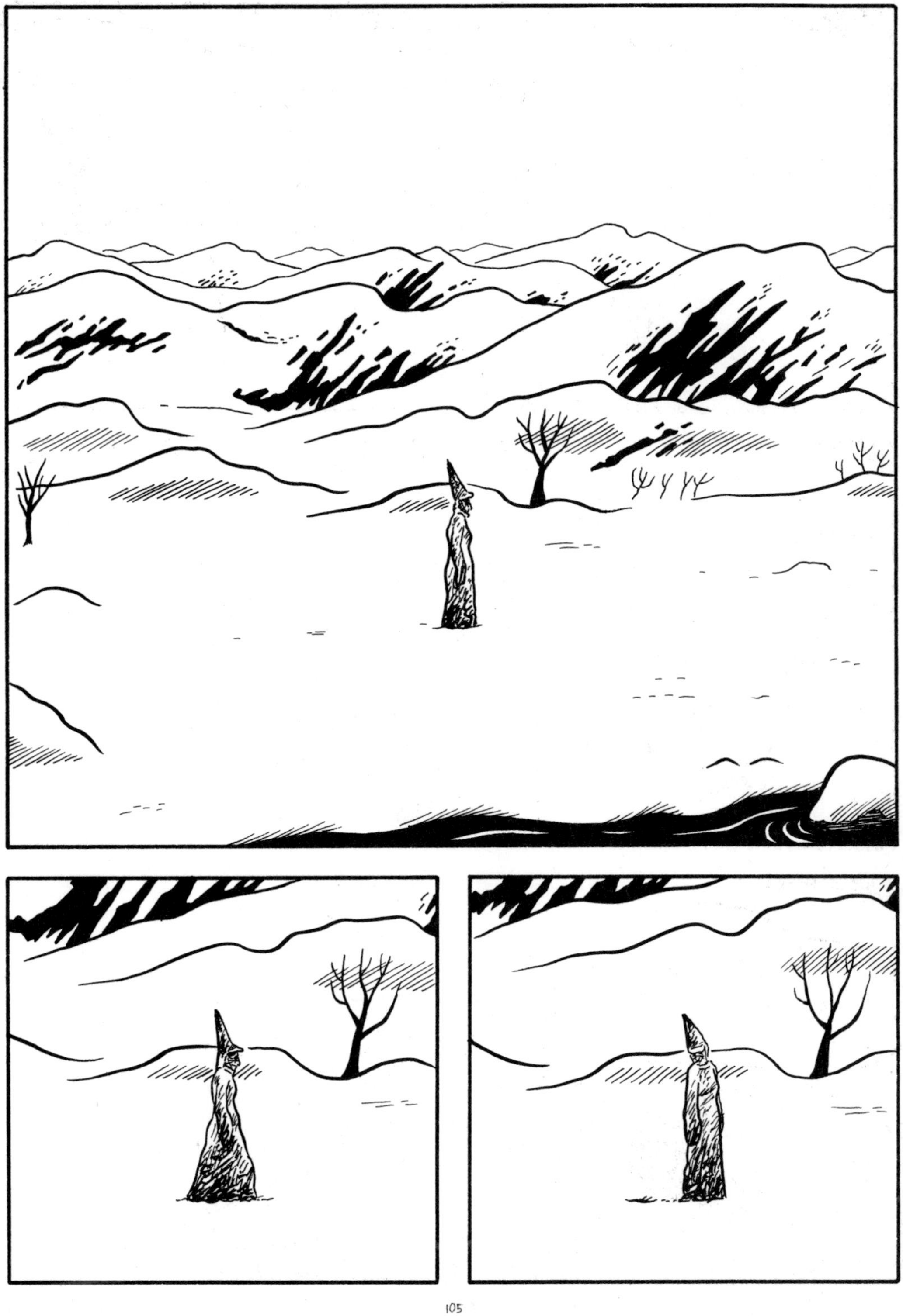

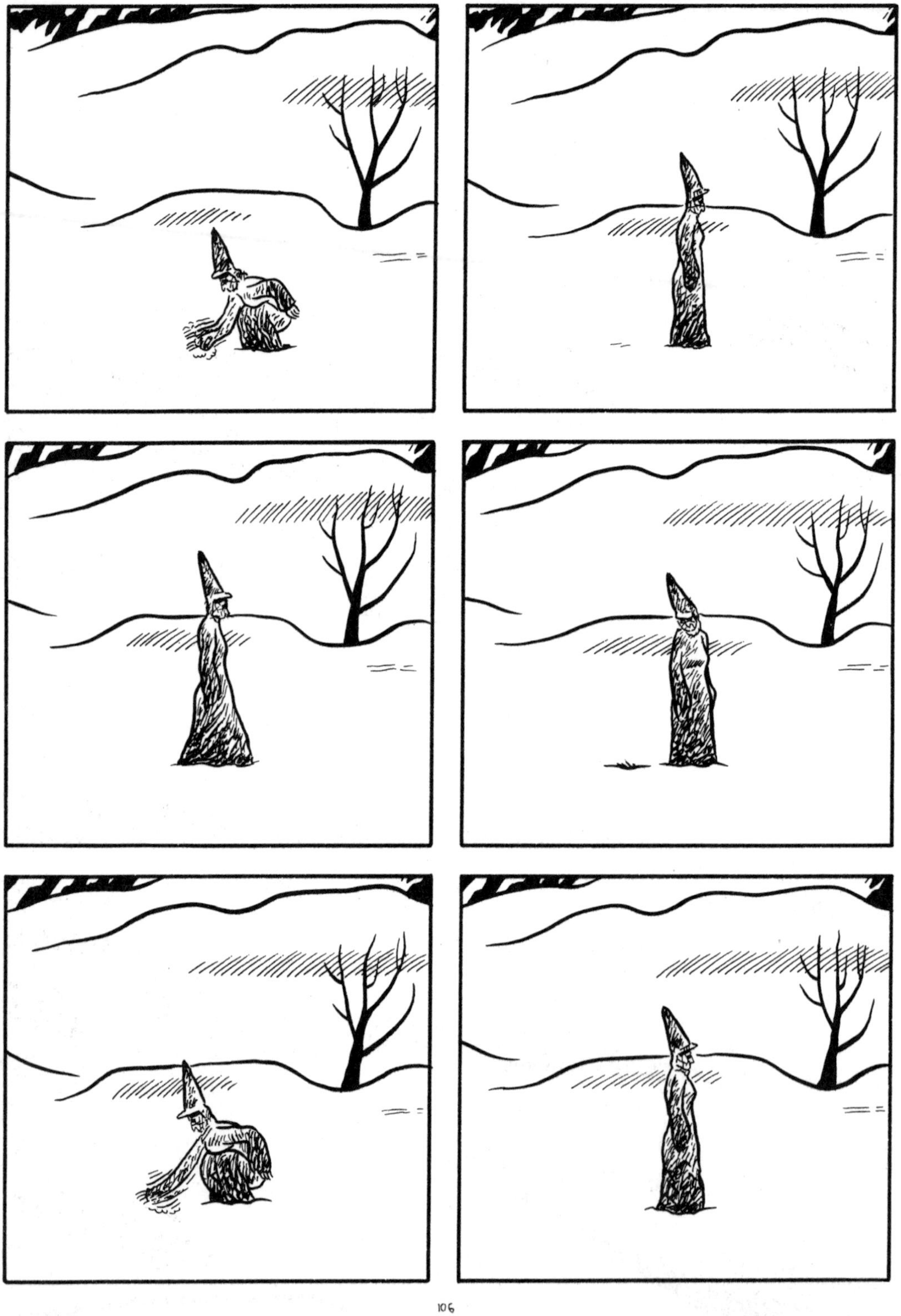

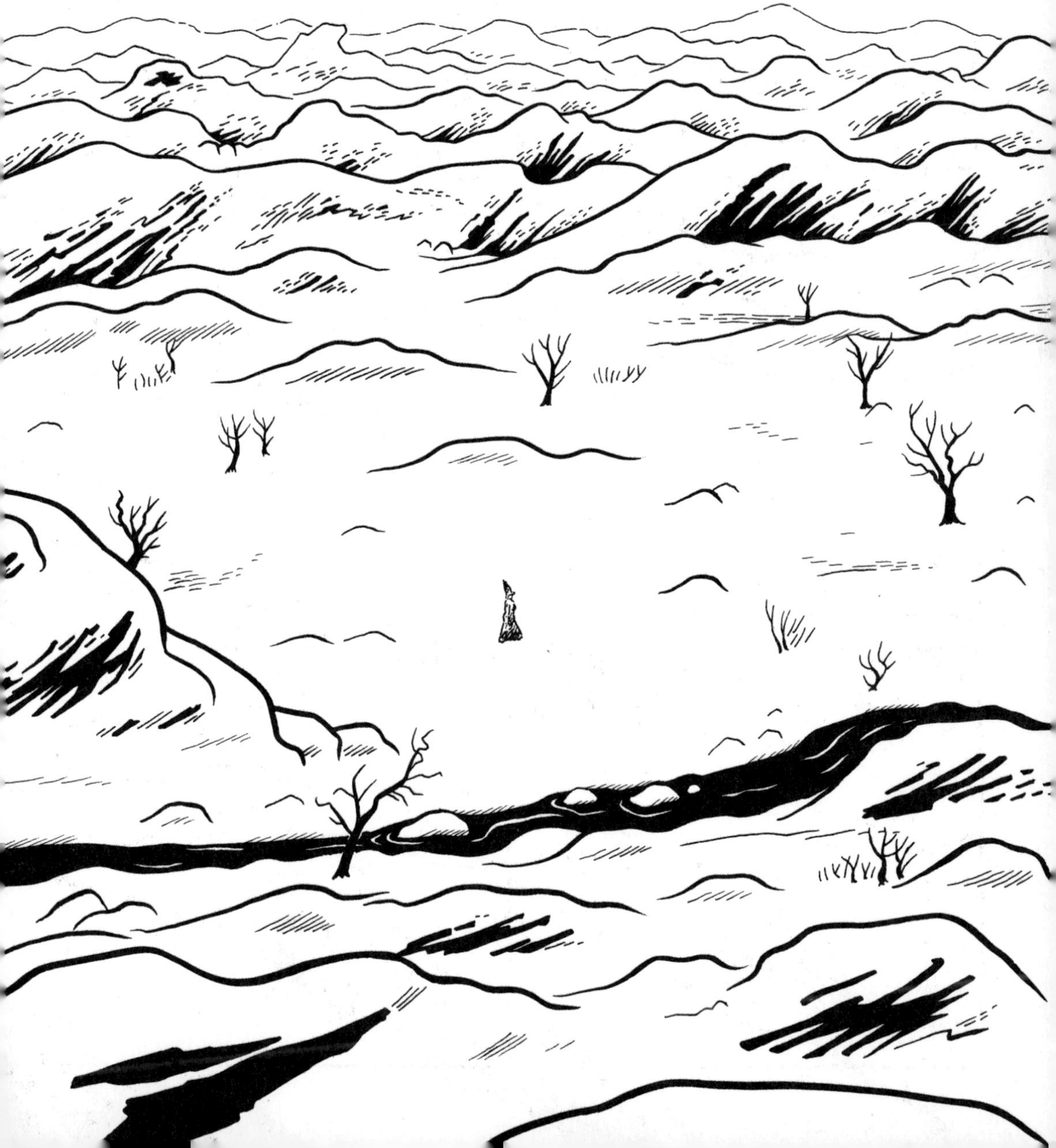

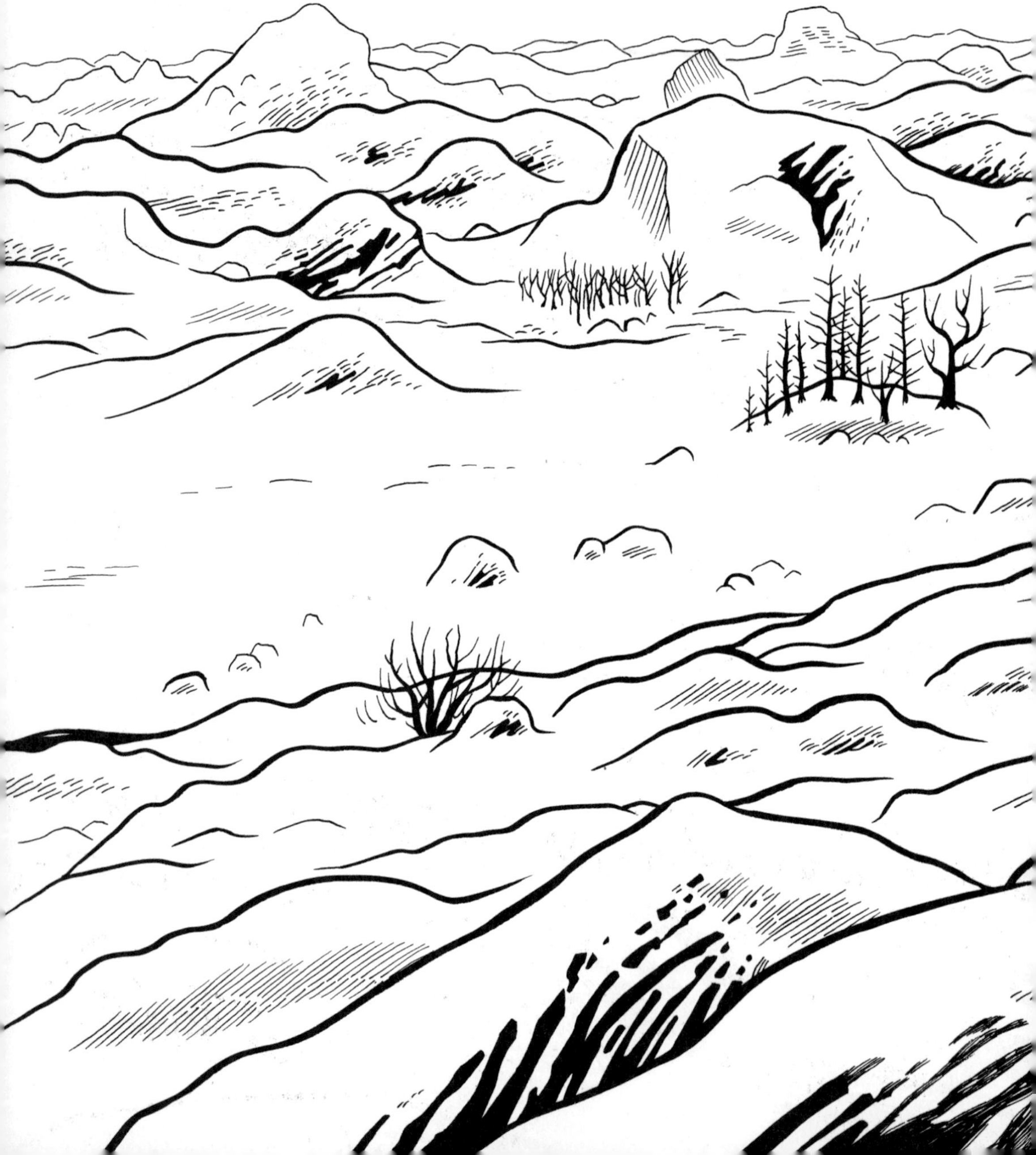

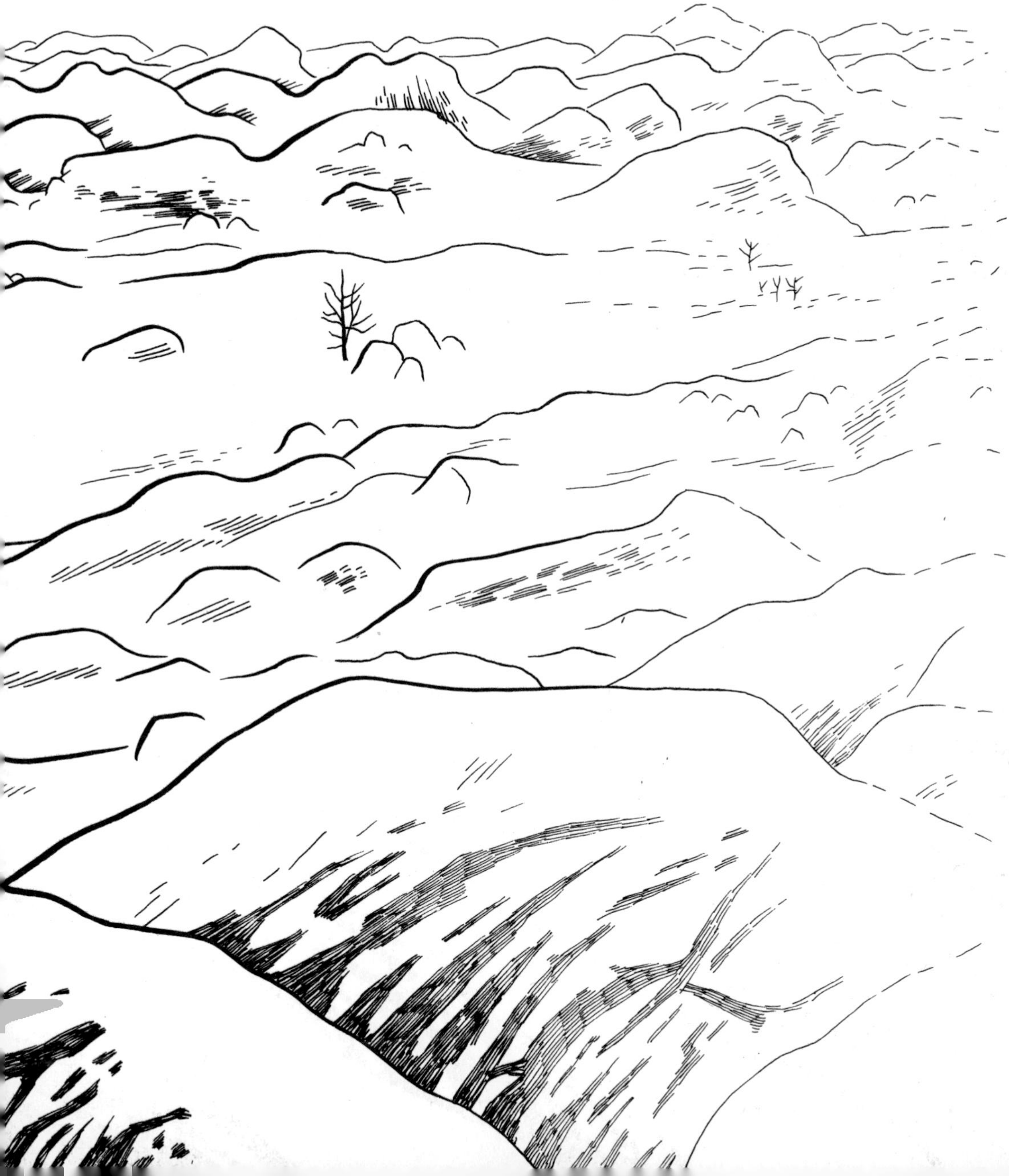